Kieren Fallon was born in County Clare in Ireland in 1965 and came to the UK to ride in 1988. He was one of the most successful flat jockeys ever, becoming Champion Jockey six times between 1997 and 2003. He rode for leading trainers including Sir Henry Cecil, Sir Michael Stoute and Aiden O'Brien, and won more than 2250 races during his long career. Among his greatest achievements was winning the Derby three times, the Prix de l'Arc de Triomphe twice and the 1000 and 2000 Guineas a record total of nine times. He retired in the summer of 2016.

Oliver Holt, who worked with Kieren Fallon on the writing of this book, is the chief sports writer of the *Mail on Sunday* having previously worked for *The Times* and the *Daily Mirror*. A former Sports Journalist of the Year, he is the author of ten previous books.

Praise for *Form*

'The most eagerly anticipated racing autobiography for many years.' *Guardian*

'Brutally candid.' *Yorkshire Post*

'I've always been fascinated by Kieren Fallon; so talented and yet so damaged. So I was drawn like a moth to a flame to his recent autobiography *Form*. It doesn't disappoint . . . It has not been a life without conflict, but if you look into his haunted, hooded eyes, that does not come as a surprise. What is unexpected, however, is the insight that one gets through the Fallon prism.' *Daily Telegraph*

'Candid and rewarding ... career highlights are left to fight for whatever space remains after honest, expansive accounts of his various scandals ... Fallon is certainly honest with himself, and that lifts *Form* out of the also-ran clutter of the genre and into the winner's enclosure ... If it were fiction, it would be a proper page-turner, Dick Francis-esque in its delivery. The reality that this is fact, a life well lived if not always lived well, makes it even more compelling.' **Racing Post**

'His story gives us a graphic picture of the downside of racing at the highest level – the pressures, the 'flipping' to keep to an unrealistic weight, the travelling grind ... For me the best pages are those in which he describes his riding methods, how he used his legs and his body while others used the whip. His story of Kris Kin's derby victory is riveting.' **Spectator**

Form

MY AUTOBIOGRAPHY

Kieren Fallon

with Oliver Holt

**SIMON &
SCHUSTER**

London · New York · Sydney · Toronto · New Delhi

A CBS COMPANY

First published in Great Britain by Simon & Schuster UK Ltd, 2017
This paperback edition published by Simon & Schuster UK Ltd, 2018
A CBS COMPANY

3 5 7 9 10 8 6 4 2

Simon & Schuster UK Ltd
1st Floor
222 Gray's Inn Road
London WC1X 8HB

www.simonandschuster.co.uk
www.simonandschuster.com.au
www.simonandschuster.co.in

Simon & Schuster Australia, Sydney
Simon & Schuster India, New Delhi

The author and publishers have made all reasonable efforts
to contact copyright-holders for permission, and apologise
for any omissions or errors in the form of credits given.
Corrections may be made to future printings.

A CIP catalogue record for this book
is available from the British Library

Paperback ISBN: 978-1-4711-6654-9
eBook ISBN: 978-1-4711-6653-2

Typeset in Bembo by M Rules
Printed and bound by CPI Group (UK) Ltd, Croydon, CR0 4YY

MIX
Paper from
responsible sources
FSC® C020471

Simon & Schuster UK Ltd are committed to sourcing paper
that is made from wood grown in sustainable forests and support the Forest
Stewardship Council, the leading international forest certification organisation.
Our books displaying the FSC logo are printed on FSC certified paper.

CONTENTS

DEDICATION

To the Thoroughbred

ACKNOWLEDGEMENTS

I've been thinking about writing this book for a long time now. There have been a great many people throughout my career who have spurred me on along the way, encouraging me to get my life story on to the printed page. But the following have all helped and supported me in different ways in the varying stages of both my professional and personal life, and my special thanks must go to them.

So, I thank all the trainers who let me ride for them, from Kevin Prendergast, who gave me my first taste of life as a jockey all those years ago in Ireland, through to Luca Cumani towards the end of my career.

I owe everything to Professor Rolfe Birch, without whose care and expertise in his field of peripheral nerve injury I'd never have ridden again after my fall. Sir Michael Stoute must have particular mention here, because through Michael Holding he found the physiotherapist Jacqueline King, whose determination set me on the road to recovery in that bleak time.

John and Sue Magnier never wavered in their support of me; likewise the great Aidan O'Brien.

I was so lucky to have the best lawyers during my legal tribulations. Early on, there was Lord Irvine QC, followed by Patrick Milmo QC, and I couldn't have had better when John Kelsey-Fry QC, Ian Winter QC and Jane Glass, the Legal Blonde, represented me in the race-fixing trial. Good things often come from bad, and Jack Ramsden introducing me to the solicitor Christopher Stewart-Moore way back in the Stuart Webster imbroglio was one of them. He and his wife Penny became, and remain, my very good friends.

Dr Adrian McGoldrick, the senior medical officer at the Irish Turf Club, helped me in a way I never would have expected. He saw the reasons for my failing energy and enthusiasm for riding and sent me to find an understanding of those reasons to St Pat's, from where I emerged healthier, happier and with a renewed zest for life.

And thanks must go to my editor at Simon & Schuster, Ian Marshall, for his understanding in overseeing the writing of this book. To Ollie Holt, whose sensitivity gave me the confidence to open up and talk about the parts of my life I found difficult to dwell on. And to Sally Partington, my copy-editor, whose love of racing and horses was second to none. Equine photographer Caroline Norris, a friend for years, has supplied many of the photographs in this book.

And, of course, I thank all members of the Fallon family, not least my parents, Frank and Maureen: by their example, they instilled in me the strongest of work ethics. My upbringing left no room for slacking, which stood me in good stead for the career I eventually chose.

And, finally, my heartfelt thanks to each and every horse I've ridden. Without those horses, where would I be?

PROLOGUE

Horses and Humans

I like chess. I would like to be really good at it. Being a jockey is like being a piece in a game of chess. In a race, all the other jockeys are the enemy. I can see them all. I know what they are all doing. I know where they are going to move. I know what they want to do. They all want to wipe me off the board. They want to capture me. And the king is the winning post. I suppose that is my life view, too. I find people hard. It's the way I was made, I suppose, the environment I grew up in, the way I'm wired.

There have been plenty of occasions when I haven't done myself any favours, either. I've made enough mistakes of my own to last several lifetimes and there are plenty of people who will always say I was my own worst enemy. Maybe there's some truth in that.

It's enough for me to say that I like horses because they have never caused me pain. They have hurt me physically when they have trodden on me but that's different. What I mean is a horse has never let me down. Horses have always brought me solace. What goes on in my outside life, I can shut it down when I am on a horse. When I am on a horse, I am happy. I am where I want to be.

I never felt when I went out on a horse and came out of the stalls that there was a gun to my head. I felt good with the weapons I had. That the horse was my army right there. I had so much trust in that. I knew I was going to get 100 per cent from the horse and it was going to do the best for me. I knew if I got in trouble, it was going to get me out of trouble. I knew that I could rely on it. I never felt like that with people.

I always loved animals. I grew up on a farm in County Clare with my five brothers and sisters, way out in the countryside in the west of Ireland. I was born in February 1965, long before the motorway was built that runs down from Galway, thirty miles or so to the north, to the airport at Shannon, a similar distance to the south. We lived what I suppose you would call an isolated existence. There was a village, Crusheen, a few miles away with a little pub called Fogarty's and a shop and a garage but it would take us a while to walk down there.

We lived higher up, among the peat bogs and boulders and the green fields. We lived up a narrow little road, the kind that has grass growing down the middle of it. We walked up the mountain to our schoolhouse in Ballinruan every morning, climbing over the stone walls, running through fields, avoiding the bulls.

We had a milking cow that was a pet. We had a bull that was a mean bastard. We used to feed calves and lambs out of a bottle if their mother died. We had a wild Connemara pony that nobody else could get near. It used to come to me and I could ride it without any tack. I could ride it bareback.

I could connect with horses even then. When you look into a horse's eye, you can see into its soul. You can tell their character straight away. You can bond with them before you get on them. I just feel at ease with them. The bond you establish with a horse works for you in a race. If you can get a horse's confidence, you are halfway there. If a horse is strong or keen or difficult and you give them a pat or talk to them, you can get their confidence. Horses can be nervous. If you spook them, they're gone.

You try and get a horse to do something that he hasn't done before like get into a horse box or into the stalls and they can be stubborn. Some are mulish. Some will look at the stalls and you can see them thinking: 'No thanks, I don't want to run down there, I'll get my back end smacked, I'd rather eat grass.'

You get others who are claustrophobic and don't want to go in the tight space you're trying to squeeze them into. They get that scared they just want to get out of there. Most of them have better senses than humans. They can sense danger, for a start. I wish I had that instinct.

Young horses, if the trainer hasn't educated them properly around the gates, they don't know what they are supposed to do and then you have to cajole them and treat them gently, because if they have a bad experience first time out, they're not going to want to do it again. Horses always remember when bad things have happened to them.

I have always been comfortable with horses but I have never been comfortable with myself. Maybe that's another reason I loved racing. I was always on the move. There was no time for people. There was no time for relationships. I was protected from people. If you're busy, it helps. You're moving on all the time, racecourse to racecourse, country to country. You don't have to interact.

I made everything secondary to racing. If anything was affecting my racing, I shut it down. I regret that now, obviously. I knew that the horses would sense it if I had had a row with my wife and I was in a bad mood, so I shut down that side of my life so the horse wouldn't feel it.

No time for my wife. No time for a life. Not outside racing. Say I'm in a 1pm race at Lingfield, you have to be there fifteen minutes before. That's the deadline. You're stuck in traffic then. I liked driving. I had a driver but I drove myself because I thought I was a great driver. I used to drive quickly. I was a bit of a lunatic in a car. If I wanted to look at the form, I'd let my driver drive. If I was late, I would always drive. If I wasn't driving, I'd be eating my nails. I'd be flat out and if there was traffic, I'd be up the hard shoulder.

Crazy things, we used to do. In the trainer Jack Berry's book, he wrote that he had once spent twenty-one miles driving up the hard shoulder on the way to Carlisle because there was a jam and he had to get to the races. You do these crazy things. I'd be going flat out up the hard shoulder at 100 mph. Flat out.

I'd be running into the course with my bag to get on the scales. Crazy. But you don't think. Then you're back in the car. If you're in the 9.30pm race at Newbury, it's nearly dark, it's 10pm before you've had a shower and you're in the car and you're trying to have a drink.

I'd have a bottle of vodka, a carton of orange juice and a bucket of ice in the car waiting for me. That was when I could have a drink. On the way home. It's the only time you get to relax. If some of the lads were with you, you'd share. If they weren't, sometimes I'd get through that whole bottle of vodka by myself in the two hours back home.

That started when I came down south when I was working for Henry Cecil in the late nineties and I was about to become Champion Jockey for the first time. It was just to unwind. However many winners I'd ridden, I'd be thinking: 'That one in the eight o'clock, if I'd done this or if I'd done that.'

Then you try and get hold of your trainers and make your phone calls. You could have twelve or fourteen rides in a day sometimes and you're having to get hold of all the trainers to tell them how their horses had run. 'They did this, they did that, thank you, whatever.' You get bollockings and you get congratulations.

I used to live about eight miles outside Newmarket in a nice big place with paddocks and ponies for the kids. But I never saw my kids. Racing is seven days a week. If I wasn't racing in England, I'd be riding in France or Ireland or somewhere. It was crazy and I could never see it.

But that was my life and for a short time, it turned me into one of the best jockeys in the world. I won the Derby three times, I won the 2000 Guineas, the 1000 Guineas and the Oaks and the Prix de l'Arc de Triomphe twice. I won sixteen Classics in a concentrated span.

Between 1997 and 2003, when I won six jockeys' championships, I felt like I couldn't be beaten. I felt like I was going to be one of the best there had ever been and ever would be. I wasn't as popular with the wider public as Frankie Dettori, the great rival I always respected, but I was popular with the punters, who knew I always gave my all.

That was one of the great ironies of my career, really.

Race-fixing allegations brought me down, but the punters knew I was the last person who would ever get involved in something like that. I was obsessed with winning, not with losing. I was obsessed with it to the exclusion of everything else. I was obsessed with it to the exclusion of my family. Losing was anathema to me.

I fought the accusations and I beat them but I couldn't beat time and I couldn't beat the depression that the struggle to clear my name and the realisation that I had lost my dominance as a jockey brought on.

It took me a long time to get to the top. I had a protracted apprenticeship in Ireland and in Yorkshire. I burned bright when I got there but I burned fast, too, and before I knew it, the light had gone out.

I don't ride races any more but I do ride out every morning. I ride up Warren Hill and gaze down on Newmarket below me. I will always ride. I'll ride even when I can't walk any more. I'll always have horses.

CHAPTER 1

Living off the Land

From as early as I can remember, I wanted to ride. I loved watching Westerns on the television and seeing the cowboys with their huge saddles and their noble horses. I loved John Wayne and films such as *Red River* and *Stagecoach* where they made riding horses look so glamorous and so wild. I watched the horse racing on the television, too, and thought that it looked like fun.

There was no history of horse racing in my family. So many of my contemporaries seem to come from a racing lineage. Their dad was a jockey or their mum was a jockey or their dad was a trainer or an owner but it wasn't like that with me. My father's father was a blacksmith in the First World War, but that's the closest I got to horsemanship among my ancestors.

There was no real tradition of riding in County Clare, either. It wasn't like Tipperary, away a little bit to the east, where the horse is king and where Ballydoyle rises from the lush green country and exists as heaven on earth for Irish racing people. I lived on a farm, sure, but it was more about cows and goats than horses.

It was still beautiful countryside where I lived, though. From my one-room schoolhouse, built on top of a mountain in a village called Ballinruan, it felt as if the whole of Ireland was spreading out beneath me with its loughs and its rolling hills and its peat bogs and its stone walls and the west coast beyond the peaks in the distance. I loved nature and I felt at ease with it.

But I loved horses most of all. Even when I was on my bike, I used to ride it as if I were riding a horse. I had a little stick and pretended it was a whip and I'd be standing up in the saddle and hitting the back wheel of the bike with it. There was a stone wall around the garden of our farmhouse up above Crusheen, too, and I would sit on that and pretend it was a horse. I'd get a rope and make out that they were my reins and lose myself in an imaginary race.

It wasn't too long before I got a go on the real thing. My dad was always buying and selling cattle and sometimes he came back from the sales and there might have been a pony thrown into the deal. There was always something thrown into the deal, even if it was just a pig or a goat or a luck penny.

Once, Dad came back with a Connemara pony. It was wild and I was the only one that could get near it. I was a small kid but I managed to get that pony close to this slab of rock that was in our field and I clambered onto her back that way. We didn't have a bridle or anything like that but I rode her anyway. I would encourage her to come across to the rock so that she was parallel with it and that was the only way I could put my leg across and get on her. So I held out a carrot or a fistful of grass. As soon as I got on her back, she set off running flat out across the field like she was a stampeding cow in one of those Westerns I loved.

I would hang on for as long as I could but then my legs got tired and I fell off. I was young and supple and my bones were not brittle like they are now and I just bounced off the ground again and again. I never got a cut or a scratch or anything. I loved it straight away, but one evening my dad was eating his meal, staring out of the windows at me, and when he saw me being flung off the pony, she was gone the next day.

Those were my beginnings as a jockey and now there is a plaque on the wall of that house. My brothers and sisters put it there after I won the Epsom Derby for the first time in 1999. There is a likeness of a horse's head and just one word: Oath, the name of the horse that gave me that victory in England's most famous flat race. The greenery has sprung up around the cottage now so you have to walk right up to the back door to see the plaque. There's no sign of the vegetable garden my mother used to tend so lovingly. My mother and father live in London now, so my brother looks after the place.

Some people would probably say we were poor but it didn't feel that way to me. We slept four brothers to a bed in one room and the two girls were in another room with the same arrangement. It didn't bother me particularly. It was what I knew and it kept us warm.

We had to bring drinking water in from the well but we had vegetables from the garden, eggs from the hens and milk from the cow. We had forty acres and we lived off the land. We lived off all the strawberries and raspberries and fruit from the plum trees and apple trees. There were hazel trees in the woods and we collected bags and bags of nuts. We took the blackberries home and my mother made jam out of them. By the time you got home, you didn't want anything to eat. It's funny how some people think of that as being poor because I have never been so healthy as I was in my childhood.

We all helped with the farm. We had one cow for milking and that was enough. We'd get a bucket of milk and the cream on the top, not like today when it's all pasteurised and 2 per cent fat. I never broke a bone in my life while I was riding and I'm convinced that was the reason. It has to be down to the fact that I was drinking so much milk and getting so much calcium. I had a few falls over the years. I severed an artery and a nerve in my arm in a fall but never broke a bone. I've got a hoof mark on my arm where a horse stood on it but it still didn't break the bone.

All us kids worked on the farm. My dad worked as a plasterer from the first light until the last light and so it was down to my mum and us to do most of the farm work. Sometimes, he'd drop us off at the bog to cut the turf and we would bring it back to load it on our big open fire.

We milked the cows and mucked out their shed and there was always so much to do that we had to pull together and help each other out. A river ran through our land, too, so we'd go fishing on it. There weren't many other people around but we had each other for company.

It was not an easy childhood in many ways, but I loved it. I never went anywhere outside Ireland for the first eighteen years of my life, but after I became a jockey, I embraced travel and I found it easy to adapt to places like Kolkata and Mumbai, Sydney, Santa Anita and Hong Kong.

It sounds strange but I think life in a tough rural environment like Crusheen prepared me for almost anything. I didn't feel particularly comfortable in sophisticated cities, but in the teeming poverty of Kolkata or the beauty of the San Gabriel Mountains in California or the manic bustle of Hong Kong, I felt entirely at ease.

It was a proper rural life. Primary school in Ballinruan was up the mountain, two or three miles away, but we never took the roads. We went across country, over the fields, skirting the bogs, jumping the ditches, watching out for the bulls.

We had a bull ourselves and it was an angry thing. He had a ring on his nose and he had to have a chain with a weight on the end of it so he couldn't run after you. That was the only way to slow him down.

Every other Sunday, after we'd been to Mass, we went to village sports days around County Clare. I loved that. My mother always won the married women's race. She was a fast runner and it was a great day out.

I didn't see my parents relax like that very often. My dad got up at 6am and you wouldn't see him again until 9.30pm. All he did was work. He never took a day off in his life. He never went to a doctor or a dentist. We just had one family ritual, which was going to Mass every Sunday, either in Crusheen or up in Ballinruan.

Religion was a big thing back then. Not like today. It's all changed now. You had to go but you enjoyed going. If you missed it, it was like something bad was going to happen. But it was a social occasion as much as anything else. It was something that bound the community together and when it was over, the kids from three or four families, including our own, rushed and chased each other back down the mountain on the way home.

When we reached a fork in the road, we went one way, the Ryders went another and the O'Briens another. We'd be messing around, pushing and shoving. It was great during the summers but horrible during the winters, wet and cold.

There were holidays, too. We always went to our granny's up in Dublin for a spell during the summer. It would take us nearly a day to get there because my father was a very slow driver in his Volkswagen or his Morris Minor. He made a series of little pit stops on the way up. He always picked the same spots for his couple of pints. The kids were never allowed in the pub so we sat in the back seat of the car and had a bottle of Coke and a bag of crisps. Everybody knew him in the pubs and I loved it when we got to Dublin. My mother's father was a gardener and they had a beautiful garden with all sorts of vegetables and fruits.

I didn't like school that much but at least my brothers and sisters were there and we could play together at lunchtime. There were four people in my class: Mary Moroney, John Culligan, Jack Mitchell and me. We sat two to a desk in that one-room, rectangular schoolhouse on top of the mountain, with some panel dividers to separate the age groups and a patch of rough grass outside for a playground. It's derelict now, that old school. I was there from the age of four until I was fourteen. The infants in one bit, the older kids in another, ready to go to secondary school at Our Lady's College down the road in Gort. Our Lady's isn't there any more, either. It's a hotel now.

The primary school headmaster was a very good Irish speaker but he was a very angry man. Taidh McNamara, he was called. He must have been angry at life because he was always bitter. He beat you if you didn't know something. He hit you with a metre stick or whatever would come handy to him.

The headmaster asked questions about what was the longest river in the world or what was the tallest mountain and you had to put your hands up. I very seldom put my hand up and yet I was the one he always asked to answer the question. I could never understand that.

There was one day I did put my hand up when he asked a question. He wanted to know the name of the mountains separating Spain and France. I didn't know the answer but I put my hand up anyway. But he didn't see my hand in time and he asked Mary Moroney, and she said it was the Pyrenees. As I was putting my hand down, he said: 'Ah Mr Fallon, you had your hand up, what were you going to say?' I said I was going to say the same. 'Ah,' he said, 'great minds think alike, fools seldom differ.'

It has always stuck in my head. Why would that be? Of all the things, of all the hidings, that one thing stuck there. He was terrible. He would take the head off you. You wouldn't go home and tell your mother that the teacher had hit you because you'd get a kick up the arse and asked what did you do to deserve it. Then you'd get another one.

That kind of behaviour was relatively common in my schooling. It was normal for that time. At Our Lady's in Gort, we had a priest called Father Larkin and he was a big man, a hard man, and he would walk up and down the rows of our classroom, threatening to hit people.

I wasn't a good student there, either. The thing that completely baffled me was algebra. I think I was dyslexic at school because a lot of things wouldn't register with me. I wasn't a very good reader, either.

But even though I was petrified of Father Larkin, he never hit me. I was a small boy and I think he knew that if he hit me, he would have killed me. When I was in the third year, I was still smaller than the kids in the two years below. I didn't get teased because I was wiry and I could handle myself and I loved sports.

I was good at badminton and soccer, and in the evenings we'd box. I loved hurling, too. There's still a picture of me in the village Under-18s team, which won the Minor Championship in 1980, staring out from one of the walls in Fogarty's in Crusheen like a pale ghost.

CHAPTER 2

After Ann Died

The time when Ann died was a before-and-after moment in our family. Things changed after my sister died. Her death affected my dad particularly badly but none of us were really ever the same again. The death of a child does that to families.

I was a middle child and I was seven or eight when Ann died. She must have been four or five. Fergus and Michael were older than me. Geraldine, Ann and Dermot were younger. Nora was born later. My mother was pregnant with her when Ann fell ill, but that time is a bit of a blur that I have tried to blot out.

My memories of that period of my life are like nightmarish visions that visit me now and again no matter how hard I try to suppress them. They are darting snapshots of a childhood trauma that has never left me, isolated things that still jolt me even now.

I think sometimes of my dad travelling in the car in the early morning to the hospital in Ennis where my sister was dying and leaving me in it while he went to visit her and me imagining what she was going through. It's difficult for a boy to see his father crying, when he's used to him always being strong.

I think of the moments when friends and relatives started to arrive at our house after Ann's funeral and none of us even knew that she had died, and how my dad took my brothers and sisters and me upstairs and told us that Ann had passed away.

I think of how Geraldine burst into tears and how I couldn't really cope. Geraldine was crying and I just walked away as if nothing had happened and I hadn't really heard the words that my father had just spoken. When I got to the bottom of the stairs, my mother was there and I seemed so casual to her that she was surprised and horrified and asked me if my dad had told me that Ann had died. I tried to pretend it was just a bad dream.

When we went to school the next day, the teacher asked us why we had been absent the day before and I told her that Ann had died. And that was the first time it really hit me that she was gone. That was when the loss hit me. But I still never really grieved. None of us did. It has affected us all in our own ways in later life. It was the root of a lot of my problems.

I have all sorts of visions like that, a man coming round to the house, trying to sell us something, I think, and my mother pushing him away and weeping and screaming that her child had just died. I try not to think of those things too much but they're always with me.

When Ann started getting sick, we didn't know what was wrong with her but she was crying all the time and it was obvious she was in a lot of pain. My parents took her to the hospital in Ennis and they kept her in but they were different times then and children weren't allowed to visit so we never saw her again.

First thing in the morning, my dad would drive to the hospital before he started work. He would be there before she woke up in the morning and then, last thing at night, he would stay with her. And he did that until she died. I think it broke his heart.

The rest of us kids didn't know how bad she was. We didn't even know what was wrong with her. She was a healthy young girl. She had never had a sick day in her life and then all of a sudden, she was gone.

They did an autopsy when she died and the poison from her appendix had gone right through her. It was the hospital's fault because they had misdiagnosed her and, of course, that made it worse. It felt like she had died needlessly.

My dad was strict anyway. He was a working man. But after Ann died, he changed quite dramatically. He stopped going to sports days and, even as a child, I was aware that he was growing increasingly distant from us.

Sometimes, people ask me if I felt the need to compete for my parents' attention because I was one of six. That makes me laugh. It was the opposite. I didn't want my dad's attention because if I was getting his attention, it usually meant I was getting a smack for something. Mainly, I just wanted to stay out of his way.

I'm not saying it was a bad way to bring kids up. He certainly had our respect. But it wasn't an affectionate house. My mum had her garden, and that was where she was happiest. She spent the vast majority of her time outside. If she had a spare five minutes, she'd be out in her rockery or something.

She more or less lived in that garden. It wasn't like she was the soft one in the family.

They weren't ones for praising. They never have been and they never will be. They came to watch me racing whenever they could over the years. They were at Epsom once, but they would never ring and say 'well done' when I won a big race. That wasn't the way they were made.

But after Ann died, there was a line that you would never want to cross with my father. He always seemed angry to me after that. If you were messing around, he would look at you once and you knew what was coming then. He would warn you with that look. My father was always very deep and very quick to fly off the handle. Whoever it was who was messing around, it didn't really matter to him. He just knew that someone would have to be punished. There was a stick over the mirror and he would grab it and whoever was there, he would lash out.

But he gave us discipline and structure and he taught me the meaning of hard work, both by example and instruction. In the summer, I laboured for him. I mixed the plaster and carried it up to him and whoever was assisting him. It was easier when it was a bungalow because it meant it wouldn't be quite as big a job. My heart sank if we pulled up outside a two-storey house.

I wanted to be a chef or a carpenter, not a plasterer. Plastering was a no-no. It was too hard. You had to mix the plaster with a stick back then and if he brought a labourer with him, you would have to keep two of them going with a ready supply. That was tough.

My dad did rescue my riding career before I even knew there was such a thing as being a jockey. I'd been chasing chickens around with a rag on our land, just flicking at them. We had hens and geese and a couple of them had got into my mother's garden where she had all of her vegetables and I wanted to get them out. I fell and I landed on a piece of broken glass and it took a chunk out of my leg. You can see the scar there still. You could see right through to the bone.

A neighbour took me to the same hospital in Ennis where my sister had died because Dad was at work. I got it stitched up, but because it hurt to move it, I didn't exercise and so it didn't mend. I went a couple of days later to get the stitches out and because I couldn't straighten the knee, they thought gangrene was setting in. They had me on the trolley, ready to take me up to take the leg off even though I'd only gone to get my stitches out. I was in the elevator on the way up to the operating theatre when my father intercepted them and picked me up and carried me out with the blanket on me and put me in the Volkswagen we had. He drove me home and within two or three days, there was nothing wrong with me.

Even though I loved riding horses when I could in our field, I didn't really think of it as a sport. Sport, to me, was hurling and boxing. When Mum and Dad were out, Michael and Fergus and I would box in the front room. We got a pair of socks and rolled them up over our hands. And then we put another sock over it for padding and then we'd get stuck in to each other.

There was a club at Our Lady's in Gort and I joined that. I was still tiny. Even by the time I was eighteen, I was five stone when I was dressed. But I liked boxing. I was fit and I'd done some weights to build myself up a bit. My dad dropped me off and went to have his pint in a pub and picked me up afterwards.

I was thirteen when I got called up for my first fight in the ring at the club. It was the first time I had put proper boxing gloves on and the coach, Jimmy Regan, who was a mentor to me then and is still someone I trust today, put me in with another kid who had just started boxing. I knocked this lad all around the ring. Jimmy stopped the fight and turned to me. 'You said you hadn't boxed before,' he said. I told him again that I hadn't. So he put me in with a kid who had had a few fights and the same thing happened again: I knocked him round the place.

Jimmy started getting annoyed with me now. I told him I had boxed my brothers when my parents weren't home with socks on our hands and that was it. I started fighting more and more after that. I was quick and I was sharp. I loved boxing. I loved the training. It's great discipline. I never felt any pain when I was boxing. I never minded getting hit because I never felt it. I suppose there was too much adrenaline in me to feel anything.

Actually, I discovered the same later in my life when I was a jockey. You often get hit by another jockey's whip when you are riding in a race and you don't feel it because you are so close and the adrenaline is running through you. You'll get back to the weighing room and you'll have red welts on your arms, but at the time you hardly notice.

And if I ever needed to fight outside the ring, it came in handy. It wasn't that I was aggressive. I'm the opposite. I am really, really quiet. I never look for trouble but if somebody comes looking for it, then I have got a terrible temper. That came later in my life. I didn't have a temper as a kid. There was no one to have a temper with. I've always enjoyed just messing about and playing silly jokes.

So I would travel around the country, fighting amateur fights. Most of my fights, I won easily. I was useful. I was on the wrong side of a couple of mismatches when my opponent didn't turn up and I was so desperate to fight that I took on guys bigger than myself.

Jimmy told someone a story about that once. He said he was worried about me boxing a bigger kid from Connacht when I was representing Munster in an Under-13s match and I had waved him away. 'He's only got two hands, the same as me,' I'd said. I knocked the kid out in the third round. I fought one guy down in Kilkenny who was a lot heavier than me. Jimmy said I didn't have to fight him but I was dying to fight. I didn't get stopped but I had a hell of a headache the next day. Jimmy thought that maybe I could have become a professional boxer but I wasn't good enough. I never really wanted that.

Even when I got into my late teens, I wasn't thinking of becoming a jockey, either. It sounds stupid but I didn't really know that such a thing existed. Where we come from, we had to walk to wherever we got to. We lived off the land. I felt like all I wanted to do was ride horses but I didn't know what a jockey was. It wasn't racing country, remember. The nearest racecourse at Galway would be an hour and a half away and, if my father was driving, that meant it would take three hours to get there. We did go once to Galway and I'll never forget it. The Galway races have to be seen to be believed.

It was 1982 and I was seventeen and we saw the Galway Plate, the biggest race of the festival. The Lady's Master won it and she was 25/1. I couldn't believe how small the jockeys' saddles were. The only ones I'd seen before were the huge big things John Wayne chucked on his horse's back. But even after I'd been to Galway races, it still didn't occur to me I could make my living out of riding horses, even though I always wanted to get away from Crusheen. I had to get away. We were in the middle of nowhere and there were no jobs.

I never thought about staying and taking over the farm myself but I got to seventeen and I knew I was going to have to find a job. One day, when I was thinking about where life was going to take me, I looked at one of Geraldine's books and there was a list of all the professions you could take up. Carpenter, plumber, doctor, lawyer: they were all there. And then, at the end of the list, it said 'jockey'. It said if you wanted to be a jockey, you could write away to the Irish Turf Club. And it provided an address.

So I wrote away and they sent me a list of trainers: Edward O'Grady, Jim Bolger, Andrew McNamara, Kevin Prendergast. My mother wrote the same letter to all of them, saying that I was seventeen and five stone dressed and that I wanted to be a jockey. Within a couple of days, Kevin Prendergast wrote back and said there was a job there for me at his yard near the Curragh and I could start whenever I wanted. I got the letter on a Friday. By the Sunday, I was in Kildare, ready to start a new life as an apprentice.

CHAPTER 3

Friarstown

If you drive out of Kildare, leaving the Silken Thomas pub behind you, and take a left down the road that leads across common land where sheep graze, you come to Kevin Prendergast's yard at Friarstown. It was the place where I spent the happiest years of my life. From being out on the edge of everything in Crusheen, I was at the heart of Irish racing now, living in a busy lively town next to the Curragh, enjoying the camaraderie of jockeys and drunk with the realisation that I might actually be good at something.

It was a hard school and Kevin was a hard man but it seemed like a majestic place to me when I arrived. The van that picked us up at our digs turned right off the main road and took us down an avenue of beech trees before it dropped us off outside the yard.

The horses' stables were arranged in front of you as you walked in, like three sides of a rectangle. Off to the left, there was a muck-heap. It was February and it was cold and I was two weeks shy of my eighteenth birthday and I knew I had no choice but to get stuck in straight away.

I couldn't ride when I arrived, but stables need staff apart from jockeys, too. I was a young kid used to working on a farm – I was perfect for what Kevin wanted. That's why he offered me a job. It was nothing to do with whether I had any potential as a jockey. Nobody had a clue how I'd turn out. Kevin thought he was getting someone who was going to muck his horses out. Even if it was just as a handyman to do the painting and fix the doors, I could be useful to him. He was probably short-staffed at the time, too. It was the winter, cold, wet and miserable, and hard to get people in.

I stayed in digs at first with a family called the McMahons. They were lovely people and I shared the digs with other apprentices: Jack Bedden, Jimmy Ryan and Chris Kelly. It was great. We'd get up in the morning, have some breakfast, go and get picked up in the van in Kildare and go to the yard.

My first day there, I got the muck sack and my fork and I was told to go and muck out three stables. I had been used to mucking out cattle with a two-pronged fork. Cow cabins with ten cows: imagine what they're like. So mucking out these stables at Friarstown with beautiful big straw beds and only one horse, that was easy to me. Most weeks, Monday was a bad day because there would always be a few no-shows after the weekend. That was always a problem for the head lad because then you have to get the other lads to do extra work and no one wants to do that.

At Friarstown, the head lad was a man called Tom Fitzgerald and after he'd given me my stables to muck out, he led the string of 30 or 40 horses up to the Curragh and they were gone for about an hour and a half. The Curragh was a couple of miles up the road, and the horses in training at Friarstown trotted up there every morning.

So I did my three stables and it took me twenty minutes. The feed man, John Fox, had stayed in the yard to organise all the feed when the horses were out so it would be ready for them when they got back. I told him I'd finished the three stables that Tom Fitzgerald gave me.

This Monday was no different from any other and so a few of the lads hadn't turned up. They must have had a heavy weekend. John Fox gave me the numbers of the three stables that each of the missing lads was supposed to do. So I mucked them out, too. Tom got back and John told him: 'The kid's after doing them, they're all done.'

Tom Fitzgerald was a strict man, always walking around whistling. Everything had to be perfect, not a straw out of place in the yard. He was one of the best head men I have been around. He always called you mister. That was always his greeting: 'Morning mister.'

When you do a box, you muck it out and the new straw is always banked around the edges like a horseshoe, with a thinner layer in the middle for the horse to roll in. You make it so that it has a nice, comfortable bed to lie on. The lazy lads or lasses in the yard only half muck them out. They hide some of the manure under the fresh bed over the top. Today, they have bins but in our day, we had muck sacks that you placed like a sheet on the ground then loaded them with straw and droppings before we pulled the four corners together, picked them up, carried them out to the muck heap and emptied them.

On Mondays, when the stable hadn't been cleaned out for a couple of days, you'd sometimes have muck running down the back of your neck and down your legs as you were carrying the sack to the heap. That didn't bother me, particularly. I'd come off a farm in County Clare. Like I said, this was easy. Tom did spot checks. He kicked the straw around to make sure it had been done properly. I couldn't believe how nice the straw was there. It felt quite luxurious. It was paradise compared to the broken three-pronged fork and the cow cabins in Crusheen.

That first morning, Tom said I could ride the stable's hack. He told me to learn to jig-jog up and down and he pointed up that tree-lined avenue that led to the main road. That was where I rode a horse with a saddle for the first time, up and down that avenue, 200 yards one way and 200 yards back.

It takes some kids a couple of days to learn to do it, to get the rhythm. But by the end of that first morning, I was able to do it perfectly. There were no back protectors then and I had to stuff my helmet with cotton wool because it was too big for me and it was falling down over my eyes. Soon, I was cantering around the field with the third lot of horses. The third lot were usually the ones which weren't much good or which were coming back off a lay-off and they just used to go round the field rather than trot up to the Curragh.

After the horses had come back, the routine was that you would brush the yard up and go home for lunch about 1pm. You'd come back for 4pm, do over your horse, sort his bed out, make sure he had a clean feed pot, check out any droppings, give him fresh water and then you would feed your horse, bolt your doors and be home for 6pm.

When I had been there for a little while, I started biking to work. I got in early and tacked my own horse up and then mucked out my three stables. I'd have my three stables done before all the other boys came in. That way, I could relax and enjoy my ride, enjoy getting on my horse, knowing that he had been groomed well.

In those days, we used to have to break the new horses when they first arrived at the yard. It was like a rodeo. We had to queue to get on them in the field. I went first, Eddie Leonard second and Steven Carroll third. Once you break them in and ride them off, they're grand. But the one who gets on them first, that's hairy.

The way I approached it, I lay across the horse's back so he could feel the weight. I knew he would turf me off sooner or later because there was no question that you'd get a chance to put your irons on. Once I got thrown off, Eddie would climb on and he got thrown off, too, because the horse wasn't tired yet. Maybe by the time Steven Carroll got on, the horse was tired and he might stay on. It was great fun. We loved it. But someone had to hold the lead rope to keep the horse from bolting off. Otherwise, he'd be off down the field at full tilt and you'd get killed. That didn't bother any of us. We'd be queuing up. We couldn't wait to get on one.

I loved the work at Friarstown. The only work I didn't like was being a labourer for a builder. That is what you call hard work. Trying to mix plaster and lift blocks all day long, every day. Racing? People would pay to do what we get paid for. I thought that then and I still think it now. Even today, when I'm in my fifties, riding out up Warren Hill in Newmarket, I turn around to the other boys in the string and tell them how lucky we are.

It was tough but I enjoyed it. There were never any worries. There was never any pressure. I enjoyed my riding. I was happy. I had money in my pocket. I was going out meeting girls, going to discos, riding winners: all the great things in life.

I liked it in Kildare. After I had been there a while, I moved into town and shared a flat above a butcher's with Charlie Swan, who had arrived a year after me and went on to be the champion National Hunt jockey of Ireland for nine consecutive seasons. Charlie struggled with his weight when he was a flat jockey but he was one of the most dedicated young fellas I was ever around. I asked him once what he had for lunch and he said: 'I made a pig of myself today. I had an apple and an orange.'

It could be a rough town, Kildare. There were a lot of jockeys and stable lads on one side and there were young soldier cadets from the army barracks on the other. They were in their uniforms and we weren't the biggest guys so it was easy to see who was who when the battle lines were drawn in the Silken Thomas and the other pubs around town.

I didn't drink in those days, but we organised all kinds of events at the Silken Thomas. We had pool tournaments and darts competitions. And then there were the scraps, of course. I loved having a good scrap on the weekends with the soldiers.

Kevin's apprentices always stuck together. We always looked after each other. Anybody who tried to pick on the younger lads in the yard, they knew about it. There was one stable lad who was a bit of a bully. He was a big strong fella and he could handle himself pretty well. He and the bigger, older boys singled out the younger lads or the apprentices and made them do the silly jobs or the dirty jobs, the jobs they wouldn't want to do. They chucked them in the muck pen, or stripped them and put them in the wash house and hosed them down or hung them on the horse walker by their belt.

Kevin had ten apprentices and we were handy little lads and we were good scrappers and because we all stuck together, the bully of the yard tried to disrupt our little army. He came into one of the boxes one day and grabbed me by the throat and stuck me up to the wall. He wanted to make an example of me and scare the rest of the lads.

So that evening, we got our horses fed and we went outside and stood by the van where it was waiting at the end of the avenue of trees. We waited for the bully of the yard to come out. He was one of the last out of the gates and as soon as he came out, we just laid into him. All of us. That was the last time he touched anybody. It was a message. It worked.

We looked after each other. If we went uptown, we always made sure there were two or three of us together, especially if we were drinking in the same pub as some of the young cadets and it was obvious there was going to be some sort of trouble.

The stable lads were great if there was a fight. That was when the camaraderie of the yard kicked in. Robbie Gallagher was Kevin's travelling head lad. He wasn't very big but he was tough. They always backed us up if something broke out with the soldiers. There were a few useful scrappers among the soldiers, too. But when you box, you don't see boxers going out wanting to fight and it was the same with soldiers. Their career was going to be about fighting, or the threat of fighting, so once they have done their training, they're not so interested in fighting with civilians. But Kildare was full of cadets and they were young lads who still wanted to prove themselves in front of their mates.

It was the same for us in a way. You had to stand up for yourself, both in the yard and out of it. Tom Fitzgerald said to me soon after I arrived that I would not succeed as a jockey if I didn't back myself. 'It's a rat race,' Tom said, 'and the biggest fucking rat wins.'

I was confronted with that reality quite often. When I first started at Kevin's, I had a little run-in with Gabriel Curran, who was the stable jockey. Everybody called him Squibs, for some reason. I quickly got a little bit of a reputation for being cocky and I think I might have said something smart to Squibs.

Squibs was friendly with the feed man and one day, the feed guy came into the box to give me a clip and teach me a lesson. I gave him a clattering and sent him flying across the place into the straw. Squibs was a lovely guy but when young apprentices are coming through and you are the jockey, it's difficult. It's normal that you feel threatened and that you want to try and protect yourself and remind the kids who's the top man. It's different now. You try and help the kids today but back in those days, it was dog eat dog. You had to grow up quickly when you were an apprentice.

I didn't get homesick, really. I enjoyed it too much for that. But we had every second weekend off and I would get the train down to Limerick and then thumb a lift from Limerick to Ennis. I liked pretending I was a proper jockey already on those visits home, the bag on my back with a whip sticking out of it so everybody knew what I was.

On the way back to Kildare at the end of the weekend, I had a routine. I liked to get the 8pm train from Limerick, which got into Kildare at 10pm. That meant I was back quite early on Sunday evening. I could get a decent night's sleep before the early start on Monday morning.

One of those journeys back to Kildare was particularly memorable. It was 21 August 1983 and my father was driving me back to Limerick in his Morris Minor. We left in plenty of time but when we were about halfway there, the engine cut out and my dad spent an age peering underneath the bonnet and fiddling about. I was getting panicky. I was a creature of habit and I was totally dedicated to the job. There was a later train that left at 10pm, but it didn't get in until midnight and that was too late. I wanted to go to bed. I didn't drink. I was a little bit sensible then. And I wanted to make sure I was ready to go for the first day back at work.

I didn't say anything about the delay making me late because I knew my father would get angry. He got the car started again after about fifteen minutes. We resumed the journey and when we finally pulled into Limerick station, I jumped out of the car, grabbed my bag and ran onto the platform. The train was pulling out. I saw the back of it disappearing into the night.

I wanted to yell and curse but I couldn't because my dad was there. My father went straight into the pub to have his pint while we waited the two hours for the next Limerick–Dublin train to come. So I got the next train and we got to a place called Portarlington, which is about fifteen miles out of Kildare, and we weren't allowed to go any further. It was clear there was some sort of major problem ahead because we were told to get off the train and get onto buses that took passengers on to Kildare and Dublin.

The main road runs parallel to the train track and as I was sitting on the bus, I could see helicopters hovering overhead and spotlights illuminating the ground below. There were ambulances with their sirens blaring. It was obvious something bad had happened but no one had any idea what it was. Eventually, I got back to my digs in Kildare and my landlady, Kathleen McCormack, was crying. When I walked in the door, she looked up at me as if I were a ghost. She'd convinced herself I'd been killed.

The train that I was supposed to have caught in Limerick, the train that I always caught on my way back home, the train I had seen pulling out of the station as I ran onto the platform, had been involved in a big accident. It had run into the back of another train at high speed near a place called Cherryville, just outside Kildare, and seven people had been killed. It was all over the news and it is still one of the best-known train crashes in Ireland's history. The whole thing sent a shiver through me, partly out of sadness for the people who had been killed and injured, and partly because of the random nature of the way I'd escaped it.

Why did that Morris Minor of my father's stop? Why did it stop for no reason? It had never stopped before. It had never broken down before but this time it had. I don't know if I believe in fate, but I always wonder whether that Morris Minor saved my life.

CHAPTER 4

Green as Grass

I knew pretty early on in my time with Kevin Prendergast that I could be a decent jockey. Within a week of being at the yard, I was riding out at the Curragh with everybody. There were some strong horses, some strong pullers and, after a fortnight, I could ride anything in the yard. I only weighed five stone but I wanted to ride stronger and stronger horses. I soon realised I had the ability to switch horses off. By that, I mean I could calm them when they were highly strung or if they were upset and unruly. The ones that other people couldn't hold, I could get them to go to sleep.

I knew then I had something. I had an affinity with horses. I still do today. I still love going up to the horses and talking to them and having a laugh with them. They are all different. They all have their own character. You have got your little two-year-old fillies who aren't sure what's going on around them, you've got the smart ones, you've got the sour ones that have been mistreated and want to kick you, and the big randy colts who want to eat you. There are others who don't know how to take you and if they can, they'll try and bite you if they think they can get away with it. They are all so clever. They are wonderful animals.

When I was in Dubai recently, there was a lovely filly there called Promising Run, one of those trained by Saeed bin Suroor. I used to give her sugar in the mornings. As soon as she heard me whistling as I walked in first thing, she'd be right at the door. I'd go looking for her and she'd come running to me.

I love the character of horses. I love the way they smell and the way they look at you. They're often suspicious to begin with and you have to earn their trust, but when they get to know you, they're amazing. There are some people in racing who are only there to get a wage and don't care about the horses. Maybe they're having a bad day or they've had a heavy weekend, but you do see the odd one mistreating a horse when they're out with the string, say, if the trainer isn't there.

You get people who jab them and rip their mouths. It makes me fume. And you don't make a tired horse go faster by hitting it. That's a lesson you learn. If you don't learn it, there's something wrong with you.

It took a long time to get my career going in Ireland. You serve an apprenticeship of three to five years and you have to get your head down and respect the governor and you have to work and if you don't, you shouldn't be doing it. If you don't, you probably won't make it anyway. Racing's a tough sport and only a very few make it. There are so many people out there that are as good, if not better, than you.

I arrived at Kevin's in February 1983 and it was a year before I rode my first race in public. I had started riding out more and more on the gallops and my first proper ride was in an apprentice race at the Curragh. That's all I remember. I don't know why but I've blanked it out. It's a blur. I can't remember the name of the horse or where it finished.

Then there was a horse called Prom that I rode at Roscommon, over in the west of Ireland. I didn't like Roscommon. It was a horrible track. There were only four runners, and the other jockeys in the race were Mick Kinane, Pat Shanahan and Mark Lynch. Kevin Prendergast told me to sit last, get him switched off because he was a bit keen and wait until I turned for home before letting him go. He was confident that I would win and I think he had a decent wager on it.

So we jumped off and I was sitting behind Mark Lynch and the other two were getting away. I don't know what Mark was doing. Maybe his horse wasn't right but we were losing touch. I was green as grass and I was a long way behind. I didn't know it but I had left it too late to make my run. In the end, I thought the front two were getting away, so I decided I had to go early and I was flying and flying and catching them up.

I finished second by a head or a neck. I should have won easily. Kevin always had the binoculars on the arm and he had a big, mad walk. He came up to the horse in the unsaddling enclosure and stared up at me with a look of disgust. 'Get down,' he said.

That was one of the worst moments in my career. I can still feel the horror of it now. I can still feel the shame and the embarrassment of having made such a mess of a race and making myself look stupid. I put my head down and walked back in.

It was 18 June 1984 before I rode my first winner. That

was on a horse called Piccadilly Lord at Navan in a mile-and-a-quarter race. He was a little chestnut colt and he was very nervous. I settled him down and rode him along at the back of the race and then let him go. I enjoyed that. It felt like a big step forward, but one thing that has run like a seam through my career is that I find it hard to appreciate success. It's easier to remember the ones that got away. It's always been like that with me, anyway. There were plenty of those in the early days.

My career was a slow burn. Nothing came easy in those days when I was starting out in Ireland. It was a bit different for Charlie Swan, as he had been brought up around the racing yard run by his father, Donald, who was a former captain in the Queen's Dragoon Guards. And although he was sent away to school in Dublin, he had been riding ponies ever since he was four years old.

Charlie, who was a good friend of mine, was a much more experienced rider than I was and had moved ahead of me in the pecking order. Squibs Curran was a friend of his family's, and he didn't have to rely on Kevin for rides, either. He'd get quite a few off his father and he was riding winners for a lot of different trainers.

Kevin liked him, too. I'd won on Piccadilly Lord but the next time out, Kevin gave the ride to Charlie in the Naas November Handicap the same year and he won on it. I was genuinely pleased for him, but it underlined to me that I wasn't quite getting the same opportunities as Charlie. I began to think I needed to move on.

Despite what I said about Roscommon, I liked all the tracks in Ireland in those early days. If I look back now, I wouldn't go round half of them. Tramore was one. Nobody wanted to ride at Tramore and I rode a treble there one day. I was leading jockey for the meeting. I'd have ridden anywhere. If there was a meeting where they were riding horses bareback around fields, I would have done it. It was wild back then. Sometimes, to get to the races, I'd have to jump in the horsebox with the horses and travel that way. I'd come home with them, too.

I got into double figures for winners for the first time in 1986. I got ten that season, which earned me seventh place in the apprentices' table. The following year, I was runner-up to Kevin Manning, who was champion apprentice.

I was very close to winning the title that year. Christy Roche left Jim Bolger's as stable jockey with about three months of the season to go and Kevin, who was Jim's apprentice, suddenly started getting all the best rides. I'm not saying I would have beaten him but we were nip and tuck.

Squibs had been Kevin Prendergast's stable jockey for years, but he was getting on now and I was hoping I might get a chance of taking over from him. I knew Kevin was looking to get a younger jockey in and I thought I ought to be well placed.

Towards the end of that season, there was a competition staged over a few races and there was a prize of a car for the trainer and the jockey who won the most points over those stipulated races. The final race was at Leopardstown and by that stage, both David Parnell and Mick Kinane had 22 points. David asked Squibs if he could get on his ride for the race because it was a decent horse. So Squibs sat out the race and Dave Parnell won the race and the car. And the next year, he got Squibs' job, too. David was in as first jockey but Squibs was still around and it wasn't difficult to see that I would be struggling to get decent rides.

I asked Tom Fitzgerald if he thought I was going to be wasting my time. 'Second jockey is semi-retired jockey,' he said. That hardened my resolve to move on and even though I felt sick about the idea of leaving Ireland, I began to think about following the path of so many other Irish jockeys who had headed over to England.

I got lucky when a journalist and commentator called Dessie Scahill, who stayed a couple of doors down from me and Charlie Swan in Kildare, recommended me to the trainer Jimmy FitzGerald, who had a great yard at Malton in North Yorkshire. It was probably the top yard in the north then, although it would soon slip into decline. Jimmy offered me the chance to be an apprentice with him and I accepted. I went home to tell my mother and father that I was going to live in England and I was in Malton a couple of days later.

It was the end of the flat racing season by then and I'd been offered the chance to ride work out in Australia for a few months with another jockey, John Egan. I had a good time out in Sydney. I rode work for different trainers, rode a winner at Wollongong and generally did a lot of partying.

I also had another narrow escape to match my brush with the train crash which became known as the Cherryville Disaster. The jockey John Egan's brother, Liam, came out to Australia for a holiday and he and I were swimming off Coogee Beach. I was on a boogie board and we drifted down towards where the red flags were. You're not supposed to stray down there but I hadn't noticed that we were drifting until it was too late.

A dozen big waves came crashing down on us and we were getting further and further out. One of the breakers ripped the boogie board strap out of my hands and Liam's as well and both boards were carried away to the shore. Liam was a good swimmer. I wasn't. He kept getting twenty yards ahead of me and then another big wave would push him right back. He was leaving me, which was fair enough. It was better that one of us got back to dry land than neither of us. We drifted for what felt like a lifetime. We kept getting hit by waves and pushed down to the bottom. It was getting harder to catch my breath. I thought we were gone. Well, I thought I was gone anyway.

And you know what, I've never before or since felt such peace. Later in my life, when I was at my lowest ebb during my struggles with the racing establishment, I remembered that peace and thought drowning might be a good way out of it all. I didn't feel as if I were gasping or choking or dying or anything that day off Coogee Beach. I don't know what it was. But I had no energy left. I just started to accept it. I felt I was gone.

Just when I had told myself that this was it and that I needed to let go, an off-duty lifeguard saw us in trouble. He paddled over on his surfboard and hauled us both on to it.

He got us back to the beach and as I was lying there on the sand, he said: 'You're not supposed to be down there, you know.' That was it. When I looked up, he had disappeared. I never saw him again. He saved my life. Even during the worst of times, I have never stopped believing that I have always been lucky.

CHAPTER 5

Kind of Wild

If Kevin Prendergast was a hard man, Jimmy FitzGerald was harder. Put it this way, I started drinking when I started working with Jimmy FitzGerald. As much as I loved him, I was still afraid of him. When he started screaming and roaring at a person, it was something to behold. He wasn't a fierce man physically but his tongue was vicious. When he started going at you, it was the way he reeled stuff off. I saw him get two conditionals up against a wall once because they were five minutes late coming back into the yard in the evening. His bollockings were legendary.

He was like a barrister giving a performance, and I've seen a few of those in my time. Or a good actor. He had all his lines memorised and his voice would get louder and louder and louder until his face turned blue and then all shades of purple. I never saw him hit anybody but, my God, when you saw him building himself up, you'd think he was going to kill them.

When I arrived at his yard at Norton Grange in the

spring of 1988 to start work as his stable jockey, I had been in Australia for a couple of months, partying and having fun, and I was out of shape. I was big, basically, and I was hoping that I would get away with it by going on a diet straight away.

Jimmy was an Irishman who was born in the Tipperary village of Horse and Jockey and he was better known as a National Hunt trainer than a flat trainer. He had won the 1985 Cheltenham Gold Cup with Forgive'N Forget and so there were jumpers as well as flat horses in the yard. There were a couple of weeks of the National Hunt season left when I got to Malton so when we went up to the gallops on my first day, I was with the flat horses at the back of the string. The gallops were called Ponte A and Ponte B because they had the same contours as the track at Pontefract.

We rode up the gallops, jumped off at the top and then led the horses back down the hill, halfway home. Then we jumped back on them again. So that day, I was leading my horse down the hill and I saw Jimmy drive up in his Subaru. Every horse that went past him, he'd ask the lad how the horse went, then drop back to the next lad and ask him the same question.

Eventually, he dropped back to me. 'Who are you?' he said. He hadn't seen me before, but I think he must have known who I was. He was toying with me. Jimmy was funny and witty and he was angry and he was mad and he was everything. He was a great man.

Anyway, he was looking at me. He had loads of conditionals, or apprentice jump jockeys, in the string and he was looking at me in this quizzical kind of way. So he saw me after I've been having a great time in Australia and I was as heavy as I ever was in my life. I was 9st 6lb, compared to the five stone I was when I arrived in Kildare.

I was big and I must have looked big. After I told him who I was, he looked me up and down. 'It's not a fucking jump jockey I want,' he said. 'It's a flat jockey. I don't want a conditional. I've got enough of them. It was a flat jockey I wanted. What weight are you?' I told him I was 8st 12lb but I said I was on a diet. I was stuttering away. He muttered something else and moved on to the next lad.

Inside the gates of Norton Grange, Jimmy was a nightmare. You couldn't please him. Everything you did was wrong. Mark Dwyer was a brilliant jumps rider for him and there was one day where he rode three winners at Wetherby and his last ride fell. As he was walking to the ring the next day, Jimmy saw him. 'What the fuck happened with that thing in the last?' he said. There was no thought of congratulating Mark on his treble. 'My mother would have stayed on that,' Jimmy said. That was what he was like.

It was a good town to live in, Malton. There were a lot of yards and a lot of jockeys and apprentices and stable lads. So it could be lively, too. In many ways, it was the epicentre of the northern racing circuit, close to Beverley and Catterick, York, Doncaster, Thirsk, Pontefract, Newcastle and Redcar.

People say it's tougher than riding down south, but I don't think so. It was more fun. And there was less travelling to do. Down south, you would spend five or six hours in the car with all the meetings.

If you are down south, maybe it's best to be in the Lambourn area because you have got Newbury, Bath, Salisbury, Windsor, Kempton, Sandown, Ascot and Epsom all within reach. But if you're in Newmarket, you are struggling. Yarmouth is closest, but that was the only flat track in that part of the country, other than Great Leighs, which became Chelmsford City in 2015. The nearest southern track in terms of driving time is Lingfield, and you need to give yourself a couple of hours each way to get there.

I didn't have it easy when I came over from Ireland. I moved to Yorkshire and there was a sense straight away that I was treading on other people's toes. Mark Birch, George Duffield, Lindsay Charnock and Nicky Carlisle were all good lads but it was their territory and they owned it.

George was one of the tough ones, too. You wouldn't cross George. I remember him picking Jimmy Quinn up by the neck when he felt he had done something wrong during a race and sitting him on the table. You have to have that sort of discipline. It's like your kids giving you cheek or thinking they can get one over on you, and if you don't put a stop to it or make them realise it's not the thing to do, they will keep on doing it and then someone will end up getting hurt.

One race at Redcar, early on in my career on the northern circuit, I was skipping up the inside and I felt I was going that well that I could go anywhere. Lindsay was two or three off the rail and rather than go round him, I tried to be clever and went up his inside and he pulled the stick through and hit me right across the face.

I won the race but I came in and I was covered in blood. He thought I was being clever, I suppose. He may not have known it was me and he said he didn't mean it but I knew he meant it and all I wanted to do was choke him. Even though I was new, the other boys knew well enough to keep us apart.

I calmed down eventually and Lindsay and I were the best of friends for many years after that, until he died at the age of sixty in the summer of 2015.

It was tough for me to break into the club in those days. Even if the other boys like you, you are stealing their bread. In their situation, you have to try to defend your position as best you can. As a newcomer, you just have to get your head down and work hard.

Jimmy FitzGerald had a house at the back of the yard and I had a room in there. I didn't have a car or anything. I was twenty-three and I could still get half fare on the train. It took a long time for people to treat me as a mature rider. It wasn't that I couldn't ride. I could. I was getting better and better, and I knew I was at one with the horse, but it was just getting the chance. I didn't really look the part.

I was kind of wild as well. I wasn't one of these A students. As dedicated as I was and as hard as I worked, I played hard as well. I wasn't a big drinker yet, but I would go out and have fun. And it was when I arrived at Jimmy's that I first started coming to the attention of the racing authorities.

When I came over from Ireland, the Ireland-England thing was lively. I was getting suspended all the time and the same stewards were doing it. I was getting suspended a lot for over-use of the whip. Part of that was immaturity and part of it was the culture in Ireland that I had come from. The older I got, the more I disliked using the whip on a horse. Partly that was pragmatic, because I was sick of getting bans, and partly because I became aware that sometimes it wasn't an awful lot of use.

Because I love and respect horses, the longer my career went on, the more it angered me when I saw jockeys using the whip when they didn't need to. But when I was with Jimmy FitzGerald a lot of the other jockeys were doing it and in those days it maddened me that they were getting away with it when I wasn't.

A few years later, I used my whip on another jockey. Lindsay had done it to me. It wasn't that uncommon. It happened at Thirsk when this kid called Keith Rutter almost had me over the rail. He was coming in and I was on the rails. If your horse is keen and you can't get back and someone else is coming over on top of you, he'll put you over the rails.

I was screaming at him to be careful, but Keith gave me the deaf ear so I picked my whip up and hit him across the back as hard as I could. And it was on camera. I got suspended for that. When the kid came in, he said: 'Sorry, Kieren, I didn't see you,' and maybe he didn't. He was one of those guys who didn't have much peripheral vision. He was a lovely guy, though, Keith, and I was good friends with him after.

A lot goes on in the weighing room, a lot of banter and there was only one jockey that I had a problem with. The stewards saw it differently, though. They saw a little Irish bully who needed sorting out.

Most of the stewards are good people; they enjoy the day's racing, with a nice lunch and maybe a drop of brandy or whatever thrown in. People like David Brotherton, a clever man, very knowledgeable. If he was sitting there in a stewards' inquiry, I knew I'd get a fair hearing. But if it was Patrick Hibbert-Foy, a stipendiary steward and a former captain in the Royal Lancers, I knew what was coming then: 'Fallon, bully, three days', and my heart sank every time I saw that he was officiating.

I'd start to worry in case I was riding any difficult horses, any that might hang or veer across the course, because then if they suspended you they would say that you 'allowed your horse to drift'. I used to see red when they said that. If that happened, it just meant I hadn't been strong enough to hold him and the horse had won the trial of strength. In a case like that, I may have caused interference but it would be totally accidental. There's nothing I can do about it. So when they said I'd 'allowed my horse to drift', all I wanted to do was get the table and heave it over the top of them.

Most of the times I got done, Mr Hibbert-Foy was involved. I didn't have a problem with authority as such. It was just the British Horseracing Authority, or the Jockey Club, as it was then. I wouldn't go in there and start kicking the tables, even if I wanted to. I would be very polite. But when it goes against you all the time, you start to get fed up.

I like a simple life but I do have a short temper. I like to try and fix things before they are broken. If I see a fight, I try to stop it. When I lived in Kildare, I saw this guy battering a girl outside the chip shop in the main street and I jumped in to stop it and he attacked me, so I ended up battering him. While I was doing that, his girlfriend came up behind me and split me across the back of the head with a motorcycle helmet. But I don't go looking for trouble. The perception might be different now, but the truth is that I always got on great with the other jockeys.

By the time I arrived in Malton, Jimmy's yard wasn't as strong as it once had been but I still got a lot more chances than I would have done if I'd stayed with Kevin Prendergast. When it came to the biggest races, Jimmy only ever used the best jockeys with his flat horses and that generally meant Steve Cauthen and Pat Eddery. I was still an apprentice so I had to fight for my rides.

I didn't ride a winner in my first eight races for Jimmy, but then I got on a horse called Evichstar at Thirsk for the Thirsk Hall EBF Stakes over six furlongs in mid-April 1988. There was a prize fund of £9000 and a decent field. Evichstar was not an easy horse, temperamental and keen, but I had ridden him a lot on the gallops and I knew him. Jimmy was a great gambling trainer and the horse had been backed down from 14/1 to 11/2. He won by a length and a half and I had my first winner in England.

There was a slightly less glorious postscript to that win. Two weeks later, I was on Evichstar in a race at Haydock when he started sweating up in the parade ring. On the way down to the start, he bolted and flung me over the rails. I had a nasty gash on my face. It wasn't my proudest moment.

I started riding a few winners, though. I won on Saladan Knight in the Houghton Stakes at Beverley and I picked up some rides from other stables, too, which is always a nice boost for the confidence because it means other trainers and owners can see something in you. In August that year, I rode my first double and I finished that season with 31 winners, which was a decent tally.

In 1989, I had one of my biggest fallings-out with Jimmy. I'd ridden a horse called Sapience, which was one of his, for his last outing of the previous season at Ayr and then again at Beverley in June, when he finished second in a field of six. But Jimmy had high hopes for him to run in the Ebor at York, one of the most prestigious of the flat races in the north, and had been building him up for that for almost two years. Jimmy and his associates had backed the horse down from 40/1 to 7/2.

It was going to be a big ride for me. I was struggling to make headway since I moved to England and a win in the Ebor was just what I needed. It was a televised race at a major meeting and it would have put me on the map. But I think the horse's owner, the Marquesa de Moratalla, had missed the price on Sapience and when Pat Eddery became available to ride him, she didn't want to miss the chance of getting the best jockey as well.

Pat Eddery vs Kieren Fallon at that time was no contest, so Jimmy FitzGerald jocked me off the horse and Pat got the ride. They did a deal with me so that I got my percentage if they won, but I didn't care about the money. All I wanted to do was ride because winning the Ebor would have kick-started my career. I was treading water and it was just what I needed.

I was at York that day, too. I had two rides and then I watched on the television as Sapience won the Ebor with Pat Eddery on his back. He won by a length or so, and every stride he took with Pat sitting on his back in the Marquesa's red colours, I knew he was going to win. I drove home in a grim mood. It felt like a crushing blow. It seemed as if my progress was stalling. That was a very low point for me.

I told myself that I just didn't have what it takes. Even though I loved horses and I loved riding and I thought I could ride anything, it just wasn't happening for me. I had been five years an apprentice and I wasn't setting the world alight. I was seeing other jockeys coming along and progressing much faster. Not getting on Sapience felt like the final nail in my coffin.

I had always admired Sir Michael Stoute and Walter Swinburn as a trainer-jockey combination and I decided that what I ought to do was abandon my ideas of becoming a top jockey and try to secure a job with Sir Michael, riding work in Newmarket.

My plan was to leave it until the end of the week after the Ebor and then ring Sir Michael and ask him if he was looking for any work riders. In the meantime, I'd ride for Jimmy and say nothing. I had a ride on the Thursday and it wasn't very good but it won. I won a race on the Friday, too.

My mood started to improve. Winning races does that for you. And so, instead of phoning Sir Michael at the end of that week, I thought I'd leave it one more week. The following week, I won a few more and my confidence started building. And so another week passed and then another week and I never made the call.

One of the races that turned things around to my mind was at Carlisle. I was in the weighing room when a trainer came in, looking for someone to ride his horse in the first. John Reid had the ride, but it was a difficult horse and he didn't want anything to do with it. If a horse is a bad ride, and you are a jockey of John's calibre, you look at some of the reports in the *Racing Post* and if you see comments like 'unruly going to post' or 'too free to post' or 'unruly in the gate', all the clues you need to see how the horse will behave are there. Maybe your agent hadn't seen it when he was booking the rides and you only realise what you've got yourself into when you're reading the paper and then it's too late and you think you're done for.

Jockeys talk to each other about horses and you either warn someone off or you reassure them. Sometimes, I'd ring another jockey who knew the horse and ask him what my ride was like and he might say 'it's not too bad', or he might say 'stay the hell away from it'.

So this horse's trainer came up to me at Carlisle because John Reid had cried off and now he needed a new jockey and he asked me if I'd ride the horse. I looked up and I could see Dandy Nicholls and a few other jockeys standing behind this trainer and drawing their fingers across their throats to try and warn me to steer clear. I scrabbled around for an excuse and said I couldn't do the weight. He just told me to put up overweight if I had to. So I got on the scale and it was fine. I got that sinking feeling. As I was going out of the weighing room, one of the other boys said: 'Be careful, it's a fucking runaway, it's mad.'

I thought I'd take him down to the start early. If you canter down with the string on horses that are really keen, they can run away with you. You can't hold them. If you take them out and walk them down, you have a bit of control. I trotted all the way around and the horse had his head over the rail and when I trotted by, I saw John Reid leaning back in a seat in the stand and he was waving at me. He had other rides later but he obviously wanted to watch me and give himself a good laugh.

Well, I popped him out of the gate and he won by two or three lengths. The horse's owner, Charlie McKenzie, gave me a roll of big old Scottish notes and I waved them at John Reid and he said 'you little bastard'. I became very friendly with Charlie after that. Every time I went up to Scotland he'd come to the races. He'd always give me a couple of hundred quid for my children. 'Give that to the kids,' he'd say.

I loved my time with Jimmy FitzGerald. We had our ups

and downs and we had some fine rows but he was a father-figure to me, someone who was always there when I needed him. When he died in 2004 at the age of sixty-nine, I felt racing would never be the same again. Everybody looked up to him. Not just around Malton, but all around England's racing scene. Everybody wanted to talk to him, partly because he had a wicked sense of humour and he made everyone laugh. He still watched out for every race I rode in. Without him, I wouldn't have lasted as long as I did in the game. When I went off the rails, he was always there for support.

I'm not glamorising what it was like at Norton Grange. It was hard work at his yard. There were no airs and graces. After we'd been riding, we'd go back to the yard for evening duties. He'd get me to school for him, too. He had this great chaser called McClure but in his first couple of runs in schooling, he would always fall. So Jimmy always put me on him to jump the four fences on the gallops. His theory was that I was light and that the horse wouldn't fall because he had a light weight on his back. Jimmy was using me as a guinea pig.

He had 30 flat horses but the main yard was for his jumpers and so a lot of the time, he let me run the flat yard and break the two-year-olds in. He would pop down in the evening and have a look at them and drive down to the field when I was doing figures of eight to help make them supple and teach them to turn in either direction. He trusted me to get them ready for the flat and when the season began, I would have all my ducks in a row for him.

He was always sparing with praise, though. I won a race on a young horse at Hamilton some time in 1991. There were two horses in front of me and I went to kick him in between them to teach him a bit about racing and what you need to do. He was halfway into the gap and he flinched a bit, so I hit him a couple of times and he went through and won.

Tim FitzGerald, Jimmy's son, had come to the meeting with me and he was delighted. Jimmy hadn't made the journey, so we went back to the house afterwards to go through the rides with him and I walked in that evening thinking I was great. Jimmy was in the sitting room with a little glass of whisky in his hand and some water on the side. Tim was afraid for his life with his dad, so he pushed me in front of Jimmy and I stood there with my chest puffed out, feeling very proud of myself.

'Evening, governor,' I said.

'Don't give me fucking evening governor,' Jimmy said. 'That fucking horse, I want that horse when he's fucking ten and you're after beating him up.'

He never moved off his chair while he was shouting at me and I shuffled away, muttering apologies. The thing was, I knew he was right. The horse was only a baby and I shouldn't have hit him. That's how you learn. That's the kind of man Jimmy was.

I got very close to him. I went racing with him all the time. That didn't stop him making sure he got a good deal out of me when he got the chance. I bought his wife's car once. The book value was £3100. I offered £2800 and I ended up paying £3500. He could sell sand to the Arabs.

He was very important to my career. I started doing well and riding winners in England and it's easy to start getting carried away with yourself. When you do, it is usually a disaster. Jimmy didn't let you get carried away. That's why he treated Mark Dwyer the way he did when he rode that treble.

That always stayed with me, even to the last day I was riding. Riding winners was great but I never got carried away. It was on to the next one, on to the next one. That was down to Jimmy. If you never met him, I wish you could have. I miss him even now.

CHAPTER 6

Jack, Lynda and Dallas Toddywalla

The fortunes of Jimmy FitzGerald began to dip in the early 1990s. There was a virus in the yard and some of his most important owners withdrew their horses from the stables. Jimmy went from having around 200 jumpers and 60 flat horses to almost nothing. It was harder and harder for me to get decent rides and even though I still rode for him a lot, I went freelance some time in 1991. It was an arrangement that suited us both.

Towards the end of the next year, Jack and Lynda Ramsden approached me to see if I would like to become the retained jockey at their yard at Sandhutton, which was about thirty miles to the west of Malton, on the outskirts of Thirsk. I was sorry to cut my ties with Jimmy, but we parted on very good terms and I knew that working with Jack and Lynda was an opportunity that was too good to miss.

They were a great team. Jack was a former stockbroker

who had become a professional gambler and I didn't see that much of him in the yard. He organised the buying and selling of their horses and decided where they ran and he generally stayed in his office, where he had several television sets showing racing from tracks around the world. He studied form and he was a great man for speed figures. Jack once said that to Lynda, a horse was a creature that ate, slept and breathed and lived in its box but to him it was a pedigree and a handicap rating that had to be placed.

He was very keen that his jockey should be a good judge of pace, so that he could gauge exactly how to execute the tactics during a race and not burn his horse's energy too fast or, if the pace was slow, leave it too late to get the maximum out of a ride. Later in my time at Sandhutton, he sent me to America to perfect my work with the clock.

If Jack was a man of figures, Lynda was the trainer. She was a brilliant trainer, too. She had started out a decade earlier with a few horses on the Isle of Man and she would send them over by ferry to compete in England and Scotland. After a little while, she and Jack moved over to Yorkshire so they could compete seriously. I quickly developed a great respect for her. She had 42 horses when I arrived and they were good horses. They were a step up from the quality of rides I had been getting at Jimmy's and I enjoyed working for her and Jack right from the start.

Lynda had the knack that good trainers have of getting a horse to reach a peak of fitness just at the right time for a big race. Her horses were always the best turned out in the paddock and she loved watching us all ride out in the morning. She would come out on her pony with her two Jack Russell terriers trotting along beside her.

Many people thought they were exactly what racing needed and that they brought a different, brainier approach to the sport but the authorities regarded them with barely disguised suspicion and often downright hostility. They were particularly wary of Jack because he was a successful gambler. The Jockey Club seemed to think that there was a betting coup around every corner. Every time a horse's odds shortened and it won, they thought Jack had had a gamble. Every time one of their horses was favourite and it lost, they thought it wasn't off, meaning that they thought it hadn't been ridden to its full capabilities.

One piece in the *Racing Post* around that time began like this: 'Perceived wisdom in the North suggests that when the Ramsden stable sneeze, a fair proportion of the betting ring catches a cold.' It was ridiculous. Lynda often said she wished she and Jack had been as clever as the Jockey Club and the rest of racing thought they were.

Jack was pally with a bookmaker called Colin Webster and the Jockey Club got it into their heads that he was gambling massive sums. They often asked Lynda in for explanations as to how a horse ran. Some of the inquiries were absolutely ludicrous. She was cleared time and time and time again, even though it felt as though a lot of the horseracing journalists, who were friendly with many of the establishment figures, would have liked to have seen a different result. They distrusted Jack and Lynda because they viewed them as outsiders who posed a threat to their cosy little world.

I know that some people believe that my own problems with the Jockey Club and, later, the BHA began because I rode for Jack and Lynda. The authorities seemed at times almost to be running a campaign against them, and because

I was now associated with them and because we had such a successful partnership, those misgivings were automatically extended to include me as well.

I had been riding in India in the winter of 1992-93, just as I had for several years previously. I arrived at Sandhutton in late February and my time with Jack and Lynda got off to the best possible start when I rode High Premium in the Lincoln Handicap at Doncaster at the end of March. The Lincoln was one of my first races for Jack and Lynda and it was seen as a great triumph for the yard. 'Jackpot Time', a headline in the *Racing Post* said after the race, the article noting that High Premium had been backed from 25/1 to 16/1 by his 'connections' on the day.

I had High Premium up with the lead in the early stages of the race and we hit the front with about three furlongs to go. There was a late challenge from the top weight, Mizaaya, ridden by Walter Swinburn, but we held it off and hung on to win by half a length. It was the best win of my career up to that point.

It was a big win for Jack and Lynda, too, especially as Lynda had brought High Premium back to full health after a series of setbacks. 'For Ramsden,' Paul Hayward wrote about the win in the *Independent*, 'this was sterling vindication of her decision not to surrender to economic logic two seasons ago.

'At that time, she and her husband, Jack, announced that they were to abandon racehorse training and put their cash to better use. Two years later, after revitalising a horse bedevilled with viral illnesses and a poison foot, Lynda Ramsden is the first woman trainer to have won the Lincoln, just as Alex Greaves made a breakthrough for women riders in this race on Amenable in 1991.'

Things continued in the same successful vein for most of the time I rode for them. We had a great relationship. I was reminiscing with them about it recently and they said they could not remember us ever having a row or a difference of opinion about instructions for a horse or the way I had ridden it. They said I never rode a bad race for them. It was a very happy partnership.

A few weeks after the win on High Premium, for instance, I rode a 54/1 double for Jack and Lynda at Catterick and in August, in my first ride at Sandown, I partnered Jack and Lynda's horse, Island Magic, to my first Group success in the Solario Stakes. It was my first big win in the south, too, and much was made of how I had beaten Frankie Dettori and Walter Swinburn in the three-horse race.

We had the odd small mishap, of course. Even on the northern circuit, there were occasional travel issues and one afternoon in May 1994, I missed riding a winner for Jack and Lynda at Ripon when the light plane I caught from an earlier meeting at Hamilton was late landing at Bagby Airfield, just south of Thirsk. I'd left Hamilton, where I'd been riding another of Jack and Lynda's horses, in plenty of time but the pilot said he had a trainee next to him at the controls and he wanted to give him some decent experience. It meant that the journey took half an hour longer than it should have done.

We had a mad dash of a drive from the airfield to Ripon and I missed the jockey declaration deadline by a minute. It didn't put me in a great mood, especially when Willie Ryan, my replacement, cantered home on the horse, Arctic Diamond.

There were other issues, too. It was while I was with Jack

and Lynda that I was banned for pulling Stuart Webster off his horse at Beverley in September 1994, and there was also the controversy over Top Cees, the horse I rode to victory at the Chester Cup in May 1995, and the familiar questions about whether it represented a betting coup for Jack.

But they were really just interruptions to the highlight reel of my time at Sandhutton. I had some memorable days on some terrific horses. Chilly Billy produced a startling turn of speed to win the Gimcrack Stakes at York in the summer of 1993. We came from last in a field of eleven to win that one and prompted one rather excitable member of the press to suggest that 'as if straight out of the Old Testament, a gap of Red Sea proportions opened up in front of Fallon and Chilly Billy'.

I won on Rafferty's Rules in the Hopeful Stakes at Newmarket that year, too, and then, as soon as my six-month ban for the Webster fracas came to an end, I won on Primula Bairn at Wolverhampton in April 1995 and the partnership with Jack and Lynda picked up exactly where we had left off.

For all the controversy surrounding it, it was a great feeling to win the Chester Cup on Top Cees. Soon after that, there was a 150/1 treble at Pontefract, which had become one of my favourite courses to ride. I was riding doubles and trebles there all the time. 'Infallible Fallon', a *Racing Post* headline read after one meeting at the Yorkshire track.

I rode 92 winners in the 1995 season and people were beginning to take notice of me. I was thirty years old and I was finally beginning to make a name for myself. There was a great kind of energy in Jack and Lynda's yard and I was responding to it. Whenever we went racing, we always thought we had a chance. It was a dream job. It was when I was at Sandhutton that I first began to believe that I could really be something as a jockey.

All those doubts that I had had when I was at Jimmy FitzGerald's about whether I had what it took ebbed away. Suddenly, it seemed a long time ago that I was thinking about jacking it all in and offering to go and ride work for Sir Michael Stoute. Now I believed that I was on the verge of establishing myself as one of the best jockeys around.

I was even getting a bit more worldly. The kid who hadn't eaten a meal in a restaurant before the age of eighteen was long gone, too. While I was at Jimmy FitzGerald's I had started spending my winters riding in India, first in Kolkata and then in Mumbai, and I had continued working there when I began riding for Jack and Lynda.

The first time I rode there was the winter of 1989-90. Another jockey, Simon Whitworth, had been riding for an owner called L.C.Gupta at the Royal Calcutta Turf Club, but Simon had taken a job in Saudi Arabia and he had suggested me as a replacement. It had taken me a long time to get out of Clare and I was keen to embrace every opportunity of travel that was offered to me.

Arriving in India for the first time is something that stays with most people who experience it. It is like an assault on your senses, the smell of spices and poverty, the sights of the beggars and the sounds of the clogged traffic and the auto-rickshaws blaring their way in and out of the gridlock that seems to be a perpetual state in most Indian cities.

My eyes were drawn to the animals. On my way in from the airport on that first day, I saw a poor little pony on the side of the road, which was being used to give rides for middle-class kids. They hadn't put a pad on his back to protect him from the hard saddle, so it was rubbing on his skin and it had created an open wound. He was just standing there by the side of this busy road amid all the chaos and the noise, tied up and resigned to his fate. There were flies all around the wound. It was so cruel but there was nothing you could do. There were scenes like that at almost every intersection.

I got used to it fairly quickly. There wasn't much choice. I was protected from most of it because they provided me with a nice apartment and I spent the majority of my time either at the racetrack or at the Tollygunge Club, which was a place for expats. It was a country club, basically. It dates back more than two hundred years, apparently, and it was like a sanctuary from Kolkata's chaos. There was a pool and a golf course, a squash court and a nice bar, and so after I had ridden out in the morning, I spent most of my days there at the Tolly.

I enjoyed my racing out there. India has five 'classic' races, which mirror the original English Classics, so the Indian 1000 and 2000 Guineas are run in December, the Indian Oaks is run at the end of January, the Indian Derby is run on the first Sunday of February and the Indian St Leger is run in October. The first four take place in Mumbai. The St Leger is run in Pune.

I didn't just stay in the Tolly the whole time I was there. I did some exploring, too. I was going out with a girl called Wendy Carter at the time and we both made a visit to Mother Teresa's convent in Kolkata to see if we could look around. We didn't realise that we might be able to meet her but when we got there, there was a bit of a misunderstanding and one of the nuns thought that we had come to offer to work for the convent. Before we knew it, we were being ushered into a little chapel and Mother Teresa walked in.

She said a prayer and asked us what kind of work we wanted to do. I told her I was a jockey and that I worked close by at the racetrack. I wanted to donate some money to the convent, but she said they had enough money and what they really needed were people to work there and help the poor.

I even saw Muhammad Ali in the lobby of one of the hotels there once and while I was riding there that winter, Patrick Swayze was shooting *City of Joy* in Kolkata with a big film crew and I got quite friendly with a couple of the sound guys.

There were a few other British and Irish jockeys out there and we would ride track work every morning, go to breakfast with our owners, have a swim at the Tolly, lie by the pool and then go back to our apartments. Amid all that poverty, there were plenty of parties to attend. One guy used to fly in from Nepal every week and he was popular because he always brought a bottle of Smirnoff with him. The local vodka was like paint-stripper.

I noticed fairly soon that if you wrapped a white cloth round your mouth in the morning when you were riding out, it was stained black where you had been breathing in at the end of the session. It was that bad you could taste the grit. For months after you came back to England, every time you coughed or sneezed or anything like that there would be black dust in your handkerchief.

The Indian racing industry has been established for a couple of centuries and the racing there was brilliant. It was restricted to Indian-bred horses and there were big crowds and a terrific atmosphere at the tracks. Gambling was a big part of the scene, too. Indian racing wouldn't be alone in this but it felt like it revolved around gambling.

Some elements of the racing there brought you up short. They still used concrete uprights for the rails so if you hit them, you were in serious trouble. It used to be that way at Epsom and other British tracks but over the years, health and safety made sure every track had plastic uprights and rails.

One time, there was a kid in Mumbai and he had got hung up on his iron. His boot was stuck in it. Luckily, the horse was just standing there but everybody was walking by and looking at them. Nobody went to help him. The first thing I did was to get off my horse and hold his steady while he freed himself, because if the horse took off with him hanging by the ankle, he'd be dead.

During that first year of racing in Kolkata, I met a young Indian trainer called Dallas Toddywalla. I rode one of his fillies in the 2000 Guineas in Mumbai and she came second to a horse that went on to win their Triple Crown. Dallas was pleased with the ride I gave her and when I was back in England the following summer, he met me at Southwell and offered me a job for the winter in Mumbai.

I loved Kolkata but Mumbai was a great place to live and work. I lived with Dallas and his family and their maid in their four-bedroom apartment in an area called Breach Candy, not far from the sea and Malabar Hill and the centre of the city. We had a lot of fun together and Dallas and I became good friends. We were so successful together. Every year I was out there, he was champion trainer. We had a great rapport and I worked hard and was well rewarded for it.

The owner-trainer-jockey relationships in India are pretty

tight. The trainer likes to keep you away from everybody. You are riding their horses and you are working for them and they want it to remain exclusive. Again, that's largely to do with the gambling. If you are seen with another owner or a bookmaker, that is seen not only as disloyal but also highly suspect and you are gone, you are sacked.

Quite a lot of cloak-and-dagger stuff went on, even when you were having innocuous phone calls with your owner about how you thought his horses might do in particular races. They were paranoid about the phone being tapped and the possibility that the information about the horse might leak out and lower the odds before they could place their bets. So some of the conversations were conducted by code. Say the owner wanted to know which horse was worth having a bet on and whether it was worth betting a lot of money or just a little, there were codes for that and for the race in which it was running.

There were only eight races at each meeting and there was a maximum field of 20 runners for each race and each of those runners had a race number. When we were talking, we used the names of airlines to correspond with each of the eight races, a travel destination for each of the 20 horses in the race and a class of travel for whether it was worth betting a lot of money or not so much.

The first race might be British Airways, the second race Singapore Airlines, the third race Cathay Pacific and so on. The horse wearing number one might be Paris, the horse wearing number two might be London, the horse wearing number five might be Rome, and so on. So if I wanted to tell my owner that a horse that was wearing number five, say, in the third race of the day was worth punting a decent amount on, I would say: 'I'd like to fly Cathay Pacific, first class, to Rome, please,' and the owner would know what the score was and be content that his information was secure.

There was a lot of wealth there in Mumbai and more poverty, and nothing in between. Those poor old rickshaw pullers, I used to fear for them. It makes you appreciate where you come from and what you have.

Working and living in Mumbai helped my racing, too. If you have got nineteen Indian jockeys on your outside and you are drawn on the rails in a five-furlong race, you have got half a furlong out of the stalls and then a big turn and then four furlongs of the straight and it is going to test you.

It was a beautiful track in Mumbai. When I was riding there, it was one of the best tracks in the world but it was also a place where you had to be alive to all manner of dangers because there were plenty of scams going on.

Often, a jockey would have instructions to try to get his horse down into a lower class of race so that it would have a better chance of winning and they had a favourite way of making sure their horse didn't win. If a horse was drawn in class two or three and an owner wanted to get him down into class four or five, they could spend a year stopping him. So, often, they would go flat out for three furlongs and then the horse would be out of gas.

When you have a bit of experience, you can see the ones who are doing it because they are driving the head off their horses from the gate. If you are riding the fancied horse, which I often was, you are on the inside and you are like a sitting duck. Time and again, I found myself with a couple of horses come straight across the track at me like a Scud missile. You know they are burning their horse out so you have to check back to avoid them, but then you have got others coming at you as well. It was difficult but it was great for developing race-craft. If you are in the army and you know there is a sniper out there, you are going to be on the ball.

They were good times. I went back every winter for five years and I loved it. Lester Piggott was often there as a guest. Mick Kinane was riding, Pat Shanahan, Johnny Murtagh, Richard Hughes, John Lowe. We were working but there was a bit of a feeling of the boys being on tour, too.

The big thing for a lot of jockeys out there was making sure your owner got the best price. Dallas wasn't worried about the price because he had most of the best horses and he would back them at 2/1 or 6/4 so it was never something I had to worry about. But some of the other jockeys developed a keen sense of how the system worked out there and they used it to their advantage. One jockey had this two-year-old that he was convinced was going to win but he wanted to get its price up before he put a bet on it.

The day before the race meeting in Mumbai, they give the horse a blow-out to clear its lungs. So you give it a spurt around the track and all the trainers are waiting by the gate with the public and the bookmakers to try to gauge how the horses are looking.

This particular jockey had a syringe of blood in his pocket and when he was around the other side of the track, he squirted it up the horse's nose. When he was walking it back in, he patted the horse so he made sure everybody saw there was blood on his hand and on the horse's nostrils. They all thought the horse had burst a blood vessel, which drains the animal of energy. In India, you don't have to do a whole lot for swarms of people to see you. The horse went from even money to 6/1 and he won easily. I loved the racing in India but it was full of little tricks like that.

I had good times out there and I would have kept going back to India for the rest of my career but then in September 1994, I rode in a race at Beverley and everything changed.

CHAPTER 7

Webster

Stuart Webster was a journeyman jockey out of the north. I had seen him from time to time at Beverley or Thirsk or Pontefract, and knew that he had a reputation for recklessness as he would ride horses nobody else would ride. He was known to be a bit erratic on the racecourse, and off it too, and everyone was always careful around him. He wasn't at all popular with the other northern jockeys, he was awkward and hard to read. But he was struggling to make ends meet, which was why he rode whatever he could, even if they were runaways or nut-nuts. That often caused problems for the rest of us, because those horses posed a real danger in races.

I was always worried about Webster causing an incident on the track, but I'd never spoken to him before he arrived at Jimmy FitzGerald's yard early one morning in the summer of 1991. He had come to ride work on a two-year-old filly whose owner he was friendly with and who had stipulated that Webster should always ride his horse. So, because he was riding her and she was stabled with Jimmy, Webster had to come in and sit on her and ride work. And we got to know each other a bit because we saw each other at Jimmy's and we were riding against each other and everything was just fine.

Then, one morning, before we rode out, we were chatting to each other about his ride. Jockeys do that. We give each other tips and exchange notes on horses, how difficult they are, how this one rears up or that one pulls or whatever it may be. I had ridden this particular filly that was owned by Webster's friend a few times and she was no good. Her owner had paid £1000 for her and I really didn't know what she was even doing in the yard. While we were trotting out to the gallops, I said: 'Stuart, she's fucking useless. She's a donkey. You're wasting your time with her.'

We went up the gallops and we jumped off together over six furlongs, testing them out and the owner was there to see his horse with Webster on it. We jumped off and we were breezing along and then we quickened. I didn't know where Webster and this little filly were because I started ahead of them and after a while I looked behind and I nearly fell off looking to see where he was because he was that far behind.

The next day, Jimmy FitzGerald came into my box in the yard and he was raging. 'Why are you fucking telling that fucker Webster that that horse is no good?' he yelled at me. He went on and on. I thought he was going to explode.

So after the conversation Webster and I had had, he had reported it verbatim to the owner. I guess he'd done it because he was worried I might get the ride instead of him. Telling the owner how badly I rated her was a sure-fire way of making sure I didn't get on it.

Jimmy was angry because he was thinking about the money. If you're an owner and you are told your horse is no good, you're liable to take it away from that yard and take it to someone who tells you what you want to hear, even if it's not true. Jimmy stood to lose £500 a week if that horse was taken away from the yard. If a horse is no good, a lot of trainers will send it home. They don't want to see it. They don't want to waste time on it. But the smaller trainers will often persevere.

So Webster had gone to the owner and said: 'Fallon says the horse is a piece of shit.' The owner said to Jimmy: 'Tell your jockey not to worry how slow it is because he won't be riding it anyway.'

I was angry Webster had done that. You don't do that to another jockey. And you particularly don't bad-mouth another jockey just to safeguard a ride on a horse that's got no chance.

To me, it looked as if Webster was trying to ingratiate himself with the owner just in case Jimmy FitzGerald decided to put me on her because I was the stable jockey. We would all cut each other's throats for a good horse but you don't stoop to that level for a horse like that. I'm not saying it's unknown for people in racing to do that kind of thing. Lester Piggott was a champion at jocking people off rides, but the horses and the races that he'd do it for were worth it. This wasn't worth it. My blood was boiling.

Jimmy could easily have said at that moment: 'You know what, Kieren, there's the fucking gate.' He could have booted me out there and then. I knew what Webster was about all of a sudden. It was then that I thought: 'You prick.'

I didn't have that much respect for him to start with anyway. If you are riding unruly horses, by the law of averages, you are going to get hurt one day. I know that if you are struggling, you are going to have to take risks but I would rather be a plasterer or take up a trade than do that. I wouldn't do what Webster did because I don't like pain. He had several heavy falls that have left him damaged in later life because of the head injuries he sustained. The level of danger he courted was a bit like being a jump jockey.

It's horrific watching the falls that happen to National Hunt jockeys sometimes. Coming down and getting back up and riding again in the next race. I couldn't do it. I rode over hurdles three times in my whole life and I had two seconds at Punchestown and a fifth at Leopardstown when I was an apprentice. That was more than enough for me.

I had never even jumped a hurdle. The first hurdle I saw in my life was when I was coming into it at Leopardstown. I knew how to sit back on the jumps and then I pinged the rest of them. When I rode in my third race at Punchestown, I didn't see a hurdle for most of the way round there. We just blasted through them. I couldn't see a stride or anything. I thought: 'I'm not that mad.'

Webster and I collided again at Southwell in the summer of 1994. I won a race there but he objected to something about the way I'd been riding and I was disqualified from first place. I was banned for what the stewards decided was irresponsible riding for seven days, too. That didn't exactly improve the relationship between us.

A few months later, on 14 September 1994, we were at the same meeting again. We were both riding at Beverley, in East Yorkshire. I was working for Jack and Lynda by then and I was having a terrific season. I wasn't thinking that the John Mangles Memorial Handicap that day at Beverley was going to be a particularly significant race for me, but that's how it turned out. The late Major Mangles was a rather stern racecourse official for many years, apparently. I don't think he would have approved.

I was on a horse called Gymcrak Flyer, which was trained by Gordon Holmes, a lovely man, who used to fly his own plane in and out of race meetings and only had a handful of horses. Webster was on Sailormaite, which was another of the horses he rode that was notoriously headstrong and wild. The race was over seven furlongs and it was a big field with 15 horses. It was too many. There's a bend at Beverley and it gets ridiculously crowded. I think they've limited it to fewer horses now but back then it was dangerous if you didn't ride responsibly.

I was drawn down the inside and Webster was drawn right on the outside. Another guy called John Stack, an apprentice from Kerry, a little Irish lad, got out fast on a horse called Royal Interval. Now, out of the corner of my eye, I could see a horse and rider coming across.

I was up near the front, third or fourth. And the horse and rider hit Stacky first and then he hit me and both of our horses stumbled badly, going down like dominoes, hitting the ground and skidding along on their knees. How we both stayed in the saddle, with ten or eleven horses behind us, I don't know.

But both horses found an extra leg and got up. The two of us carried on but by then we were at the back of the field. I didn't know it was Webster who had done it at first. All I saw were the colours. I was in pink and the jockey who had almost brought down me and Stacky was in green and purple with a white cap. I was fuming. I wanted to find whoever had done it.

When we crossed the finish line, I hunted through the field

and I saw the green and purple colours up ahead. It was my bad luck that the jockey who flattened us won the race. That meant the cameras were following him as he trotted back. That meant the cameras would be on me, too, as I pulled up alongside him. I didn't care. I had the red mist.

I rode up alongside him, me on the right, him on the left. I looked over. It was Webster. It was typical of his recklessness. 'You wanker,' I said. 'You nearly killed us.'

If I do someone in a race, the first thing I do is say sorry. You have got to hold your hands up. Webster chose a different tack.

'Fuck off,' he said.

I reached out with my left hand and grabbed him by his silks. I shook him and he fell off his horse. It wasn't that big a deal. He landed on his feet. He didn't hurt himself. But it was all on television. It didn't look good.

'I'll see you when we get back inside,' Webster said. He meant he'd see me in the weighing room. It was obvious he wasn't for backing down.

He was leading his horse by this time, so I cantered back to the unsaddling enclosure and spoke to Gordon Holmes and said the guy had nearly killed us. Gordon was sympathetic and that was it. I went back to the weighing room and sat down by my peg.

There are seats all around the weighing room at Beverley, grouped around a table in the middle. Webster's seat was near the door, on the left as you came in. My seat was opposite the door and you had to walk to the right and around the table to get to it. Webster came flying in. Instead of walking through the door and turning left, he hurried round to the right. He still had his saddle in his hand. I was waiting.

He slung the saddle on the table and then turned and launched himself at me. I ducked and then split him with my head. That was lights out. It smashed his nose and he was on the ground and I can't say I regretted it.

He went to the toilet to wash the blood off his face and then they took us into the stewards' room. He was in a bit of a state, still bleeding, and I had a small plaster across my forehead. The stewards said nothing like this had ever happened before and they didn't know how to deal with it.

It was funny them saying that nothing like it had happened before. I've seen loads of fights in weighing rooms. It happened all the time back then. Jockeys think: 'If you do me, I'll do you.' Then you have a ding-dong, bang-bang, someone will separate you and you shake hands and go home. You don't go and rant in the stewards' room. But you don't get jockeys pulling another jockey off his horse in front of the television cameras very often. That was what I was in trouble for. The stewards referred the matter to the Jockey Club and we were both summoned to their headquarters at Portman Square in London.

I didn't really think it was that serious. Honestly. Like I said, I saw fights all the time in weighing rooms. But the fact I'd pulled Webster off his horse had caught the imagination of the press and they were making a big deal of it. Some people were suggesting that I should be banned for a very long time.

Jack Ramsden did a ring-round for me and got people like Kevin Prendergast to send references as to my character. That made Kevin laugh, I know. 'I told them he was the sweetest apprentice who had ever ridden for me,' he told someone recently. He had a very big grin on his face when he said that. So we went down to Portman Square and now it was obvious it was a big deal. There was a lot of attention, a lot of photographers. It was a bit of a scrum. Jack Ramsden said to me later that all publicity is good publicity, but I wasn't sure about that.

One good thing came out of it. It was the first time I met Christopher Stewart-Moore, the lawyer that Jack had hired to represent me. Luckily for me, he had a lifelong interest in horseracing, and he and I became very good friends. And I've kept him busy.

Once we were inside the Jockey Club, we were taken up to a room and we all sat around it: me and my barrister, Lord Irvine, who was shadow lord chancellor at the time, Webster and his barrister, Christopher, other representatives and the stewards. Another jockey, Lindsay Charnock, was there, too. He was quite friendly with Webster but he came down to testify on my behalf. I had a great deal of respect for him for that. He was willing to tell the truth and say that I had been provoked by Webster.

He was the only one, though. There is a culture of *omertà* in the weighing room. What happens in there stays in there, and no one else was prepared to come down to London to give evidence. Maybe that worked for me in some ways, too, although I knew I had only acted in self-defence.

Some outlandish claims were thrown around in that room. Mrs Dana Brudenell-Bruce, one of the stewards, put it to me that I had once head-butted a horse behind the stalls before a race. Lord Irvine responded to the effect that he thought there would only be one winner in that exchange. That seemed to settle that.

There was one inadvertently funny moment when Webster claimed that another jockey had been so horrified by the damage I caused him that he had been physically sick when Webster appeared in the toilets. It turned out the jockey had been in the process of making himself sick to avoid putting up overweight for his ride when Webster happened to stagger in.

I think at one point, I tried to argue that I was actually helping Webster back onto his horse rather than dragging him off it. They played the video evidence. It didn't really support that argument. Even I had to admit that.

At the end of it, they banned me from riding for a total of six months, three for pulling Webster off his horse and three for the fight. The suspension was to run from 30 September 1994 to 30 March 1995. It was the most severe punishment given to a jockey since Billy Newnes was banned for three years for receiving money for information in 1983. It didn't stop Peter Scudamore beginning his comment piece for the *Daily Mail* the next morning with the line: 'Kieren Fallon is a lucky man.' He said that he and 'many others' felt that I might have received 'a career-threatening suspension'. Part of his point was that I wouldn't actually miss much of the English flat racing season and he was right about that.

The whole thing put me on the map. Not quite in the way I'd hoped for but there you go. It was one of the items on the *Ten O'Clock News* that night. Lord Irvine was so startled by the amount of media outside the Jockey Club at the end of the hearing that he escaped out of a back entrance.

It could have been worse for me. As Scudamore had pointed out, the flat season was nearly over so most of my suspension was going to be served when I wouldn't have been riding in England anyway. Jack and Lynda sent me over to the States so I could learn more about timing with some of the greats of the sport. That was one of the best things that ever happened in my career.

And Webster? He didn't do much after that. He was at the end of his career anyway, struggling to get rides, riding lunatic horses. He dragged out another year or two because he got on a good horse called Blyton Lad. He won six times on that and that kept him in the game a bit longer. But his career petered out and all those terrible falls he had had began to catch up with him, sadly. A few years later, the *News of the World* published an interview with him and attributed some of the signs of dementia he was suffering to his fight with me at Beverley. They apologised later for that.

I was in the public eye now, though. That kind of attention wasn't about to go away.

CHAPTER 8

The Gift of the Clock

When my ban for pulling Stuart Webster off his horse kicked in, Jack Ramsden made it very plain to me he thought I should use the time to go to America during the winter and learn more about the clock. I didn't need much persuading. I probably would have got into mischief if I'd stayed in England. I thought it was a great idea. So I headed out to the West Coast with a few other jockeys and spent a couple of months learning about timing and pace with the American trainer Rodney Rash, who had been an assistant to the great Charlie Whittingham, America's master trainer.

It feels like an enchanted time to me now. It was like heaven on earth. The smell of the air in the winter California sunshine, riding for a brilliant man like Rodney Rash at a wonderful track like Santa Anita and gazing up at the majesty of the San Gabriel Mountains framed against a blue sky every time I climbed on a horse's back. I never got tired of it.

I learned so much in that time in America. In many ways, it transformed me from someone who was struggling to rise above being a journeyman into a jockey who felt like he was finally a master of his trade. My fortunes had started to improve when I went to ride for Jack and Lynda but this accelerated the process.

I soon realised I hadn't a clue about riding. Yeah, I had ridden a few winners, but I started learning about horses racing on the right lead and how to pace a race. I was a different rider when I came back from Santa Anita. It was like a finishing school for me and my results started to show it very quickly. Santa Anita is the place where I learned most of my trade. I went there when I was just out of my apprenticeship and every piece of work was like riding a race. I still count myself fortunate that Rodney, who was to die tragically young, agreed to take me on for a little while.

In the States, they expect you to work over a specific distance, say five-eighths of a mile, in a specific time, to the second. They're not too keen on guesswork. They told me that some of the best riders out there at Santa Anita would be able to tell you to within a fraction of a second how quickly they had gone over a given distance. The idea was that if you're in front in a race and you're going too quickly for the capabilities of your horse in terms of how he's going to be able to finish the race, then you know it. You know where to be in a race and how to pace it. You know if others are going too quickly and you can afford to lay off the pace.

I learned about the clock. I learned to judge how fast I was going. It's a bit like when you're driving your car, you've got an idea of how fast you're going without looking at the speedometer. Imagine you've got to know to the exact number of miles per hour how fast you're going in your car. That's what learning about the clock in racing is about.

It takes a while. Some people will never be able to pick it up. In America, you've basically got two long straights at most racecourses. A horse going flat out, his maximum speed is going to be about 40 mph and if he's doing that, you're going to know that he's right on his limit. Then, it's about who is the smartest jockey, who is the best judge of his horse, who can gauge how fast he is going the most accurately.

If a jockey's making the pace and the pace is too quick, he's going to struggle in the final furlong. If it's too slow, then he is going to have to quicken off the front and that way, he will be taken out of the reach of horses who might want to travel more slowly and save everything up for a fast finish. That's why you need to know. That's why you need to have a clock ticking inside your head.

If they are going too quickly up front, you sit back and enjoy it. Go to sleep and relax. Don't use up your gas. In cycling, you slipstream. Then you pull out and you're gone. It's the same with horses. If there's a headwind, I want to be tucked in behind the leader. I don't want to be up front, sheltering the others.

It's why Steve Cauthen dominated when he came over from America to England. He had a great clock in his head. He'd learned the knack with the best. He used to go into the lead off the best horse and if he slowed him down, he would kick off the front like elastic and he'd be gone. If he was riding a keen horse and it was out of control, he would sit in behind. I'd always know where all the boys were going to be. Richard Hughes liked to be up front, Jamie Spencer sat at the back, Pat Eddery was very good from the front. Frankie Dettori would always be in a smart position.

But learning the clocks helps you to be adaptable. It helps you to respond better to the circumstances of each race. It all happens in the first couple of furlongs. It's very important to get your position and know how quickly they're going, know when to kick and when to sit. If a horse kicks too soon, they drag the field along. A lot of jockeys follow suit. Guys like Frankie and Ryan Moore take it to a different level. They can make changes as they gauge the race. Most of the jockeys, most of the time, they can't.

I don't know how Rodney Rash put up with me for the first few weeks. I didn't have a clue about the clock but he and I got on very well from the start. He let me ride all his good horses and he put me out with the leading jockeys over there, like Gary Stevens and Chris McCarron, to try to help me. To begin with, I was doing the following, trying to learn from Gary and Chris. Rodney sat in the stands, flicking his cap and shaking his head, and I knew that was a sign I had got my times wrong. I picked it up in the end but I think Rodney was losing patience with me.

After about a fortnight, I caught on and then it was all fine. It was a joy working there. There's nothing better than Santa Anita, with the mountains behind you, the sun coming up at 7am, going to Clockers' Corner, the famous café at the top of the stretch, for coffee in between work and seeing some of the best horses in the world gallop past you.

I enjoyed it so much in the States that I went back the next year and rode a few horses for another great trainer, Bobby Frankel, who had a really good work-rider. I learnt so much from him about pace, too. When you grasp it, it all seems so easy. If I had not gone to America for those few months during my suspension, my career would have been very different. I don't think I would have become champion jockey. I could easily have got lost.

When you're working for top trainers like Rodney and Bobby Frankel and you're riding good horses all the time, you can't help but improve. I became a better judge of pace, my balance improved and I came back a much better rider.

I got into a few scrapes of course. That was par for the course at that time for me. When I went over to the States, I didn't have a visa and the authorities were always on the lookout for people who were overstaying their welcome. You were supposed to have a different visa if you were coming to work.

Some jockeys didn't even make it into the country. Paul Burke, who I knew from Malton and who was a lovely kid and a great little rider, got on a plane to America and when they went through his gear at customs, they saw his boots and his whip and his helmet, so it was a bit of a giveaway. They put him on the next plane home. He had time for a cup of coffee at the airport and then he was heading back to England. He said it was the most expensive cup of coffee he ever had. He was a good lad. He died a few years after that in a road crash in America when the horse transporter he was riding in was involved in an accident.

Those of us who did make it into the country were always ducking and diving because we didn't have a work visa. We went into Santa Anita through a back gate and were generally as clandestine as we could be. Rodney and the rest of the American guys used to make fun of us because of it, but one night we were all at a Mexican restaurant and two policemen turned up.

There was one each side of me and they said they were

arresting me for being an illegal immigrant and that they were going to have to deport me. A lot of things started going through my head: things had been going so well, I was riding with Gary Stevens, Chris McCarron, Mike Smith, Pat Valenzuela and all the great riders, I was feeling great, the horses were running for me and I was learning so much. And now this. They started picking me up to drag me out of the restaurant and I was weighing up whether to make a run for it. Then suddenly everybody burst into laughter. Rodney had set it all up and they were just stable lads in fancy dress cop uniforms. Everyone was falling about.

And then there was something that wasn't a joke. After the track work in the morning, we had a routine. We'd go back to the digs and go down the road and have a couple of beers. We'd play a bit of pool and then head down to the restaurant in Sierra Madre. It was heaven.

This particular day, we pottered off down the road to the restaurant for lunch and as we were walking down there, one of us must have bumped into someone. It was totally innocuous. Nothing was said and we went on to the restaurant and had something to eat. As we came out, a police car skidded in front of us and a cop jumped out. It was a real cop this time. He told us to get against the wall and slammed Carl Hodgson face first into it and asked for his ID. He put the cuffs on him and then he asked me for ID.

I pulled out my little racing licence. He said that wasn't ID and he went to slam me against the wall, too. I slipped away from him and took off running. I didn't realise in America that they can shoot you for that. I kept running. I was sharp and quick and the cop was a big fat guy. He was yelling at me, but I whipped down a side street and went a roundabout route back to the house I was sharing with Dave Duggan, Frank Dalton and a couple of other good friends of mine.

They slung Hodgy in the cop car, asked him who I was and took him to the police station. They said we had been drunk and disorderly and somebody had reported us. They kept Hodgy in the slammer for two days, trying to find out who I was. They went to the track, where they denied all knowledge of me, and then they came knocking on my door and I hid under the stairs in a cupboard. They searched the premises but they couldn't find me and that was the last I heard of it.

The work in America made a huge difference to me. Look at my record before I went and after I got back, and I was much improved. Apart from learning the clock, I was better out of the gate, too. If I got a bad draw, I wanted to be out and get across.

I went back as often as I could after that. I think Santa Anita is my favourite track anywhere in the world. Some of the memories are tinged with sadness, though. Less than a year after I had left to return to England, Rodney Rash died of a rare blood disorder. He was only thirty-six. Bobby Frankel is dead, too. They were both great men. I owe them a lot. They are a big part of the reason why I became a champion.

CHAPTER 9

Top Cees

I loved Top Cees. He turned out to be one of my most famous rides but for all the wrong reasons. He was a beautiful horse and of his 39 races on the flat, I was on his back 11 times. I rode him in his last race at the Roodee in the Chester Cup in May 2000. I had to pull him up on the far side of the course on that occasion and he was taken to the racecourse stables and fitted with a splint to his near fore. For a while, it looked as if he might have to be put down. I was so upset that I gave the vets a mouthful when they came down to treat him on the course. I got fined for that.

The reports on his final race pointed out that even though he had not been an outstanding racehorse, Top Cees had garnered more attention than many great champions. That was mainly because of what happened when I rode him in two races in quick succession during the spring of 1995.

Everything was going well for me then at Jack and Lynda's. Things were taking off in my career and in that April, Lynda asked me to ride Top Cees in the Swaffham Handicap at

Newmarket. I hadn't ridden him before, either on the gallops or in a race, so I looked at his form. He'd finished sixth the month before in a big field at Doncaster and I looked at the jockey who had ridden him that day and thought that if Top Cees could finish sixth with him on his back, then there was probably room for improvement. I think that jockey barely rode one winner in his life.

He started as the 5/1 favourite for the Swaffham. Lynda gave me the instructions and there was nothing out of the ordinary. It was fairly simple. Nine times out of ten, Jack liked you to hold his horses up, come late, don't win by too far, the usual stuff. That was as far as it went. Top Cees was going well enough down the Rowley Mile until we were going down the hill, down by the bushes, and a horse stopped in front of me. Top Cees changed his legs and I picked him up and he ran on. If I had got the run of the race, he probably would have won, but I tried to switch him between two horses a couple of furlongs out and the gap didn't open. We had a bit of bad luck and I rode a bad race. We finished fifth.

The stewards had us in and asked me if there were any excuses. They looked at the footage and they saw that the gap stopped in front of us and that there was no way through. They accepted my explanation. No action was taken. I was disappointed in my ride but I thought that was the end of it.

That evening, I went to The Old Plough pub in a village called Ashley, near Newmarket, for a drink and a bite to eat with friends. When I was coming back from the bar at one point in the evening, I bumped into Derek Thompson, the presenter of *Channel 4 Racing*. I didn't really know Derek at that time. I was still a northern jockey then, so I rarely stayed down in Newmarket or the south. I was only staying over this time because I had more rides at the course the next day. I knew that everyone liked Derek, though. He was a nice fella and we had a quick chat about Top Cees and I told him what had happened. Then I went back to my table.

Three weeks later, I was on Top Cees again, this time in the Chester Cup at the Roodee. We were quite optimistic about him. The Swaffham had been over a mile and six furlongs and if I had ridden a better race, he would have won. The Chester Cup was two miles and two furlongs, so the only doubt was about his stamina and whether he would stay.

He had been bred for a mile and a half, but it turned out there was no problem with his stamina. It was a very smooth race. I started out with identical tactics to the Swaffham, running towards the back of the field and trying to ease through. This time, I had none of the problems I'd had at Newmarket and coming round the home turn, I moved to the outside and Top Cees started to fly. He scythed through the field.

We were clear in the last furlong and the commentator mentioned that Top Cees was coming home to 'a mixed reception'. There was already talk that this had been set up to be a gambling coup for Jack. We won by five lengths. We had barely crossed the line when the commentator said: 'There are going to be some ructions now, I can tell you.'

He was right about that. There were some of the biggest ructions racing had ever faced. Channel 4 had trained a special camera on Top Cees all the way around the course and John McCririck, their racing tipster, didn't help matters by ranting and raving and saying how terrible the result of the race was. 'How can punters back horses with confidence after that?' McCririck asked on Channel 4. 'All right, it was a half-mile further than the Swaffham and I fully accept the distance made a huge difference to Top Cees. But with the way it was ridden and the way it ran at Newmarket, it is quite extraordinary for it to come out now and win the Chester Cup.'

Even the cartoonists had a field day. One sketch in a national newspaper depicted a choirmaster upbraiding a young chorister, who is singing at the top of his voice. 'And why couldn't you produce Top Cees like that last week?' the choirmaster is saying.

That was one thing but the real problem came in the next day's edition of the *Sporting Life*. In a comment column under the headline 'Contempt For The Punter', written by Alastair Down, the newspaper's associate editor, it was alleged that Jack and Lynda and I had been cheating when Top Cees had finished fifth at Newmarket in the Swaffham. I wouldn't say I was immune to this kind of thing by now, but the Stuart Webster case and other brushes with authority had made me try to ignore stupid accusations like that. I hated the hassle of the legal process and the way it made you the centre of attention.

But Jack and Lynda were appalled by the article. They felt very upset by it. They had turned a blind eye many times before when there was innuendo about their horses in the papers, but this was different. They felt that it had damaged their reputations. They were determined to do something about it and decided that they were going to pursue the paper for damages.

Jack pulled me into the office at Sandhutton one day and said they were involved with a civil case against the *Sporting Life* and that I was part of it, whether I liked it or not. He said I would be entitled to damages, too. He asked me if I was okay with that and I said I was. I didn't want to get involved but I did it out of loyalty to Jack and Lynda.

My first winner on Piccadilly Lord, beating John Hyde at Navan in June 1984. He was nervous before the race, but I settled him down and felt the result was an important step forward for me. *(Caroline Norris)*

As a fresh-faced apprentice working out of Kevin Prendergast's yard in 1987. At the end of the season, I decided to move to England to join Jimmy FitzGerald. *(Caroline Norris)*

Kevin Prendergast, the man who gave me my first opportunity in racing. *(George Selwyn)*

Jimmy FitzGerald was capable of dishing out some of the most spectacular bollockings, but despite that I loved my time working with him in Malton. *(George Selwyn)*

Top Cees on the way to a controversial victory by five lengths in the Chester Cup in 1995. *(George Selwyn)*

Flanked by Jack and Lynda Ramsden, leaving the High Court in February 1998 during the libel trial, after we had been accused of pulling Top Cees to stop him from winning. *(PA)*

Having joined the powerhouse stable of Henry Cecil, I knew I was expected to win the big races, and happily Sleepytime took me to my first Classic success in the 1997 running of the 1000 Guineas. *(PA)*

Our different racing styles clearly visible, Frankie Dettori got the better of me in this one, but I would soon end up beating him in the race to be 1997 Champion Jockey. *(Getty Images)*

Bosra Sham wins the Prince of Wales's Stakes in June 1997, but it was her loss in the Eclipse the following month that put my position with Henry under scrutiny. *(Getty Images)*

With Pilsudski and Benny the Dip ahead of us, it was a case of Bosra Shambles in the Eclipse. *(George Selwyn)*

In a tight finish, Wince came through to win the 1000 Guineas in 1999 (run on the July course that year), beating Ray Cochrane, one of the hardest jockeys to overcome at the finish. *(Getty Images)*

A job well done. Oath wins the 1999 Derby, but it was immediately time to move on to the next thing. *(PA)*

The tension in the air is clear. Henry Cecil looks on at Goodwood in July 1999 after the *News of the World* printed stories that a top jockey was having an affair with his wife. *(Getty Images)*

Thanking Alva Glen for providing me with my 200th winner of the 1999 season, so becoming the first jockey since Gordon Richards to reach the landmark in three successive seasons. *(PA)*

Sir Michael Stoute and I celebrate after King's Best, one of the finest horses I rode for him, wins the 2000 Guineas in May 2000. *(Getty Images)*

But the season, which had been going so well, came to a shuddering halt when I fell in the Ascot Stakes. For a while the shoulder injury I suffered put my career in danger. *(George Selwyn)*

Jack and Lynda instructed Christopher Stewart-Moore to take action against the *Sporting Life* and I became the third claimant. If Jack and Lynda had lost, it would have cost them a fortune in legal fees and other expenses. They were in pretty deep but they were sure of their case. Apart from anything else, Jack had wagered quite a lot of money on Harlestone Brook to win the Chester Cup. It had finished second. Why would he have done that if he had been preparing a betting sting on Top Cees?

The libel trial took place in the High Court in February 1998. I was champion jockey by then and riding for Henry Cecil. Henry didn't want me to give evidence because he thought it would bring bad publicity for all of us, but I was already committed. I wasn't going to change my mind now.

The *Sporting Life* did not back down. Its owners, Mirror Group Newspapers, denied libel. It said the article was true in substance and in fact, and also fair comment on a matter of public interest. And when Alastair Down gave evidence, he said he stood by every word he had written. Referring to the Swaffham, Richard Hartley QC, for the *Sporting Life*, asked Down: 'What did you think of Kieren Fallon's riding?'

'I thought the horse was not off,' Down said.

'Meaning?' Mr Hartley asked.

'Meaning he did not try,' Down said.

The trial lasted for nineteen days and I was told later that the defence team hoped that I would be the weak link for Jack and Lynda, particularly under cross-examination. Mr Hartley wanted to make a big thing of my poor disciplinary record. I think he was assuming I would contest the idea that I had a poor record, but I didn't make any attempt to conceal my failings in that regard. I told him I was ashamed of my record and that seemed to take the wind out of his sails. My guess is he had to rip up a lot of questions after that.

There were some embarrassing moments for the *Sporting Life*. They had claimed that the switchboard at Chester racecourse had been inundated by complaints about Top Cees' victory straight after the race, but two of the ladies who worked the phones told the trial they had barely received a single complaint.

The defence also tried to blacken my character by asking me about an incident involving my brother, who had been arrested for drink-driving some time earlier. He had picked a girl up and told her he was me because he thought that would impress her. So when the police stopped the car, they asked the girl who her companion was and she said: 'He's Kieren Fallon.' The newspapers reported that I'd spent the night in a police cell and when the BHA asked me about it, I didn't deny it because I didn't want to get my brother into trouble. It subsequently became clear that I had not been driving the car because I had been riding in Scotland at the time.

That also, though, made it obvious that I hadn't been telling the truth to the BHA and so Mr Hartley raised the issue in court and said I had lied about the incident. I admitted that and so Mr Hartley said that if that were the case, why should the court believe my evidence now. I grabbed hold of the Bible that was next to me on the stand and held it up. 'Because I'm on the book now,' I said. I was serious, but it got a few laughs from the public seats.

There was only one time when Jack's resolve weakened, I think. I know he found it very difficult when Lynda took the stand on the first day of the case and Hartley really went for her. He called her a cheat and a liar. Jack asked Lynda if she wanted to call it a day and she said she was made of sterner stuff than that.

In the end, the case hinged on evidence given by Derek Thompson. Thompson was not a declared witness in the trial but the *Sporting Life* had to seek permission from the judge to amend its case to include his evidence. My team believed it was because Hartley had thought he would destroy me on the stand and, when he didn't, they had to change tack.

Thompson was a reluctant witness. 'I didn't want to repeat this in court,' Thompson said of the exchange we had had. 'It was told to me in confidence. I asked him what happened because I thought the horse would win.

'He said: "I thought it would win as well but when I got in the paddock Jack told me to stop it." He didn't say anything else. The conversation lasted no longer than two minutes.'

Thompson was away in Dubai at the time of the trial, but our lawyers believed that he had been strongly encouraged to come back by Mirror Group because he was the source of Alastair Down's comment piece in the *Sporting Life*. Thompson agreed that during a Channel 4 production meeting the morning after our encounter in The Old Plough, he mentioned the conversation in front of John McCririck, Brough Scott and Lord Oaksey, but was not sure how many people heard him.

So much for his protestations about the fact that the conversation had been held in confidence, then. He denied boasting that I'd told him I'd 'pulled Top Cees' and said he had been speaking in hushed tones at that Channel 4 meeting. A lot of people seem to have heard his hushed tones, unfortunately for him. It was our case that he had fabricated part of the conversation and repeated it in the company of others and now he was being called to account for it.

Our QC, Patrick Milmo, was worried about Thompson's evidence because he knew it had the power to sway the jury of five women and seven men against us but Thompson, who kept saying he wished the trial had never happened, didn't come out of it well. Mr Milmo emphasised the absurdity of the allegation. The court was hushed when Mr Milmo was questioning Thompson. He was on the stand for about two hours.

'You are asking the court to believe,' Mr Milmo said to Thompson, 'that, in a chance encounter in public, Mr Fallon made a confession to you which would put his professional career at risk and that of his trainer?'

Thompson clearly didn't want to be there. At one point he said, 'I feel very sad that the case has reached court. I gain nothing out of it ... I was encouraged to stay in Dubai as long as I wanted because I couldn't be subpoenaed there. But I knew I had to come back. I didn't do so willingly. I am here under duress.'

He was asked if he bore me any ill will. 'None,' Thompson said. 'That's why it is so difficult to be here.' He said he had taken it seriously when I supposedly said I had been told to stop the horse. 'I hope I'm wrong,' he said. 'It might have been said flippantly. He might have had one too many. I don't know. But I took it seriously.'

At that stage in his evidence, I was called back to the witness box. Mr Milmo asked me if Jack had told me to stop Top Cees.

'I have never been told to pull a horse by Mr or Mrs

Ramsden ...' I told the court. 'It would be terrible for a jockey to do or say anything like that. You would jeopardise your career.'

Then Mr Hartley asked me questions.

'You were under instructions to make sure you didn't win, to pull your horse,' he said. 'Your orders were not to win that day?'

'It was worth winning,' I told the court. 'It was a ten-grand handicap.'

'I suppose if you are asked not to win, you would follow those orders?' Mr Hartley said.

'I would risk my licence if I pulled a horse,' I told the court.

'It is easy for a horseman of your ability to stop a horse, isn't it?' Mr Hartley said. 'Find trouble, don't take a gap, don't urge him on – the easiest thing in the world?'

I told him what it was like being in a race. 'You are riding at forty miles an hour, four inches from the hooves of the horse in front,' I said. 'You don't look for trouble. You avoid it.'

'You can deliberately make the wrong decision, can't you?' Mr Hartley said.

'I have never done that in my life,' I said.

When Thompson returned to the stand, Mr Milmo questioned him about another detail of his evidence. I'm friends with Jack and Lynda now but when I rode for them, they were my bosses and I treated them as such. I never called Jack by his Christian name in those days. I always called him 'Mr Ramsden'.

So Mr Milmo asked Thompson if he was sure I had referred to Mr Ramsden as 'Jack' when we spoke in the pub. Thompson insisted that was the case. Mr Milmo pointed out how unlikely that was and mentioned that the transcript of my evidence would show I had only ever referred to him as 'Mr Ramsden' in court.

Mr Milmo also cross-examined Thompson at length about his tipping line the day before he gave evidence. On that particular day, every horse that he tipped lost. Thompson had also claimed that he had spoken to the trainer Arthur Moore, but my legal team had contacted Moore and he had told them he did not know Thompson. Mr Milmo had a lot of fun with that.

'You do not know Arthur Moore any more than you know the Pope, do you?' he asked Thompson.

'That's not fair,' Thompson said. 'I never said I knew the Pope.'

There was another very telling piece of evidence against Thompson's version of events. One of the reasons he said he had come to give evidence was because he felt it his duty as a racing journalist to expose skulduggery in the sport where he could find it. At that point, Mr Milmo showed him an extract of himself on Channel 4's *The Morning Line* programme, where he was sitting next to the leading Jockey Club steward, Anthony Mildmay-White. In the footage, Mr Mildmay-White was defending the Jockey Club's record on cleaning up racing and he said to Thompson that the real difficulty was getting substantial evidence on which you could convict.

Their conversation on the programme post-dated the conversation in The Old Plough between me and Thompson so Mr Milmo asked Thompson why, immediately after the programme, he had not told Mr Mildmay-White about what I was supposed to have said to him. Thompson didn't have any convincing answer.

It was clear by now that Thompson's evidence had been

discredited and the *coup de grâce* was administered by the judge when he asked Thompson whether I might have been joking when I said what he had said I said. Thompson agreed that I might have been. At that point, Mr Milmo immediately halted his cross-examination and offered no further questions.

In his summing up, Mr Justice Morland warned the jury about Thompson's evidence. 'You should treat this evidence with caution,' the judge said. 'Only after careful consideration must you act on it, when you are satisfied of its truth and accuracy and that it amounts to a confession.'

He said the reason for the warning was that the alleged conversation had taken place nearly three years ago and Thompson had not made a note of it at the time. Mr Justice Morland also pointed out discrepancies between the reported conversation and the one which had been submitted to the court as part of the preparation for the case.

The judge reminded the jury that Thompson had earlier given the defence a statement that was inconsistent with his later evidence. In his first statement, Thompson had claimed that I said Jack had told me: 'We have missed the price. Today is not the day.'

'You may well think,' he said, 'that these inconsistencies throw serious doubt on what he said.'

The jury did not take long to reach their verdict. They decided unanimously that the words complained of were neither substantially true nor fair comment in Lynda's case. They returned the same verdict for me and Jack by a majority verdict of ten to two. The jury awarded me damages of £70,000. Lynda got £75,000 and Jack £50,000. The paper closed soon afterwards, although the Sporting Life name lives on online.

After the case, Jack described Thompson's part in the case as 'contemptible', and Thompson said he had been made a scapegoat. I felt a bit sorry for him because he is basically a nice fella. Everyone likes him but he got it wrong and he couldn't backtrack. I didn't feel any great sense of satisfaction when I heard the verdict. We won the case but it was one of those situations where there were no winners. Racing didn't need it. I certainly didn't need it, even though my name had been cleared.

Jack and Lynda packed it in as a training team soon after that, too, and moved to France. They came back but I don't think their heart was ever quite in it again. They definitely felt that the racing establishment was against them. They sensed the establishment would never stop treating them as outsiders. Even in the immediate aftermath of the judgment, they believed that people were still casting aspersions on the performances of their horses in new races.

I wasn't in court for the verdict. I was told of the decision at Lingfield just before I rode Master Caster, an even-money favourite. We came home first. I was on two winners in the space of fifteen minutes that day.

CHAPTER 10

Warren Place

Towards the middle of the 1996 season, when I was still the stable jockey for Jack and Lynda Ramsden, I rode in a race at Doncaster on a horse trained by Henry Cecil. I was on a roll that season and I had already ridden a couple of winners that day. Henry ran three horses in this particular race. Willie Ryan was on one of them, Tony McGlone was on another and I was on the third. I was on the outsider of the three, which was normal given that Willie and Tony were both attached to Henry's yard at Warren Place.

I picked it up during the race and I won nice. Afterwards, I rang Henry to say what a good horse it was and we had a bit of a chat about it. Nothing out of the ordinary. It was a bit of a thrill for me to speak to him because I had never actually met him and he was horseracing royalty.

I had spoken to him on the phone earlier in the day to take instructions for the race, but that was the only previous contact I had ever had with him. I'd been doing so well for Jack and Lynda that the racing press had begun to speculate that I might be in line for a big job in the south, but most of the speculation centred on the idea that I would be offered something by Sir Michael Stoute.

That evening, I was out having dinner with a friend when my phone rang. The voice at the other end of the line said it was Henry. That was how he always referred to himself. Just 'Henry'. And that was what everyone else always called him in return. He got straight to the point. 'Would you like to come down south and ride for me?' he said.

I honestly believed it was a joke at first. I thought it was one of my friends ringing to wind me up. I wondered if someone had seen some of the speculation about a big job being in the offing and thought it would be a laugh to try and get me going by pretending to be Henry Cecil. But the voice at the other end of the line was adamant it wasn't a joke and it gradually dawned on me that this was real. This was real. It was one of the best moments of my life.

Henry Cecil wanted me to go to Newmarket to be his stable jockey. I couldn't believe it. It was every jockey's dream job. You don't think about the money. You just think: 'I've arrived.' You have taken off. You think about all his Classic winners, all his Derbies and his Royal Ascots.

No northern jockey had ever done that. No one had made that big a move to the south. A northern jockey is just that, a northern jockey. They struggle to get rides down south. I wouldn't say southern jockeys are the best jockeys. But they are the most successful. They get the opportunities. The big stables are all in the south, the big money is there, the fancy lifestyle.

If any northern jockey was going to make a big move south, people thought it would probably be Kevin Darley. He was a bit like Pat Eddery: never late, always smartly dressed, crossed his 't's and dotted his 'i's. He was doing really well, too, but it was me who got the job.

Now that I can look back on it, I preferred the atmosphere up north. Little tracks, nice people. Yorkshire people are different, so laid back, no pressure. There is always tomorrow. You stroll on to the races. Down south, it's M25, M11, A1. Your head is fried. You're on the hard shoulder for ten miles, trying to get to a meeting and it's absolutely crazy. Up the hard shoulder, cutting people up, road rage. All to get in to ride a horse round Kempton at nine o'clock on a Friday night and your head is melted.

For what? Often it didn't feel worth it, just to have someone give you grief. 'Fallon, you're late.' There are a lot of great days, too, of course, but some of the crazy things we do . . . in the ledger of racing, there are more crazy things than sensible things. The M25, any day of the week, the odds are there's going to be something bad.

But I knew Henry had good horses. I knew he had a potential Classic winner in Sleepytime. I knew this was a passport to the big time for me. I knew this would change everything.

When I got to Henry's palatial yard at Warren Place, I felt like a fish out of water. Most of the northern trainers combined farming livestock with training racehorses. This was very different. I drove into the yard and my horse was tacked up for me. I was used to tacking it up myself up north. I did it because I liked to do it. I don't like arriving at the gallops and jumping on and jumping off. When I got the job, I said to Henry that it was important to me that I rode out every day. I wanted to get to know all the horses and all the staff. It was a big team thing.

Everybody was predicting the working relationship between me and Henry would be a disaster. They said it would be over very quickly. Henry was public-school educated, a man from an aristocratic background with a lot of posh middle names, and I was portrayed as a hooligan who dragged other jockeys off horses. People didn't give us much of a chance, but Henry saw something in me.

My first day in the yard, I was riding a horse called Anytime. He was a lovely big horse and the string pulled out together. All the colts were in front and the fillies were in behind. Henry was on his lovely big white hack, a stately ex-showjumper and he sat there and watched us from the top of Warren Hill, like a king on his steed.

It was a Monday morning and the first four went off and then the next four and then there was a gap of 100 yards until the next four. I was the last one of the four jumping off in front. It was four furlongs up Warren Hill and Henry was at the top of the hill on his hack, waiting. He had said that we'd do a steady canter and then an ordinary canter. The steady canter is like a warm-up and then you go back down the hill and ride back up. So we jumped out on the steady canter and the horses in front of me went off like bullets.

I was taken by surprise. The horses behind me caught me up quickly and I didn't keep pace with the horses I was supposed to be in a group with. They had pulled about 100 yards clear of me and Anytime by the time we reached the top of the hill. So we all pulled up at the top and Henry came flying over on the hack and asked what was wrong.

I said: 'You said steady canter, ordinary canter.'

He said: 'Bloody hell, that is our steady canter.'

We went back down and I made sure I was right up there

with the rest of them for the ordinary canter. It wasn't that we didn't have good horses up north but they were Toyotas and Volkswagens and Minis. Henry's were Ferraris, Lamborghinis and Rolls-Royces. They oozed up that hill.

It was a culture shock and part of me was still thinking: 'What the hell am I doing here?' Not for the first time and not for the last, I wondered if all the people who were saying it wouldn't last were right. I was way out of my comfort zone.

One of my first rides for Henry was at Pontefract. I had had a lot of success there and I was on a lovely big horse but the ground was very firm and that worried me, so I rang Henry and asked if we should run it. He said I should let the horse take his chance. That was an eye-opener. The previous trainers I'd ridden for, if there was any little thing at all that might cause a problem for the horses, they wouldn't even think about running them. In a small yard, you have to wrap them up in cotton wool if you get a good horse; it might be the only one you have. But if you have 150 or 200 horses, and so many well-bred youngsters, you're not depending on just one or two to earn your bread.

I felt some pressure, of course, but it was eased by the fact that I was riding against boys like Pat Eddery, Frankie Dettori and Steve Cauthen, and I had been riding against them and winning in the previous months and years when I was with Jack and Lynda. I was riding a lot of winners and I was riding with so much confidence.

I thought that when I got the ammunition that Henry was going to give me, I would be able to use it. The only thing I was slightly intimidated by was Henry Cecil himself, the man he was. Everyone was in awe of him. It was like when

I went to meet Mother Teresa. I didn't know what to say or do. But once I was on his horses, I was fine.

I also knew that I needed to win a big race quickly. I couldn't afford too many failures. I needed to win a Classic, basically. That was what was expected of me as the stable jockey for Henry Cecil. People were after me straight away. Every failing was pounced upon. I rode Sleepytime in the Fred Darling Stakes at Newbury. She was the favourite for the 1000 Guineas at that stage and a short-priced favourite to win this particular race, but we got boxed in and could only finish fourth.

People called it the first serious test of my association with Henry and they were far from complimentary when the race had been run. People were raising their eyebrows but even if I hadn't done anything wrong, they were going to do that anyway. The horse didn't perform on the ground that day and that was that.

Henry didn't have a horse in the first Classic of that season, the 2000 Guineas. I rode Musical Pursuit in that race and came in dead last. When I rode Sleepytime in the 1000 Guineas the next day, I pretty much knew I had to win. If I didn't get that first Classic straight away, I don't think I would have lasted. If that makes the owner–trainer–jockey relationship sound precarious, that's because it can be. Here today, gone tomorrow in racing.

Little Harry Bentley rode Limato through 2016 and won two Group Ones on him: the July Cup at Newmarket and then the Prix de la Forêt in France. The winter after, he ran in Dubai, the ground was a little bit loose, the horse didn't like it, he finished fourth and Harry's off him. Someone else got the ride. One bad race and you're gone.

Owners can sometimes be difficult. A lot of them don't know much about racing. Someone introduces them to a bloodstock agent and they think 'I'll have a horse'. Then, if they see it running badly, they sack the trainer or the jockey.

Another example is Silvestre de Sousa. He was riding lots of winners and he got the Godolphin job but he didn't win any of the biggest races. Then he had one bad ride on Cavalryman in the Dubai Gold Cup, got boxed in and couldn't get out, should have won but didn't. And that was it. He was out at Godolphin.

I knew it would be the same with me and Henry. If I rode a bad race, all the owners would be saying 'I told you so' or 'I don't want him on my horse'. Only a trainer with the power of Henry Cecil could have picked me out of the north and been able to tell his owners I was riding for them. Most trainers wouldn't have that authority over his owners that Henry had. They wouldn't be able to impose a relatively unknown northern jockey on them. So Henry had a lot on his plate. If I didn't do well, he had egg on his face and I'd be looking for another job.

So the 1000 Guineas was probably one of the biggest wins of my career. It was a smooth race. Sleepytime started as the third favourite and we had a few problems with traffic in the opening stages but I held my nerve and things opened up. We hit the front about a furlong from home and opened up a gap to the rest of the field. We won pretty comfortably in the end. It was Henry's fifth victory in the 1000 Guineas and my first. I was delighted to win my first Classic for Henry, but I didn't celebrate outwardly because that was not really my way.

I knew it was the biggest win of my career up until that point, but I wasn't thinking about that. I was thinking about the next race and the race after that. I found it hard to get a real buzz out of those wins. It went back to my grounding with Jimmy FitzGerald. I'm not one for getting the crowd behind me. For me, it's not a performance; I feel like it's my job. You feel great but you think 'job done, on to the next one'.

The one that I really allowed myself to enjoy was North Light winning the Derby in 2004. I knew there was no pressure that day. It was easy to ride but when you are riding horses that need to be held up, you are thinking, thinking all the time, watching everything around you, what everyone else is doing and then the race is over and it's just a relief that the job is done. It's a pity, but sometimes you can be so driven that you can't actually enjoy the moment. They say that about a lot of sportsmen and women. I was always thinking of the next day, the next race.

For Frankie, maybe, it was a bit different because his father was a great jockey, he came into the racing world and it was expected of him to be a champion. He was always bubbly, a funny guy. He saw it a different way and his career took off straight away but mine was in turmoil. Once I'd won the Oaks at Epsom on Reams of Verse at the beginning of June 1997 to bring me my second Classic, my confidence grew. But even then, I was just thinking that it had bought me some time. As things turned out, I'd need every little bit of credit in the bank I could muster.

CHAPTER 11

Bosra Shambles

Henry Cecil had a filly called Bosra Sham and, oh, God, he loved that horse. She was his pride and joy. He talked her up and talked her up to the point where I think he actually believed that she really could no longer be beaten. I understood how he felt. He loved his horses and he had so much passion for them and that was his life. His life revolved around the yard and the jockeys and the world of horses. I understood that because that was my life, too. I had kids that I loved there with me in Newmarket, a beautiful house, everything I ever needed, and all I wanted to do was get on those horses. The horses brought me a bit of peace.

She was something else, Bosra Sham. It was true. She wasn't built like a filly. She was built like a colt. She was big and strong and robust and she had everything. Her performances and her figures speak for themselves and tell you of a horse that was majestic and grand. Getting on her back was like getting behind the wheel of a top-of-the-range Ferrari. She was the nicest, smoothest, strongest machine that I ever rode in my career.

She won her first four races, including the 1000 Guineas in 1996, but she had problems with injuries. Her feet bruised very easily and she had to take a lot of time off, and when she came back she was beaten by Mark of Esteem in the Queen Elizabeth II Stakes at Ascot on the day in September 1996 that Frankie Dettori won all seven races.

I rode her for the first time in May 1997 in the Brigadier Gerard Stakes at Sandown Park and she won by half a length, but she was breathtakingly good when we won again at Royal Ascot a few weeks later. This time, she destroyed a decent field in the Prince of Wales's Stakes on the opening day of the meeting and won by eight lengths. It was the kind of luxury ride that made you feel lucky to have access to Henry's horses.

But there was a lot of disappointment at Warren Place that I could only finish last but one on Lady Carla in the Hardwicke Stakes on the Friday of Royal Ascot when many had expected her to win. The gossips in racing were already starting to predict my demise as Henry's stable jockey.

A few weeks after that, on 5 July 1997, I rode Bosra Sham again in the Eclipse Stakes at Sandown Park. It was seen as a decent test even for Bosra Sham because she was up against the Breeders' Cup Turf winner, Pilsudski, and the Derby winner, Benny the Dip, but she was so good we all expected her to win.

There were only five horses in the race and Bosra Sham was a hold-up filly. I needed to switch her off at the start, which I did, but unfortunately the rest of the race didn't go to plan. I was annoyed with myself afterwards because I didn't see it coming. I was a bit naïve, I suppose, and the boys from the south taught the new upstart from the northern circuit a hard lesson.

Sometimes, it's like that. When I rode in the north, we gave the southern boys a bit of a hard time if they came up to ride on one of our usual tracks and now that I was riding for Henry, the boot was on the other foot. They weren't going to make it easy for me in races like that.

Mick Kinane was on Pilsudski and he jumped out fast and Willie Ryan was alongside him on Benny the Dip. I was tucked in behind them, but I was aware very quickly that Michael Hills was sitting on my outside on Sasuru and had me boxed in. I felt I had been done up like a kipper straight away. So I'm in a pocket and I'm wondering what to do. I didn't want to start forcing my way out early on and running deep. It's a long straight at Sandown so there was time but I knew that for all Bosra Sham's talents, she didn't have instant speed. She needed a little time to get going and I was think-ing 'I don't want to be in here'.

Michael Hills sat there on my outside, effectively saying 'you're going nowhere'. He had me covered. I'm not saying they ganged up on me or that they talked about it beforehand, but everyone knew who the best horse in the race was and they were all clever jockeys and, one way or another, they figured out a way to beat Bosra Sham.

I did glimpse one chance about two furlongs out when Pilsudski moved to the left a little and a gap appeared down the rails. I went for it, but I was trying to kick past a Breeders' Cup winner and a Derby winner, and then two things happened simultaneously. Mick moved back over to close the gap and I realised that I was about to be cut off by the false rail that makes a right to left kink in the straight at Sandown. If Bosra Sham had had instant speed, I would have been through the gap and we would have won the race, but it took her a furlong to reach top gear and so we didn't make it.

It was a disaster in terms of the race. I had to halt Bosra Sham's run and switch her to the outside, we lost all momentum and Pilsudski and Benny the Dip were away. Bosra Sham started to accelerate and make up ground but it was too late. Pilsudski and Benny the Dip were fine horses and we just couldn't catch them. We got close but not close enough and finished third. What a mess. When I was asked about it later, I called it the 'Bosra Shambles'. The term stuck.

Most of all, I was just annoyed with myself that I didn't see it coming. I let my guard down and I paid the penalty for that. I'd allowed myself to get boxed in and I'd been right where they wanted me to be. People say I never accepted it was my fault, but of course I accepted it was my fault. I even went into the yard the next day and apologised to everyone for what had happened. The head lad said they'd not seen jockeys do that too often.

I'd tried to do something about it by kicking down the inside but if I had just sat there behind Willie, they weren't going to change positions. I knew that Bosra Sham had to be gone in plenty of time because there was a little bit of a gap between putting your foot down and getting the acceleration. I knew I was in trouble soon enough, but I didn't know in time to get us out of it. I could have killed myself. Inside, it was eating me up. But there was no point in blaming anybody else. It would have made it worse.

Henry was okay. If it had been any other horse apart from Bosra Sham, not as much would have been made of it, but everyone knew that that horse was his favourite and it was hard for him to deal with the disappointment. Henry had made no secret of his belief that she was practically unbeatable and that she was the best horse he had ever trained and that brings dangers of its own. Sir Michael Stoute always hated you heaping praise on his horses before they had retired and that was one of the reasons: you are there to be shot at if you talk them up.

Henry refused to speak to the press after the race and when he finally forced himself to comment about the Bosra Shambles, he made it clear he wasn't overly impressed. 'She's had a hard race for no reason and I don't think she will be able to run again until York in August,' he said. 'I have never had her better than she was on Saturday but she never had a chance. It would have been far better if she had stayed at home. I'm not going to blame anyone but anyone who didn't see what happened in the Eclipse would be better off watching theatre. The whole thing was appalling.'

There were some people waiting for me to fail and now they all came bounding up with an 'I told you so'. Wafic Saïd, the owner of Bosra Sham and Lady Carla, insisted that I was taken off them both and Henry had to release a statement saying it was 'in the best interests of the fillies if Kieren Fallon is replaced'.

I had to go and pick myself up. The press were slaughtering me. I generally had a difficult, combative relationship with journalists, although I trusted a couple of them. I loved Alan Lee, who worked for *The Times* – I was so shocked and sorry when I heard he had died suddenly at the end of 2015. Anyway, I knew I didn't have many chances left. I was also struggling a bit to deal with the instructions that Henry would give me for races. Henry would always say to me 'be handy but get a lead, sit second, third or fourth, be in the box seat'. That was the only instruction I would ever get. When I got to Royal Ascot, I met up with Steve Cauthen and asked his advice. I should have done it earlier.

I told him what Henry was telling me and Steve said he used to say exactly the same to him. 'Look,' he said, 'you are riding the best horse, you know the best thing to do, you go out and do it and nine times out of ten, you will get it right. The odd time, it might not work for you but you have to do what you think.'

So I started doing my own thing and it was easy after that. Steve wasn't exactly saying I shouldn't listen to Henry, but he was telling me I had to have the confidence to adapt to circumstances.

No one ever saw my side of the story in the Eclipse but the truth is, I walked into it. They didn't want to see me doing too well, the southern boys. I had come down from the north and straight into one of the top jobs in racing and they weren't sure they liked it. The Bosra Shambles race was just a part of my welcome to the beautiful south.

CHAPTER 12

Twin Peaks

I don't know how close I was to getting the sack after the Bosra Sham debacle. I knew that Henry must have been thinking about it. When Wafic Saïd told him he didn't want me to ride his fillies any more, that was serious. Quite often, when one owner puts down a marker like that, others queue up to follow and your position can become untenable.

I was riding plenty of winners and I was leading the jockeys' championship for the first time in my life, but I understood that even that wasn't enough when you were riding for Henry Cecil. It wasn't sufficient any more to be racking up winners at Beverley and Thirsk at run-of-the-mill meetings. I had to be winning the biggest races.

The thing was, I liked riding in the big races. Some jockeys panic when they ride in a Classic or another high-calibre race and the horses can sense that. A horse senses danger, so it is not going to perform to its highest level if it can feel your fear. Anything I got on, I could just blot it out. The horse is all I can see in the race and that was all I concentrated on.

After the Bosra Shambles, my price for the jockeys' title was pushed out, too. The bookmakers, who had had me as the favourite, decided it was more likely that either Frankie Dettori or Pat Eddery would win the championship in 1997. Everyone's faith in me seemed to be draining away.

Then, less than a week after the Eclipse, everything changed. On the second day of the July meeting at Newmarket, I rode a four-timer. I started off with a winner in the opening race, a maiden, on Light Programme and then followed it up with three more on Bold Fact, Memorise and Daggers Drawn. In the week after the Eclipse, I rode 11 winners, but that day at the July meeting was the day I knew everything was going to be okay and that I was going to keep my job with Henry. I could go home knowing I'd done a good job.

It was one of the only days in my career that I thought that. There was something about that day. It even started well. Prince Khalid Abdullah, one of the sport's most influential owners, rang me when I was on the way to the course to let me know that he had full confidence in me and that gave me a huge boost.

I even got lucky with my car journey. The tank was showing empty. In fact, it was showing less than empty. It was right at the bottom of the reserve tank. When we were still a few miles away, it said there was only enough petrol for one mile. I was starting to think I might have to coast downhill some of the way, but we got there without turning the engine off.

The mood around me changed after that day at Newmarket and all my critics backed off. I reached 100 winners in early August and opened up a lead of 14 over Frankie and Pat. Even on that day when I rode four winners, though, I got done for excessive use of the whip in the last race. I wasn't a whip jockey and yet I found myself getting in trouble quite a lot and serving various suspensions for it and so I resolved to do something to change it. Instead of hitting the horses, I started to whistle. The rules had changed so that you were allowed fewer hits anyway and I knew I had to find a new way to get my mounts to quicken and lengthen without using the whip.

When most jockeys get a horse to lengthen and stretch, they change their hands and get on the shoulder. The whistling was a psychological ruse that I thought of. The horses were alarmed by it and so the effect would be that when I leaned forward and whistled in their ear, they wanted to try to get away from the whistle and they quickened. It was the opposite of drawing a horse to water by smooching it and it started to work for me. It was all about getting them at the right time when you're stretching and getting them to stretch further. Lengthen, lengthen, lengthen and because you're over their head and you're not far from their ears, they can hear it.

It became one of the things I was known for. Some of the other jockeys were intimidated by it, I think. It got so that if I was gaining on them in a race, they could hear my whistle coming and when they heard that, they knew they were in trouble.

It all stemmed from the fact that I understood horses. I liked them and I knew how their minds worked and what their natures were and what they responded to. I knew how to switch them off, to get them calm at the start of the race when they are sometimes wide-eyed and wild and raring to go. If you can switch a horse off, it is because it trusts you. You need to get its confidence. You can see it thinking. You can see the eyes. You can see it thinking: 'What is this fella like?'

Perhaps the stable lad who is looking after them doesn't give them any affection or attention and that has made them sour and made them want to bite you, but when you start patting them and talking to them, straight away they think 'oh, this is different'. For a lot of the stable lads, it's work. They don't understand. If a horse is sour, it's because it's not been given any attention. See how they change when you give them some attention. It's like being a student of psychology. No one really knows how clever horses are. They are one big clever machine.

Equally, when I wanted to step things up, I would use my body or my legs as well as my whistle. Mostly, everything is through the hands and the reins and it is all about feel and instinct. Most jockeys want a tight rein on a horse so you are travelling with them, but I have a long, loopy rein because I always maintain that if you have a tight rein, the horse is using more energy. Frankie Dettori rides much shorter, American style, he gets down behind his horses and uses their neck. I use my lower body and my legs. I could throw the rein away and ride a horse.

Everything is behind the shoulder. When a horse is getting tired in the last two furlongs, you want to keep them going and stop them slowing down. That's why we have the stick to persuade them, but while Frankie pushes them with the neck or the head, I pushed from behind the horse's shoulders. I could work on a horse from behind the shoulders to keep them at their maximum speed for as a long as possible. The whip was the last thing I used.

Around the time I joined Henry Cecil, I gave an interview to Sue Montgomery at the *Independent on Sunday*. She was another journalist I respected, and we talked about my riding style. I told her I just liked being on a horse, whether it was riding work or riding in the country. But when you're racing, you get the ultimate feeling, the rhythm and flow of a race, getting deep into your horse, getting him to stretch, becoming one with him.

I like to throw them their heads, on the buckle end of the rein. I ride the horse, not just its head. You use your legs and your body to keep a horse balanced, not your hands. Some jockeys just push the reins and when you see that, you know they could be getting so much more from that horse.

Willie Carson was always criticising me for not getting hold of their heads but to me, that's gagging them, stopping the forward movement. He said I would have looked the part better if I did, but my view was that I'd rather be in the winner's enclosure than look pretty riding.

If you can get a horse to flow a bit, that's better. What used to perplex other jockeys was that they would never know how well I was going because when you have a loopy rein, your rival jockeys can't tell whether you're travelling well or trying to get a horse to lengthen. It's like when you are watching cyclists or runners and you can see the ones that are travelling strong and the ones with the stress. If another jockey was on a tight rein, I could see whether he was travelling well and whether he was one I wanted to be following.

You also know that if a jockey on a tight rein has to ask the horse with half a mile to run, they are going to be dropping back and you don't want to be behind them because there is a danger they will impede you. You want to be behind the one that is travelling the strongest, so that it carries you with it towards the finishing post.

A lot of the time, you will be riding a hold-up horse and

you know the pace is not strong, but you also know that if you let your horse go, it might hit the front and think it's all over. It's like switching off the ignition on your car. They cut out on you.

Even though horses are racing, they can spot things and that's why they put blinkers on so they can focus better. The best thing is to get your horse in the slipstream of the leader. It's a bit like cycling with its pacemakers and its slipstreamers.

I admired Frankie's style as a rider and, in a way, I envied the ease with which he was able to play to the crowd and make the most of his big wins. I could never really do that. It wasn't my character. I would have felt self-conscious doing what he did. I would have felt presumptuous. It was a relief for me to win rather than a triumph. I hadn't been brought up to expect praise, and you carry that with you.

Frankie and I had been apprentices together, but it took me about ten years to get to the top and it took Frankie one. He had got Sheikh Mohammed's job, which catapulted him miles ahead while I was still pottering away up north. Now, I had caught up.

It wasn't just that I was Henry Cecil's stable jockey. I was also lucky to have a brilliant agent called David Pollington, who booked all my rides. I started to work with him when I came over to ride for Jimmy FitzGerald. He was one of the first agents and he was unbelievably knowledgeable. He was a serious man on form.

I spoke to him every morning. He went through my rides with me and told me I'd be going to Salisbury that day and I'd ask him why I'd want to go all the way to Salisbury when I could go over the road to Beverley. 'We're riding one for Sir

Michael today,' he'd say. He always seemed to send me to the right meeting. The only one little blot on his copybook over all those years was when Benny the Dip won the Derby and David told me afterwards we could have ridden him because John Gosden had rung him the Tuesday before the race to offer me the ride.

I rode Symonds Inn for Jimmy FitzGerald in that race who was 33/1 or something and Benny the Dip was second favourite. David didn't tell me because he knew I would have put my foot down and ridden Benny the Dip and there would have been a hell of a row with Jimmy FitzGerald. I was angry about it for a couple of minutes when I found out, but I let it go.

For a while, it was a close race between Frankie and me in the jockeys' championship in 1997, but after that four-timer at Newmarket, it was all plain sailing. To win the championship was expected of me and so, once again, I didn't feel a great deal of elation when I won it for the first time.

Sure, winning the jockeys' title brings you a lot of satisfaction. People always ask whether I got more satisfaction out of winning the Derby or the jockeys' title and even though there's only one Derby, to win a championship it takes a lot longer and it's hard work for months and months on end.

I accelerated away from the rest of the field in the second half of 1997 and rode 202 winners altogether. I rode 909 turf rides that season and won nearly £2m in prize money. It was 9 November when I was confirmed as the Champion Jockey. It had taken me sixteen years to get from my arrival at Kevin Prendergast's yard and jig-jogging down that tree-lined avenue to the top of my profession.

Winning the jockeys' title was one thing, but the other

achievement flat jockeys crave is triumphing in the Derby. I didn't come close in 1998. I finished halfway down the field, but I won the jockeys' championship again that year, this time with 204 winners. I like to think I had some talent, obviously, but no one worked harder than me and I took real pride in that. I had 972 rides that second season with Henry and I became only the fourth jockey after Fred Archer, Sir Gordon Richards and Frankie Dettori to ride 200 winners or more in consecutive seasons. I used to keep myself to myself. I was up at 6am and home at 9.30pm. That was my life.

Only 57 of my winners came from horses trained by Henry, which showed there were plenty of other trainers and owners who wanted to use me. I was riding a lot for Barry Hills and John Gosden as well by then so I could have stayed in the south if I'd wanted to, even without the patronage of Henry.

I was confident I would win the jockeys' championship again in 1999. As I've said, it was expected of me. I hoped that this would be my year for the Derby, too, and I started the season by winning the 1000 Guineas on Wince, although I was still angry with myself for the way I'd lost the 2000 Guineas on Enrique the day before when we were baulked just as we were starting to make a run.

A month later, I won the Oaks on Ramruma the day before I rode Oath in the Derby. I didn't feel as if it was a good omen particularly, but it did remind me how well I felt I knew the course at Epsom and the challenges it set for the horses and their riders. I had only ridden in the Derby three times, but there was something about Epsom that brought the best out in me.

The first furlong at Epsom is uphill and then there is a

little chicane and that chicane is one of the keys to having a chance in the Derby. You can't win it there but you can lose it. A lot of horses veer across at that point because they don't want to ride into the kink and so it's chaos at the start of that chicane. The horses are young and excitable and full of the adrenaline of the race and if your horse gets a bump, it's like if you're running for a ball and someone gives you a dig in the ribs: it's going to knock the wind out of you. Once you get through there without any interference and get across to the rail, you can relax a bit.

You have to be aware of everything around you. It's like being on the M25 at rush hour with cars flying around everywhere, switching lanes, trying to dart up your inside or cutting you up. You have got to anticipate what other people might be trying to do.

Coming down the hill isn't as bad as people think. There are a lot of horses thundering down towards Tattenham Corner and you have to hold your nerve, but if your horse is travelling well and you have got a good hold of its head, it's a piece of cake really. But all the time, you're also thinking about being where you want to be when you turn the corner and go down the straight.

I knew Oath was a decent horse who had great finishing speed because he had won the Dee Stakes easily, but it was a strong field that year with horses like Daliapour and Dubai Millennium both well-fancied. Henry was worried that Oath would sweat up before the start and use up all his energy before the race, so I broke the parade early and took him down to the stalls quietly and steadily. I was fined £2500 by the stewards for that. Henry had said he would pay it but he never did.

We got a decent start and he travelled well. I used to study Lester Piggott, who was the master of Epsom, and watch how he approached the Derby, and he always seemed to get in the box seat, just behind the front runner, getting cover on the inside. Oath was round the inside that day, not staying on the rail but one off. You have to leave yourself options in case the horse in front of you comes back. It's like having two positions. Other jockeys don't like it when you have two positions because you are in and out, in and out.

I just wanted the race to run smoothly and I got through the kinks at the top of the hill without any problem. When we got to Tattenham Corner, we were close enough to Daliapour to cover him when his jockey, Gérald Mossé, made his move two furlongs out.

When I asked Oath to quicken, he responded beautifully and we surged past Daliapour and into the lead. We won by more than a length and now I was a Derby winner as well as champion jockey. It felt unbelievable. It was a job well done, but that was all. Time to move on to the next thing.

That's what racing is like. There is no time to pause for thought, although maybe that was partly because I didn't want to pause for thought. I rode in another race at Epsom that afternoon and then rushed back to Newmarket to ride in the last race of the evening meeting.

That was the way I approached things. I did not want to stop for rest because I never felt settled. I never knew what was coming round the corner. It turned out I was right to feel like that. A few weeks later, when I thought my partnership with Henry was as strong and formidable as it had ever been, I was out of a job.

CHAPTER 13

Fairytale of Newmarket

The first time I saw Natalie Cecil, Henry Cecil's second wife, I was in the kitchen in the house at Warren Place. Henry was at the stove, frying up some mushrooms, and Willie Ryan and I were sitting at the table. We had been riding work on my first morning as Henry's stable jockey and when it was over, Henry invited us in for breakfast.

I had seen Natalie from a distance before. She had been a stable girl when Henry met her and she was more than twenty years his junior. His first wife, Julie, the daughter of the great trainer Noel Murless, was a lovely woman and Henry had left her for Natalie, who was only twenty-three when they got married. Julie was well liked in Newmarket and so Natalie always found it hard to gain any kind of acceptance. She had some dressage horses that she looked after, but I knew that she wasn't popular around the yard and that her increasing tendency to interfere in how it was run was causing tensions among the staff.

A couple of years earlier, in fact, many people had blamed

Natalie for Sheikh Mohammed's decision to remove his 40 horses from Warren Place, a move which dealt a crushing blow to the yard and which it struggled for a long time to recover from. Natalie had made some criticisms of the Sheikh, and not long after that he had suggested that Henry was not surrounding himself with the best or most qualified people and had added that everyone in Newmarket would know exactly who he was talking about.

There were other issues, of course. Henry and Sheikh Mohammed had had a disagreement about an injury to a horse called Mark of Esteem. They were both strong-minded men and there were other tensions between them, too, but it was clear Natalie's arrival as a person of influence did not help.

I'm not saying that I took an instant dislike to her, but even though she was an attractive woman, my first impression was that she was someone who had gone from being a stable girl to a person with a lot of airs and graces. This will seem ironic given what was to happen later, but I didn't like the way she treated Henry. Neither did a lot of the lads who saw the way she was around him. I didn't think she was very nice to him. I felt that she mocked him and some of what she did could appear quite insulting to him. Maybe that was just me being conservative but that was my impression.

Henry was rather reserved. He was a genius with horses and king of his own world, regarded throughout racing with affection and respect. But he didn't like confrontation, and his way of avoiding it was to be as indirect as possible. Natalie was much more direct and confident. In many ways, she behaved as if she were the boss. It made me feel uncomfortable, the way she treated him. I didn't like to see it. Before long, I started making excuses to avoid going into the house for breakfast. I'd say I was going to ride work for someone else after I'd finished for Henry. I'd say I had someone to see.

But Natalie was around more and more. She started riding out with the string in the morning and when we were on our way out to the gallops, she would trot along next to me. I didn't mind to talking to her in some ways because she knew about horses. But it soon got to the point where I thought she was openly flirting with me right under the nose of Henry, who was sitting up at the top of the hill on his white hack. I wouldn't have liked it if my wife was doing that to me and it made me embarrassed. I felt self-conscious about it. I was married and she was married to my boss. She was married to the man who had given me a dream job and I soon started to worry that her behaviour was putting it all in jeopardy.

I couldn't tell her to get lost. She was Henry's wife and he was clearly smitten by her. I didn't want to make an enemy of her because I knew how much influence she had with Henry. I wanted to say to her: 'Don't you realise your husband is watching you?' but I didn't feel I could.

Then Henry made things worse. For some reason, he put Natalie in charge of finding a house for me, my wife, Julie, and our children to buy and move into. That was what really ruined things. Now, she had an excuse to be around me all the time when I had finished riding out. So I would get back to where my car was parked at Warren Place and she would have stuck one of those yellow Post-it notes on the side window with a message on it. It would be the time of an appointment at the estate agents or a list of arrangements about when and where we were to meet to view a house somewhere.

Most mornings after riding out, it would be the same,

a little sticker on my car saying we had an appointment to look at a property at 10.30am and that I should meet her at a certain place. I had realised by now that this was getting dangerous and so I always asked my driver, Tony, to take me to these appointments so that I would have company. It started to wear me down. 'Come and see this house, Kieren' or 'come and see that house, Kieren'. I didn't like it, but Henry had put her in charge of doing it and so she had all the excuses she needed to write me as many Post-it notes as she wanted.

She even got me to go to Laura Ashley to look at wallpaper once. Me, in a branch of Laura Ashley. Can you imagine that? When I told some of my friends about it, they thought it was hilarious. I was obsessed with riding horses, not picking out a floral pattern for a pair of curtains.

In the end, with her help, I decided to buy an old chapel in a beautiful little village outside Newmarket, called Dalham. It was a lovely spot, a small community with the little River Kennett running through it and a pub called the Affleck Arms on the bridge. The chapel, all red brick and stained-glass windows, was right on the road. It was a very short walk to the pub and not far at all to The Old Plough at Ashley, where I had had that fateful encounter with Derek Thompson a few years earlier.

Natalie Cecil got all her carpenters and workmen to do it out and it did look great. It was a bit small and there was no garden to speak of, but I think Natalie was more concerned about the interior design element of things. It wasn't really a family home. I stayed there for my first year with Henry and then my wife and kids moved down.

I was soon aware that people had started gossiping about me and Natalie. I told my friends that she was driving me bloody mad. Mostly, they still just thought it was funny. But things got worse. She had never really come out on the road before, but now she made it clear she wanted to travel to race meetings that I was riding at. These were quite often fairly obscure meetings. So she'd suddenly be at Windsor on a Monday evening to saddle the horse or something. There was always some excuse, some stupid reason, why she said she had to be there. And there was always a reason why she had to get a lift there with me and a lift home.

On the way back from meetings, she would often suggest that we stopped off at a pub for a drink or that we went to have something to eat. I'm not going to say she was chasing me but it was all a bit uncomfortable.

And I had a wife, too. Julie was still living in Yorkshire with our daughter, Natalie, and our newborn twins, Cieren and Brittany. She'd been pregnant with the twins when I got the job with Henry and moved down to Newmarket, and it was around a year after that by the time the new house was ready.

I'd met Julie in Malton when I was riding for Jimmy FitzGerald. She had been an apprentice jockey to Captain Jim Wilson and then she moved to Malton to ride for Nigel Tinkler. She was a good rider. She used to ride a horse called Crofter's Climb; he was a good horse and she won plenty of races on him.

She was determined and gutsy, too. She was several months pregnant with Natalie when she rode her last winner for Gordon Holmes on one of his Gimcrack horses. But by the time I had got the job with Henry, the work had already started to take its toll on our marriage. I was just always away. I was always at work. The way I worked, I was up at six in the morning. I was getting on my first horse at half six and riding out and then I was rushing around, getting ready to go racing.

You are trying to get home to have a coffee or a bit of toast or something. You are jumping in the shower, you are running around, you are flat out all the way, you are trying to eat your bit of breakfast, trying to get your clothes off to get changed.

Julie used to say I left a trail of destruction. She knew where I was because of the mess I left behind. And then, when you've left the destruction behind, you're in the car and you're gone and your wife is almost literally picking up the pieces after you've disappeared.

I was the Antichrist to be around when I got back in that car after a race meeting. Say I was at Lingfield and rode four winners and two seconds; all that was happening in my head was that I could have had six winners if I had done something differently. By the time I got home, it would often be 10pm and I would have had a few drinks. All I wanted to do by then was go to sleep. And then it would be the same the next day. Or I'd be travelling abroad, to Hong Kong or Australia or California. You are always moving on.

The kids were still young when we eventually broke up. They were in a good school near Newmarket and sometimes I made it to their sports day and that was something else. But I was seldom there, either for them or for Julie. We were married for a decent time before we divorced but it was inevitable that we drifted apart.

The truth is I have never been confident around women. I have never been confident around people in general. But I liked to have a good time and when I was younger, up in

Malton, I was out a lot, partying. I was a bit shy but you have a few drinks and away you go. That was another reason why I found the whole thing with Natalie Cecil so difficult. When people started speculating there was something going on between me and her, it was my worst nightmare, my worst fear. All my dreams were wrapped up in this job and I could see it was in jeopardy.

And then, in the late summer of 1999, a few days before Glorious Goodwood, it all came crashing down. Perhaps I was fortunate it hadn't happened earlier but it still came as a shock when I drove out of the house one morning to go and ride work for Henry and saw a black car blocking the country lane outside.

I was living in a bigger place near another village near Newmarket called Cowlinge by now and we had to drive down a single-track road to get to the main road. That Saturday morning, a friend of mine called Frank Dalton was driving me and when we left about 6.30am, we saw this black Audi parked in the lane. Frank put a couple of wheels on the grass and we pulled up alongside it. He wound the window down to remonstrate with the driver, who was just sitting at the wheel doing nothing.

He looked at me and said: 'Kieren Fallon, I'm from the *News of the World* and we're running a story tomorrow that you have been having an affair with Natalie Cecil.'

My mind started whirring. I was thinking: 'That golden thing is gone.' I was thinking: 'The best job in racing is gone.' I was thinking: 'Derbies, Guineas, everything, all gone.'

I knew Natalie Cecil had been constantly bombarding me. And now someone else knew. I knew they'd say no smoke without fire. I thought of Julie and the kids. You can't imagine the panic and the dread that was coursing through me. What should I do?

I was late for work now, too. I hate being late. I cut it fine but I hate being late. My father used to do it. We'd get to Mass at one minute past eleven. We'd be sitting in the car waiting for him and he'd potter along and we'd be one minute late.

I said to the guy from the *News of the World*: 'There is no affair but if you want to talk to me, I'll see you in the Heath Court Hotel when I finish work.' He had his photographer with him. They said they'd be there.

I rode work for Henry. I didn't say a thing. I came back down to the hotel. I sat down with the reporter and the photographer. The reporter said a friend of Natalie Cecil had told them we were having an affair.

I think that by then everyone knew Natalie wasn't happy in her marriage to Henry and she wanted a way out. But I told them again there was no affair. They wanted to take pictures. Frank, who had come with me to the hotel, wanted to kill this guy with the camera.

I told them that if they ran the story on me, they would be sued because there was no affair. I went and rode my horses in the afternoon's races. My mind was blank. I couldn't tell you now where I was that day. I didn't know what to tell Julie. I didn't know what they were going to run. My mind was everywhere. I didn't know what they had been told.

I thought there was no point saying anything to Julie before I knew if there was even going to be a story. Julie had a short fuse as well. People said we had a tempestuous relationship and I think that was a fair description of it. But later that day, after racing, I got a phone call from Henry. He wanted me to come to see him. No prizes for guessing what he wanted to talk about. I went up to Warren Place and he seemed fine. He invited me into his office and we had a beer.

There was a moment of awkward silence and then he asked me about his wife and what there was between us. I told him about her coming racing and leaving notes on my car, I told him about her asking me to choose wallpaper and I told him there was no affair.

At the time, I wondered whether someone else who worked in the yard had been putting poison in Henry's ear. Later I realised that, after they'd spoken to me and I'd told them flat out that there was no story, the *News of the World* must have rung Henry and asked him if he had heard the rumours and what he thought. They may have told him what they told me, that it was going to be in tomorrow's paper.

He asked me again what was going on and I told him again that there was no affair. It seemed as if he believed me, but he hated confrontation and that kind of conversation was his worst nightmare. I think he probably just wanted it to be over, but I left the yard thinking that everything was fine and that he was satisfied that I had done nothing wrong.

I got up on Sunday morning and went to the newsagent to get a copy of the *News of the World*. The headline said she was having an affair with a top jockey. It didn't name me. It didn't name anyone. In racing circles, there were rumours about other jockeys and Natalie Cecil as well. Not just me. I still don't know if there was any truth to any of them.

The details were fairly lurid, as you would expect. The story was presented as if it had come from one of Natalie's friends. She had confided in this friend and the friend had confided in the *News of the World*. Presumably for a reasonable amount of money.

The friend said that Natalie had become friendly with a married jockey and that she had enjoyed the friendship. She said he was someone she could laugh with and share a drink with at a time when she was feeling vulnerable in her own private life. She also said that the friendship had become something more and that she and the married jockey had had a one-night stand during a working trip to Ireland and that they had had sex in a shower. The account did not leave much to the imagination.

I never rode for Henry again. Not really. I think I rode one horse at Goodwood and another at Deauville in France four or five days later. But to all intents and purposes, that was it. He never called me to tell me it was over. He never contacted me personally. He just cut me loose.

I knew it was over when my agent called the yard the next day to ask which horses I was riding at Goodwood and Henry's racing manager said I wouldn't be required. I knew then that was the end of it.

Then at Goodwood, Henry released a statement saying I had been fired for 'personal reasons'. So now everybody assumed even more than ever that I was the 'top jockey' that had the affair with Natalie Cecil. The media had a field day. It was a feeding frenzy.

That was fairly devastating professionally. And personally. Julie assumed something must have been going on. And that was a huge blow to our marriage. We didn't get divorced until some years after that, but we didn't really recover from that furore. We didn't have a big row about it or anything. We didn't see enough of each other to have big rows by then.

I was obsessed with my riding and I didn't make room for anything else.

Christopher Stewart-Moore advised me that I had a good case to take action to recover the rest of the money owed from my contract as Henry's stable jockey. He resisted and proceedings were issued in the High Court to pay the outstanding sums due under my retainer.

In those proceedings, Henry alleged that I had had sex with his wife. My lawyers asked for what I believe were known in those days as 'Further and Better Particulars' of that allegation, and specifically where and when the sex was supposed to have taken place.

We were a little surprised when Henry's lawyers provided those particulars. There were about six occasions alleged, I am told, and my lawyers went through each and every one. It was easy to establish my whereabouts most days because of my racing commitments and we were able to show that I could not have been in the vicinity of the alleged 'breach of contract' on any of the occasions mentioned. Soon after we had pleaded our reply to the Further and Better Particulars, Henry settled the case and paid the money.

I didn't speak to Henry for a while after that, but some time later I started riding for Paul Howling now and again when I was available and Paul lived in one of the cottages at the back of Warren Place. We'd be out in the yard, having a coffee and Henry would come up and sit down and chat to me and say: 'What are you riding today?' Nothing was ever said about Natalie. Nothing. It was strange. As if nothing had ever happened. It was as if he had erased it from his mind. It was as if I never really rode for him. He was polite and nice and I thought maybe he'd put me up again because I was champion jockey most years. But that never happened.

Henry fell on hard times for a while and he and Natalie divorced. More owners left him and his yard fell into a steep decline but then, to general rejoicing in the racing world, he made a great comeback, starting with Light Shift winning the Oaks in 2007. Frankel gave him some of the most glorious days of his career in the autumn of his life and he married for a third time, happily, before he succumbed to stomach cancer in 2013. He was seventy years old.

As far as Natalie Cecil was concerned, it was just a case of out of sight, out of mind. Once I left Warren Place in 1999, I never saw her again. I think she walked out of the yard that week as well and never came back. It would have been better for all of us if she had never crossed the threshold in the first place.

CHAPTER 14

The Big Flip

By the time I stopped riding for Henry Cecil, I had started to adopt a new attitude to the issue that dominates the lives of most jockeys. Like many riders, from the time I was in my early twenties, I had been engaged in a constant battle with the weighing scales. The horror of putting up overweight was always with me, but I was starting to learn new tricks.

Making the weight is an ever-present discipline for jockeys. Boxers have to make weight for every fight so they might have to face the scales in public every few months. They can let themselves go a bit in between fights, or at least in the periods when they are not in training camp. There is no window of indulgence like that for a jockey. We have to make weight for every race, pretty much every day of our working lives. The dark art of starving yourself or getting down to the weight by any means necessary is known as wasting in racing.

There is no down time as long as you're riding. There is no time when we can let ourselves go. There is no time when we can forget about the scales. The hub of every racecourse for us is the weighing room. That says it all, really. The result is that most jockeys have to take extreme measures to get down to the required weight and over the years those extreme measures, those abuses of your body, begin to seem like the norm.

In the mid-1990s, 8st 6lb was the weight that most flat jockeys were required to ride at. I was a real lightweight when I was eighteen years old, but after my trip to Australia in the winter before I came over to England to ride for Jimmy FitzGerald, I had filled out. I came back from Australia weighing 9st 6lb and ever after, it was a nightmare for me to get back down to 8st 6lb.

Putting up overweight just wasn't done. That would kill your career. You'd have a black mark against you straight away with your owner and your trainer because you would effectively be handicapping your ride more severely than it was already handicapped. Extra weight means extra time getting around the track and seconds lost mean the difference between winning and losing.

If you put up a pound overweight and the horse still ran well, then it would be even more harshly handicapped the next time out and so there really was no upside. Putting up overweight was a real no-no. You might get away with it once if you'd been stuck in traffic, say, and not had a chance to sweat off a bit of weight in the sauna at the track but if you did it more than once, you would start losing rides quickly.

The problem, I suppose, for most jockeys, was that we were trying to get down to weights that were unnaturally low even for men with smaller frames. So it was a grim struggle. A lot of jockeys just didn't really eat. Others were incredibly frugal with their diets. Others found ways of getting the weight off.

I know that jockeys like A.P.McCoy spent a lot of time in

hot baths, sweating and sweating. Other jockeys swore by time in the sauna. Some of them seemed to spend half their lives in one. I couldn't do that. I'd have a couple of minutes in the sauna and then find I couldn't breathe properly. So when I was riding for Jimmy FitzGerald, I had these torturous methods of getting the weight off. I had five or six different sets of long johns and T-shirts and I would put those on and then pull on a plastic sweat suit over them. Then I'd put a tracksuit over all that and go for a run.

Still wearing all my layers, I'd get in the car and head off to the races at Thirsk or Beverley or another of the northern circuits. If it was a hot day, I'd leave the windows up and let myself bake in the car with the sun's rays beating through the glass. If it wasn't a hot day, I'd switch the heaters up to full blast, turn the music on loud and just try and get through the journey without thinking about it too much. I might allow myself a bit of Lucozade with some ice in it and sip away at that a little bit. And if I wanted to treat myself, I'd wind the windows down for a couple of minutes when I was driving across the moors.

Some drives were more draining than others. Going to Ayr was the worst because it was the greatest distance. There was one occasion when I knew I had to shift three or four pounds on the journey from Malton and so even though it was a hot summer's day, I turned the heaters up as well for maximum effect.

I got to the end of the A74 on the drive up there and I felt like I was going to pass out at the wheel. I had been in the car for a couple of hours already by then and I had sweated out a lot of fluid. I looked over to my right and I saw a big lake shimmering in the sunshine. I was almost delirious by that stage and I thought I might have been hallucinating and that it was a mirage. When I had satisfied myself that it was a real lake, all I wanted to do was pull over and run the hundred yards across the field to that lake and dive into it. I knew I couldn't do that because I still had another pound at least to get rid of.

I know it sounds extreme but this was how my mind was working: I knew the horse that I was due to ride that day at Ayr was fancied and that I could win and I wanted to ride it more than anything else. I wanted to ride it even more than I wanted to dive in that lake. I wanted to ride it badly enough that I was willing to risk passing out behind the wheel. I had another forty-five minutes to go and it was a bad road for the last part of the journey but I gritted my teeth and drove on.

There were a couple of more times on that journey when I thought I might faint but I made it. I turned the shower on cold in the weighing room and just sat there for about ten minutes. Then I had a drop of tea with a bit of sugar and that was it.

It's not really a case of having to liven yourself up before a race if you've been wasting hard like that. You don't need to do that. When your colours are on and your helmet's on, then the adrenaline starts and you forget all about the wasting until you get off the horse. When you are wasting that hard, you can drink but you can't eat.

I wasted nearly every day of my riding career. For years and years, I put that sweat suit on, got in my car and drove off. Years ago, it was even more primitive than that. Jockeys used to go to the muck-heap in the yard and bury themselves up to their neck in steaming horse manure. That was a do-it-yourself sauna, I suppose.

In the end, though, I grew tired of driving for hours in my

car with the windows up and the heaters on in the height of summer, and I decided to try a different approach. A lot of the other boys had found a new way of getting down to the required weight. They called it flipping.

You eat as much as you can and drink as much as you can and then you stick your finger down your throat and pop the lot out. It was a hell of a lot less effort than the sweat suits and the running and the car journeys. I did it pretty much every day for the rest of my career.

Some people would call it bulimia. I realise that there are a lot of people who are concerned about the lengths that jockeys go to in their pursuit of weight loss and the effects it has on their long-term health. But I don't think flipping is the same as bulimia. It shares some of the same characteristics, particularly the bingeing and then the purging, but there are important ways in which it is different, too.

I am not an expert on bulimia but my understanding of it is that it is a product in part, at least, of body consciousness and a person's desire to look thin, often caused by the images that are beamed at us from the pages of style magazines. Flipping has nothing to do with that. Flipping is not about body consciousness. Flipping is a purely pragmatic device to allow a jockey to work. It is a means to an end. It is a way of ensuring that he can get the rides he needs to make a living.

I'm not saying it's pleasant. At the start, I found it hard. My eyes were popping through their sockets, my stomach was red raw and I was spitting blood because the acid cut my throat. It was unpleasant and there's a stigma attached to it. But you get more efficient as you get more experienced. I made sure I threw up straight after eating, for a start. That way, you reduce the amount of acid that is forming in your stomach and coming back up with your food and so it has a minimal effect on your stomach lining and your teeth.

People say that the acid can rot your teeth and make them fall out, but not if you get rid of the food straight away before the stomach has had a chance to go to work on it. I haven't had any long-lasting problems with the after-effects of flipping.

If I were in a restaurant, I would go and throw up before I had even finished my meal. Sometimes, a restaurant might only have one toilet in the restroom and I worried that other diners might hear me or that it might leave a smell and so I'd go out into the car park to throw up there instead. That was a common practice with jockeys.

I've been out in restaurant car parks with other jockeys, all of us throwing up in the dark. It wasn't a pretty sight or a nice sound, either. One of the other leading jockeys had this unbelievable technique. He would eat as much as he could and drink a whole litre of Coke and then he would flip it. He'd projectile vomit it across the car park. It was like watching a scene out of *The Exorcist*.

The more you drank and the more you ate, the easier it was to flip it. And the longer I did it, the easier it became. It wasn't a case of having to force your fingers down your throat any more. My brain started to know what was coming. If I just touched my throat somewhere around my Adam's Apple, it would be enough to pop it all out.

Flipping was satisfying psychologically, too. I imagine that is one of the things it does have in common with bulimia. Part of the reason you eat food is that you love the taste. You don't lose that with flipping. You just don't gain the weight. So in some ways, you get the best of both worlds.

Everything is in your head when it comes to how much you eat and eating less is about controlling your mind as much as your stomach. You get up in the morning and you have breakfast because it's breakfast time, not necessarily because you are hungry. You have lunch because it's lunchtime even though you might not be hungry. Dinner? Yeah, I'll have some dinner. You are full but you keep eating.

Flipping is just another psychological trick. It stops you craving food. When I went out to be sick, I always made sure I left something on my plate, so that I could come back in and end up with a nice taste in my mouth. I might have a bit of chicken waiting for me and then just drink the juices.

I always had a piece of chocolate afterwards, too, because it's sweet and it makes you feel good and gives you a bit of energy. You feel light-headed if you take absolutely everything out of your stomach. You have got to be smart about it.

I didn't notice any impact on my health. I had problems with stomach ulcers when I was younger, but that was because I wasn't eating enough and I was drinking too much alcohol. That didn't do my insides any favours but it was nothing to do with flipping. If anything, I felt better when I was doing it. The Romans used to do it, too. They had a banquet and then got rid of it. If you feel uncomfortably full, it's a normal instinct to try to want to make yourself feel better.

I felt embarrassed about doing it. Of course I did. It's not part of our culture. It's something that's frowned upon in modern society. I think all the jockeys who do it probably feel embarrassed about it. But most of them did it and my guess is that most of them still do.

They won't say that, though, because no one likes to admit it. We all did it and we all knew we all did it, but there is still a taboo about admitting it publicly. Maybe some jockeys see it as a sign of weakness. I just saw it as a way of helping me to reach my goal.

The truth is, it's part of the job. It's the same with hydration. If you're a jockey, you're always going to be dehydrated. You are so dehydrated that your urine is the colour of amber. It should be straw-coloured or paler but if you're a jockey, it never is. It got so that it was only a shot of vitamin B12 or a shot of vodka that could properly revive me after I had been wasting. You drink to give yourself a boost. And to stay sane. Because it's not normal to be on hunger strike and that's effectively the state we keep ourselves in for most of the year.

As far as the flipping goes, I wouldn't say I'd recommend it. I am aware of the dangers of it getting it out of control and now that I'm retired, I don't do it any more. I still eat relatively sparingly because old habits die hard and my stomach shrank so much that I don't have a huge appetite. I get uncomfortable if I eat when I'm full but I don't flip any more.

As for it causing long-term health problems for jockeys, though, my own belief is that it is better to keep your weight down, even if it is through flipping, than to be overweight or obese. You are storing up way more problems if you are too heavy than if you are keeping your weight in check.

In the end, there's only one excuse for flipping: it's not body image, it's being able to do your job. You do what you have to do to get on those scales and see the red figures on the digital read-out tell you that you don't have to put up overweight. In our world, there's more shame in that than popping your meal out in a restaurant car park.

CHAPTER 15

Stoute Party

When I lost my job with Henry Cecil, I was in turmoil. For about seventy-two hours. And then, I had the kind of stroke of luck that most people can only dream of. A few days after the Natalie Cecil 'revelations' hit the newspapers, Gary Stevens, who was the retained jockey for Sir Michael Stoute, rang me.

He said he was going back to America. He said he was leaving. He said, basically, that there was a vacancy with Sir Michael Stoute. And so, less than a week after I had lost one of the two best jobs in English racing, the other one had become available and I knew I had to be in with a good chance of getting it.

I had had some contact with Sir Michael in the months before I was approached by Henry and I had ridden plenty of winners for him while I was still retained by Jack and Lynda Ramsden. In fact, back then there was some speculation that I was going to be offered a job at Freemason Lodge, Sir Michael's yard in Newmarket.

Henry Cecil was like a god to all of us and I had always admired him but, as I have said before, the group that I always thought of as the Holy Trinity of horse racing was the Aga Khan, Sir Michael Stoute and Walter Swinburn, the perfect combination of owner, trainer and jockey.

It was my dream to ride for Sir Michael and when I was struggling to make progress in my career when I was riding with Jimmy FitzGerald, I was ready to settle for the job of being one of Sir Michael's work riders. That would have been enough for me in those days. That was still something to aspire to and now it was intoxicating to think that I had a chance of getting the top job itself.

It was music to my ears when Gary Stevens phoned me with his news and within a short time, Sir Michael got in touch and offered me the job at Freemason Lodge for the start of the 2000 season. I had plenty of moments of ill-fortune in my career. This was not one of them.

I loved working with Sir Michael right from the start. He was different from Henry. Henry and I were both great around horses, but neither of us was very good at communicating and our exchanges could be a little awkward. We sometimes had quite fundamental misunderstandings: we were talking about Ramruma once, quite a while before she won the Oaks at Epsom in 1999 and I ventured fairly cautiously that she didn't seem to be a great horse.

'Oh, so we'll run her in a seller then, shall we?' he said, but of course he was joking.

The joke was that a seller is a poor-standard race followed by an auction for the winner that you might use so someone could come in and buy her for £6000 or something like that. You wouldn't run a filly with a pedigree in a seller no matter how bad they were. I learned that you always had to think before you said anything to Henry.

He asked me how I was one morning and I said 'not bad'. He was immediately alarmed and wanted to know what was wrong. I had to explain to him it was just my way of saying I was fine. So we sometimes struggled with communication.

Sir Michael was much easier. He would let you find your own feet and he would discuss things about the races ahead in a more informal way. Henry was less private with his instructions, often giving them in the parade ring in front of the owners.

Sir Michael talked to you about the race the day before. We might even talk about it over a glass of wine in his house the night before. There were no owners around then, no stewards tugging at your tack, no fuss, no cameras. It seemed like a good way of doing it to me.

Sir Michael's work was impressively detailed. His work was more important than his races. That is one of the things that makes him such a great trainer. He had excellent work riders when I was there and Sally Eddery was always on the lead. She was one of the best work riders I've been associated with. Sally rode most of the lead horses for Sir Michael. In work, you are building a horse to get it ready for the peak on race day. That's why it's important that the work rider doesn't go too quickly or too slowly when you're riding out and Sally was a brilliant judge of that.

I'd ask her what a horse was like when I got on it and she was very knowledgeable and astute. I loved working with her and she was the key to a lot of Sir Michael's success. Her timing seemed to be perfect and Sir Michael put a lot of trust in her.

In the five years I was to ride for him, there was really only one time we had a blip. It centred on the fact that I was horrible around Windsor. If my strike rate at any given track wasn't around 20 per cent, I'd be disappointed. It might dip to 17 per cent or 18 per cent from year to year. But at Windsor, I was appalling. I was 8 per cent or 9 per cent. It was dismal.

I think it was because Windsor wasn't a track where you could use your head to ride. It was about the speed of horses riding into the bend. You came into the bend, pulling them up, and then you took off again. It just didn't suit me. I didn't like the rhythm of riding there. It suited jockeys who liked to be front runners, like Pat Eddery and Richard Hughes.

Sir Michael and I were at breakfast at Freemason Lodge one morning after I had ridden another disappointing race around Windsor the evening before. The filly I was on had been in season, which makes them more difficult to get a decent performance out of, but Sir Michael didn't know that at that point. I was sitting in the kitchen, lifting a bit of egg into my mouth, and he suddenly smashed his fist on the table and said he had had a 30 per cent strike rate at Windsor before I started riding for him. He found out the horse had been in season later, but that was really the only tense episode we ever had.

It was good timing when I joined him. I was thirty-five and racing people were saying I was at the peak of my powers. I had finished my wider apprenticeship as a jockey. I had done my time on the northern circuit and my years with Henry had taught me how to win the biggest races. I'm wary of saying I was the finished article by the time I started working with Sir Michael, because I don't believe you are ever the finished article. You can always get better. But I was a decent jockey capable of doing a job for a big trainer.

I could talk to Sir Michael. I knew what he wanted. I knew that he was happy to plan for the long term. If we had a nice horse, I knew that Sir Michael wouldn't want me to spoil it by beating it up the first time out, trying to get a win, and then it would never want to race again.

Kevin Prendergast wouldn't let you touch his two-year-olds with the whip and Sir Michael had something of the same philosophy. It's like a child going to his first day at school – if the teacher comes out of the door, gives the kid a whack round the head and shouts 'go on, get in there', the kid is going to be like a rabbit in the headlights next time he goes in. He's not going to enjoy it. He's not going to want to go back to school. You treat animals the same way you treat humans. It's not difficult.

Sir Michael's a trainer that likes to take a horse to the very top. He's not thinking about today. It's about the long term. You have these young animals and you know that if you do look after them, they will reward you. That's what I liked about him.

It is hard to separate him from Aidan O'Brien and Henry Cecil, but I do know I was very lucky to ride for all of them. Sir Michael could put up with a mistake but you wouldn't last if you kept making them because there was a queue of people to fill your boots.

You could go and have a glass of wine with Sir Michael the night before a big race and often we would talk about anything but racing. I'd go round to his house and you could let your hair down rather than being in the paddock when you've got twenty owners around you and everyone is pushing and shoving. We did our homework, but we did our homework with a nice glass of red.

It was obvious he trusted me, too. Fergal Lynch was his second jockey and now and again, Sir Michael would be talking to me about a particular race that was coming up and he'd say: 'Tell Fergal how to ride that horse.' He made it clear he valued my input.

Our partnership started well even before I had officially taken over as his retained jockey. I was leading the jockeys' championship when I parted ways with Henry in August and I was 50 winners clear by early September. It was later that month when I was officially confirmed as Sir Michael's stable jockey for the following season.

I rode my 200th winner of the season when I won on one of Sir Michael's horses, Alva Glen, at Nottingham. It was the third season in succession that I had clocked up a double century of winners and I sealed my third jockeys' championship soon afterwards. I was the first jockey since Sir Gordon Richards, fifty years before me, to ride more than 200 winners in three successive years.

When the 2000 season started, I thought I would cruise to a fourth jockeys' title. I had been lucky with the horses that I was given to ride when I was with Henry and I was in the same privileged position with Sir Michael. One of the first horses I rode for him, and one of the finest, was King's Best.

I'd been on the wrong end of a beating by King's Best already in August 1999 when I rode a horse called Shamrock City, which was a horse I liked, for Paul Howling at York. He was outclassed by King's Best with Gary Stevens on board. I sensed then what a good horse he was.

I rode work on him a lot when I joined up properly with Sir Michael and I was struck by how sweaty and gassy and keen he was. He wasn't an easy horse to manage and it took a lot to get him to settle.

We went for the Craven Stakes at Newmarket in April 2000 and he travelled really well, but I kicked too soon and he got tired and Richard Hughes on Umistim caught us and beat us by half a length. I was furious with myself. I rode a bad race and I beat myself up about it.

It is rare that a horse loses the Craven and wins the 2000 Guineas, which is only just over a fortnight later but Sir Michael never had his horses 100 per cent for the trials. If they are 100 per cent for the trials, there is only one way to go and all good trainers know that.

I wanted to ride him as often as I could after the Craven, come in and talk to him, get him used to me, get him to trust me and really develop a rapport with him. When the day of 2000 Guineas came along, I was confident we'd get it right.

There were 27 runners and only one pacemaker, Primo Valentino, ridden by Pat Eddery. Primo Valentino was a sprinter and he shot out of the stalls and came across to the stands side and the whole field followed him. That's what happens: they follow the speed. At halfway, the whole field was in front of me and it looked as if I was going to be in trouble because you can't go around the field and Sir Michael doesn't like that anyway. He said later that he thought I was in such a hopeless position that he was already starting to plan my next race.

There were good horses ahead of us, too, not least Giant's Causeway, who was being ridden by Mick Kinane. Mick had kicked on on Giant's Causeway and it looked like he was clear and away. But I stayed calm and when things started to open up and I asked him to quicken, King's Best was like a knife through butter.

It was one of those races where it seemed like there was no way through but then suddenly a gap appears as if the waters are parting and when I gave him a couple of flicks, King's Best just surged through it. Part of it is luck. Part of it is instinct and that day it all worked beautifully.

Giant's Causeway had gone too quickly and as we picked up and picked up, he started to feel the pinch. Because King's Best had been doing nothing apart from conserving energy, he had better finishing speed and we ran by Giant's Causeway easily in the end, winning by three-and-a-half lengths. That was one of my best-ever rides because King's Best was such an amazing horse and it got everything off to such a great start with Sir Michael. At Freemason Lodge that night, we had a drink with the lads in the yard to celebrate a job well done.

When you get a horse as a yearling, a lot of work and a lot of love and a lot of effort and a lot of money goes into getting it to win a Classic, and it's something that the head lad and the travelling head lad and everyone in the yard works towards. It is racing's equivalent of winning Olympic gold when you win a Classic.

My job was easy. I just steered him. But I had enough experience to know by then that it makes the year for the yard when you win a Classic, whatever happens next. It just gives everyone a huge boost. That night, William Haggas, another fine trainer, came in and clapped his hands as a mark of respect for Sir Michael.

To get King's Best to win the 2000 Guineas was a great training performance. A lot of analysts didn't think the horse was good enough and he had been beaten in the Craven and so for Sir Michael to be able to pick him up within a couple of weeks and for him to win like he did was a great achievement. To see another trainer applauding him gave me goosebumps.

I was excited about what King's Best could go on to achieve, too. The next big goal was the Derby and I knew King's Best could win it. He was getting better and better and better on the gallops. One day, not long before the Derby, I was riding him and we were following a horse called Little Rock, who was a proper horse himself, a Group Two winner. Deckie O'Shea, who was about seven stone, was on Little Rock and King's Best had me on his back, weighing 8st 7lb. So Little Rock was not just an older horse but we were giving him a stone and a half advantage as well.

Not long after we set off, Deckie O'Shea looked round to see where we were and I was on his heels. I didn't even have to ask King's Best to quicken and we went by him and after what felt like a matter of seconds later, I looked around to see how far ahead I was. I nearly had to turn my head around like an owl to see where Little Rock had got to. He was a dot on the horizon, about a furlong behind me.

King's Best would have won the Derby that year. No question. But about a week before Epsom, he went wrong and tweaked something and couldn't race. It was a dreadful shame. He was a force of nature, that horse. He was so strong and so fast, and it was so hard to pull him up that we almost ended up in the cricket pitch at the end of the gallop in Newmarket once.

That was a big disappointment but I still felt delighted with the way my season was going. The transition to riding for Sir Michael had been seamless and I was happier than ever with my race-riding. I was as hungry as ever, too, and by the time

Royal Ascot came around, I was already a long way ahead of my nearest challengers in the jockeys' championship.

I was taking it for granted that I would win that fourth consecutive title that year. In fact, I was feeling so confident that I saw title after title after title stretching out ahead of me. I was starting to think I couldn't be beaten. But it's dangerous to take anything for granted in sport. It has a habit of punishing you for making assumptions. It was a lesson I was about to learn the hard way.

CHAPTER 16

The Fall

I always loved Royal Ascot. Most flat jockeys do. The Classics are special and they are the pinnacles of racing, but there was still a kind of glamour about Royal Ascot that you don't get anywhere else in England. It felt a bit like the Breeders' Cup to me. It had that kind of allure. I suppose it's the flat's equivalent of the Cheltenham Festival.

Part of the magic was the presence of a lot of foreign jockeys. It had an international feeling. I got more of a kick out of beating Frankie Dettori at Ascot than anywhere else, and he and Mick Kinane were two of the best jockeys in the world at that time, but Royal Ascot offered the opportunity to test yourself against riders you didn't get to face too often and that gave it something extra.

When I arrived at the meeting in 2000, I already had plenty of happy memories of previous visits. In my second year with Henry Cecil, I had won the St James's Palace Stakes on Dr Fong and it was one of my favourite victories because I'd damaged the ligaments in my knee a week earlier.

I didn't want to tell Henry about it because I knew it would lose me the ride and I also knew that Dr Fong was going to win so I had to go to elaborate lengths to keep the injury a secret from Henry. This got particularly difficult when it came to the immediate preamble to the race because Henry had a sort of superstition about always being the one to leg his jockey up on to the horse in the paddock.

The thing was, he wasn't very good at it. He was a bit clumsy and I knew it would hurt like hell if he did it with my injured knee and that I wouldn't be able to disguise my discomfort. So I told the travelling head lad what the situation was and we waited until Henry's attention was diverted by talking to someone in the parade ring and then the travelling head lad legged me up. Henry wasn't very happy about it when he saw me up on Dr Fong, but there was nothing he could do about it by then. I had to ride a little bit longer on him because I couldn't bend my knee but we won well enough and I told Henry about the injured knee after the race.

I didn't have any worries like that when I arrived at Royal Ascot this time around. I felt at the top of my game and my rides on the first day reflected that. I won on Kalanisi in the Queen Anne Stakes, the first race on the card, and then on Dalampour in the Queen's Vase, both for Sir Michael.

I rode two more winners on the second day, Caribbean Monarch in the Royal Hunt Cup and Celtic Silence, trained by Mark Johnston, half an hour later in the Chesham Stakes. I was down for one more ride that Wednesday, in the last race of the day, the Ascot Stakes, but I didn't want to be there.

I was due to ride a horse called Alhawa for Karl Burke but I had told my agent, Dave Pollington, that I didn't want to ride in the last. Partly, that was because I had ridden Alhawa before, a year earlier at Doncaster, and he was a lazy horse. We'd won the race but I had had to push him all the way.

But the main reason was that there was an evening meeting at Kempton that day and Sir Michael had two nice horses running in it. The Ascot Stakes didn't go off until 5.30pm and I knew that coming out of the course after that would be like trying to leave a football match at full time. The crowds would be swarming, the traffic would be snarled and I would be in a race against time to get to Kempton. But I was desperate to ride those horses. That was the way I was. I was miles ahead in the race for the jockeys' championship, but I was just addicted to the buzz of winning races.

It didn't matter that I was riding at Royal Ascot that day anyway. I wanted to ride at Kempton, too, even if they were inconsequential races worth a couple of thousand quid in prize money. I wanted to ride wherever there were winners.

That's what I mean when I say I wanted to be champion jockey every year and I wanted it more than anybody else. It was easy for me then. I was always hungry. I always wanted to win, even when I was small. It used to kill me if I didn't win. I was a useless runner but if I was in a race, I used to run my heart out.

So I was nervous about the idea of trying to get out of Ascot after the last race and I told Dave to get me off Alhawa. Karl and David had a chat about it, but there was some misunderstanding and Karl looked at the times of the races and thought, for some reason, it would be easy to make it from Ascot to Kempton. He must have looked at the short distance between the two courses but he probably didn't think about the traffic. There are only fifteen miles between Ascot and Kempton but there would be race crowds and it was rush hour. It was the kind of stress I hated.

The thing is, a trainer can use a jockey's code to enter you for a race and so Karl put me down and submitted the entry about two minutes before the deadline. There was nothing malicious about it, but by the time Dave Pollington saw what he'd done, it was too late to pull me out.

The only option available to me was to say that I couldn't ride in the last at Royal Ascot that day because I was dehydrated. But that wasn't really an option because if I said that, then I wouldn't be able to ride Sir Michael's horses later at Kempton. So the die was cast. I made arrangements to have a car waiting to take me to Kempton and went out on Alhawa in the Ascot Stakes.

It was a big field and the race was over two-and-a-half miles. There were 24 runners and as we came round the final bend, I was right in the thick of it. Then, right in front of me, Prairie Falcon, who was being ridden by Michael Hills, slipped and fell. In a race like that, that's always going to be serious.

Other horses went down around it. Generosa, ridden by Seamus Heffernan, and Natural Eight, with Alan Daly on board, both hit the deck. I had no chance to react. There was absolutely no way I could avoid it and Alhawa and I went over the top of them.

It was like a motorbike accident and I went head first into the ground. I was speared into the turf and my head was whipped away from my body because it couldn't hold the weight of it. Really, I should have broken my neck but because of all the milk I had drunk over the years, my bones were strong. I have never broken a bone in my life, thank God. That's probably the reason I wasn't even more seriously hurt or killed that day.

I was flung onto the turf and I rolled for a bit. It was like being in a washing machine. One horse stood on me and I had a little bit of bleeding on my arm. I felt a kick on my left shoulder, too, as another horse ran past and over me. There was no pain at first, but my left arm just flopped beside me. I couldn't pick my arm up. I was feeling nothing. I thought my arm was detached from my body and I wondered where all the blood was. I thought I might have severed my arm completely.

The doctor and the paramedics were there pretty quickly and tried to give me that stupid gas and air. I whipped the mask off and said, 'Just effing knock me out.' It was as much use as an ashtray on a motorbike. The other boys had got up but I was lying there, still. I told them I had a pain in my shoulder and the paramedics removed my silks and my body protector so they could have a look. When the pain kicked in, they gave me some morphine and I felt like I was floating.

My shoulder was already starting to swell and the doctor was worried that I had internal bleeding. There was a hoof mark on my shoulder, which was a decent clue as to how the injury had happened. The skin can stretch but arteries can't and I tore an artery in my shoulder and severed a nerve.

I was carried from the track to the racecourse ambulance on a stretcher and then taken with a police escort to Wexham Park Hospital in Slough. I asked the doctor straight away whether I would be able to ride again and he reassured me that I would, but I could tell that he was worried.

I was soon transferred to Stanmore Hospital in north London. I was in intensive care and I lost three-and-a-half pints of blood from internal bleeding. But I had been taken to Stanmore so I could be placed into the care of Professor Rolfe Birch, the head of the Peripheral Nerve Injury Unit.

I was told he was one of the best neurological surgeons in the world and the only man qualified to perform the operation that could save my career. He was an expert in nerve injuries and how to repair them, and everyone was confident that I was in the best hands. Nerve endings die within twenty-four hours and Professor Birch knew to operate on me without delay. I'll always be grateful to him. Without him I'd never have ridden again.

It was such a complicated operation that there is an account of it in the *British Journal of Sports Medicine* so that medical students can refer to it. Its title is: 'Rupture of the axillary (circumflex) nerve and artery in a champion jockey'.

The report began by saying that 'rupture of the circumflex artery and nerve, without fracture or dislocation, is a rare traumatic event', which backed up my theory, in my mind at least, that I had unusually strong bones.

'At operation,' the report in the journal went on, 'a haematoma of about 750ml was evacuated from around the shoulder. The circumflex artery had ruptured 1mm from its origin from the axillary artery and was tied off.

'The axillary nerve was ruptured and repaired using a three-stranded cable graft from the medial cutaneous nerve of the forearm. The medial and posterior cords of the brachial plexus were visibly contused. No intraoperative nerve action potentials were recorded.'

They were pleased with the way the operation had gone

and I was determined that I would make a full recovery; but Julie told me some time later that they had said to her I would never ride again because I had lost feeling in my arm and it was unlikely I would regain the full use of it.

I'm glad I didn't know that because the process of recovery was tough psychologically anyway. I had told myself initially that I would be back in time to make sure I won my fourth jockeys' championship in a row. I had such a commanding lead that I thought I might only need to ride for the last couple of months of the season to make sure of another title. I soon realised I was being way, way too optimistic.

I was sitting up in bed and watching the rest of Royal Ascot soon enough and Julie came in on the final day of the meeting to say she was going to see the Queen to accept the Ritz Club Trophy, which is given to the leading jockey there each year, on my behalf. Despite the fact I had missed the last two days, no one had beaten my total of four winners. There is an irony in the fact that it was the only year I ever won that trophy. It was not an irony I was able to appreciate for some time.

The road to recovery was long and hard. At first, I couldn't grip at all with my left hand. I couldn't close my fist. I couldn't hold anything for months and months. And when I went home from hospital after some weeks, the pain in my shoulder was so bad that I found it hard to sleep at night, even with the painkillers I had been prescribed.

Six weeks after the fall, I took Julie and the children to Barbados. Sir Michael had suggested the trip and helped to organise it and he had also contacted Jacqueline King, the physio for the West Indies cricket team, to work on trying to restore movement and strength to my left shoulder and arm.

I appreciated the fact that Sir Michael was standing by me, for a start. Racing is a ruthless, ruthless business but he made it plain he wanted me back as quickly as possible and that he was willing to do what he could to help with my recovery and rehabilitation.

That trip to Barbados might have been good for Julie and the kids, but it was no holiday for me. It was more like slow torture, but I knew the work had to be done. I worked two hours every day, from 9am to 11am, with Jacqueline, lifting weights, doing shoulder exercises with pulleys and working on making a fist. Sir Michael had told me she would help me and I put my trust in her.

But it was hard. I worked with Jacqueline every day for three weeks and I did exercises in the pool for seven hours every day, too, and it still wasn't getting any better. I had some movement in my left arm but not much. I couldn't even straighten it. I worked so hard. I took a ball of putty with me everywhere I went and I was constantly trying to squeeze it while it was in my hand. The pain was unbelievable. I asked for stronger painkillers at one point, because I still couldn't sleep at night, but the doctor said I was already on a big dose.

He said he could put me on a bigger dose, or he could put me on different painkillers, but that I had to be aware that they might cause long-term damage to my kidneys. That was the day I stopped taking the painkillers altogether and I was in no more and no less pain afterwards. Sometimes, pain is all in your mind.

There was a time in Barbados, though, when I thought to

myself: 'I can't do this any more.' Progress was so slow and the pain was so great that it was difficult to see a way past it.

There was talk at one point that they might have to do another operation because my arm had tightened up. By then, the realisation had also set in that this was going to be a long lay-off and that I was going to lose the jockeys' title. I went through a spell where I struggled to see any positives.

But the kids were in Barbados, too, and they were jumping and leaping around. One morning, when I was thinking seriously that I would just jack it all in and retire, Brittany and Cieren, our twins, came dashing in and started to play and I looked at them and knew I had to carry on. If not for me, then for them. We had bills to pay. I had to think about things like their schooling and their livelihoods. I had to think about their future. It was the kids that inspired me the most but it was probably for me, too.

Deep down, I knew that I would find it tough without racing at that stage of my career. Things had been going so well. I told myself I just had to push through and I could get back to where I was. There was no point feeling sorry for myself any more.

When we got back from Barbados, I started to see some signs of improvement. I recovered a measure of grip in my left hand and the pain in my shoulder eased a bit. In September, I went back to Freemason Lodge and rode out for the first time since the accident. That felt like a significant step forward.

There were other things that kept me motivated, too. Kevin Darley, Pat Eddery and Richard Quinn were locked in a battle for what I thought of as my jockeys' title and it was tough to watch them vying for it, knowing that I was powerless to do anything.

It also annoyed me when Terry Norman, Kevin's agent, said Kevin should have got the job at Sir Michael's ahead of me anyway and began to speculate about whether my career was over. 'If Kieren Fallon's injury doesn't clear up, which I sincerely hope it will,' Norman told the *Guardian* in mid-September, 'there would be the Stoute job going, yet Johnny Murtagh, who has been on a roll for that stable, would probably get that.'

It's always nice when you see people squabbling over the spoils when the body's still warm. Kevin won the title that season but I didn't forget what his agent had said. It drove me on.

At the beginning of November, I headed out to Dubai to try to get fit during the winter and be ready for the start of the 2001 season. That was my new target. I rode out for the American trainer Kiaran McLaughlin and, four days after Christmas, I rode my first race in public since my fall at Ascot on 21 June.

I got a decent cheer from the crowd when my name was announced at Nad Al Sheba and I rode one of Kiaran's horses, Hunting Tiger, in the Silver Charm Stakes. He bolted up and won by three-and-a-half lengths. The win didn't mean that much. It felt like a bit of a fluke. But it was good to be back on the track.

I said at the time I was blowing harder than the horse was after the race and that was true. But there were a lot of other familiar faces in the race like Richard and Michael Hills, Willie Ryan, Seb Sanders and John Carroll. It wasn't like racing in Britain but it was the next best thing.

A few months later, I was nearly ready to race again in the UK. I was subjected to a thorough physical by Dr Michael

Turner, the Jockey Club's chief medical adviser; they stuck a big needle into my shoulder and tested the muscle reaction with electric shocks that nearly lifted me off the ground. I passed it fine.

It was Tuesday 27 March before I rode a race in public in Britain. My first race back was the Henry Royce Maiden Stakes on an all-weather card at Wolverhampton. It was 279 days since I had crashed to earth in front of the packed grandstands at Ascot. The crowd at Wolverhampton was not quite as big.

I rode a horse called Wintertide, trained by Richard Fahey, and lost by a head. Straight away, I had people jumping on my back, saying it had been a timid ride and that I would never be the same. They said I looked frail. They said I looked weak. They said I looked frightened. They said I looked shot-shy. After one race. After one race on the all-weather at Wolverhampton. It was typical of the negative way some people in racing thought.

I was interviewed a few times that week and I told them the only way I wouldn't be champion jockey again was if I had another injury. I was convinced that was true. But when I rode at Nottingham, Southwell, Lingfield, Nottingham again, and Southwell again, all without a winner, the doom-mongering increased.

I wasn't bothered. Honestly. There was not a doubt in my mind. Maybe I had come back a little bit too early but it was only a matter of a week here or there. I had been out for the better part of a year. I was always going to need a little bit of time to get back into the swing of things.

It took me ten days to get my first win after my comeback; that was all. Not so bad after 279 days out. It was an Irish horse called Regal Song in the second race at Musselburgh on 7 April that gave me my first winner in Britain since my accident. It was the Scottish Racing Is Fun for Everyone Handicap that provided me with that victory and it was certainly fun for me that day. I rode another winner in the last. I was up and running again.

CHAPTER 17

Panorama

It might have been hard for the critics to handle, but the truth is that, after the return from my fall, I picked up where I had left off with Sir Michael Stoute. I won the 2000 Guineas, the first Classic of the 2001 season, with Golan, and my career took off again. I rode a series of winners that put down a marker that I was going to be the man to beat again in the jockeys' championship as well. Those who were hoping that I would be a different rider after my injury clung to grains of hope, but for the most part they were sorely disappointed.

Some things changed, though. I started to feel a subtle shift in my fortunes at that stage of my career and my life. I was thirty-six now and I wasn't a man on the up any more. I was a jockey trying to stay at the top. It wasn't that I had lost any of my hunger or any of my confidence or any of my ability, but I wasn't the upstart any more. I wasn't the surprise package from the north. I was the guy that the others wanted to beat and that did bring a different kind of pressure.

I was drinking a bit more, too. Alcohol was at the heart of

a lot of my time away from the racecourse and even though I didn't really notice the effects of that, I think I suffered because of it. I often drank a bottle of vodka on the journey back to Newmarket when I was being driven home from a race meeting a distance away like Newbury or one of the northern racetracks. I wouldn't admit it at the time, but it can't have done me much good.

It was also in those years that I started to become the focus of more controversy. I had had plenty of scrapes with authority before, but after the BBC broadcast a *Panorama* documentary in the autumn of 2002 that sought to expose wrongdoing in racing, I became mired in a series of increasingly serious legal issues. Over the years that followed, I won a series of libel payouts and court cases. It sometimes seemed that the Jockey Club, and later the BHA, and I were incompatible.

I never grew tired of racing, I never grew tired of battling Frankie Dettori or Ryan Moore, Jamie Spencer, Richard Hughes or Paul Hanagan for the jockeys' title, but I did grow weary of defending my name. I brought plenty of my problems upon myself but when the accusations were false, that gnawed at me and sapped my energy. It cost me championships and Classic wins. It wore me down.

I didn't see any of that coming when I won on Golan, who was an 11/1 shot in the 2000 Guineas. That afternoon in early May was a glorious moment for me. Yes, I found it hard to celebrate victories like other people, but even I could appreciate the psychological importance of winning the first Classic I had competed in since my return from such a serious accident.

It lifted all the pressure off me in one go. It shut everybody up and gave my fans something to shout loudly about. There was a deafening roar from the stands at Newmarket when we surged past the winning post. I got plenty of praise for that win on Golan, particularly as I had been given an unfavourable draw, wide on the outside, and came from a long way back to win.

Red Carpet and Nayef had set the early pace but I started to make my move through the field with five furlongs to go. We hit the front two furlongs out, surging along the outside, past the leaders on the rails, and winning by a length-and-a-half from Tamburlaine and Richard Hughes, with Pat Eddery a neck back in third on Frenchman's Bay.

The press did have a field day later that month when Lord Carnarvon, the Queen's racing manager, criticised my ride on Her Majesty's horse, Flight of Fancy, when we could only finish fourth in the Musidora Stakes at York. He said I rode 'an awful race'. I did my best to remain diplomatic for once. It was the Queen's horse, after all. I think I wondered aloud, as gently as I could, when was the last time that Lord Carnarvon had ridden competitively. I also pointed out that Flight of Fancy would now be in perfect condition for the Oaks. I was right about that. We finished a close second.

But all that was really just a distraction. I had a golden run of wins on a lovely horse of Sir Michael's called Medicean that summer, too. We won the Lockinge at Newbury in May, the Queen Anne Stakes at Royal Ascot in June and the Eclipse at Sandown in early July.

I was riding well. I thought I was as good as I had ever been and I had the benefit of more and more experience. I had a tough fight with Kevin Darley to win the jockeys' championship back but I didn't mind that. It showed I still had the appetite to win and to work harder than anybody else.

I rode 166 winners on the way to my fourth title and I told the press it felt special because I knew what it had taken just for me to be riding again. I knew how hard I had had to work to regain the feeling in my left arm, I knew I had had to push through the pain barrier and then force my way back into the arena.

Despite the season I'd had and the way I had won the jockeys' championship, the exchange with Lord Carnarvon had created a torrent of speculation about my position with Sir Michael and the doubts that some owners were supposed to harbour about my ability. It seemed a strange time to be harbouring doubts after I had just won my fourth jockeys' championship. The press were convinced that Sir Michael and I had had a falling out and that we were barely talking, but that simply wasn't the case. Apart from the fist-on-the-table incident, I don't remember a cross word between us.

There were some minor issues with owners but that is not unusual in racing. Sir Michael felt the need to put out a statement at the end of the season. 'Not all of my owners wish to use Kieren Fallon,' it said, 'but his association with the stable will continue with those that do. Kieren assures me that he is keen to do so.'

That was it. The racing press interpreted that as meaning I had been sacked. Maybe I was just putting a positive spin on it, but that wasn't my interpretation. Technically, I was not retained by Sir Michael any more after the end of the season and I rode as a freelance, but practically that made no difference at all. As far as I was concerned, I was still his leading rider. I still got the rides on most of his top horses. Our professional and personal relationship remained unchanged the season afterwards. And the season after that. And the season after that.

The press also made a big play of the fact that the Aga Khan no longer wanted me to ride his horses. Well, that may have been true but the Aga Khan was not the player in the sport he had once been. Since 1990 he'd largely withdrawn from the English racing scene, concentrating his interests in Ireland and France, and his patronage was not nearly as important.

I was happy with my arrangements with Sir Michael. If I was sacked, it was the happiest sacking I've ever endured. It is a strange kind of sacking when you don't notice you've been sacked and you still get the best rides and you win the jockeys' championship again. If every sacking were like that, no one would mind getting fired.

The racing press couldn't contain their glee, though, and a lot of the old prejudices came spewing out. 'To outsiders,' one of the press boys wrote in the *Guardian*, 'it will seem more than strange that the best jockey in the business has got the boot from the country's best home-based stable but the truth among all the conjecture is that Fallon's rough edges could not be ironed out.

'He remained the recalcitrant schoolboy, when he should have grown up. The fact was that the boy from County Clare did not fit in and did his cause no good by continuing to be his own worst enemy. The rebel in him has rarely been far from the surface.'

To some of them, I never stopped being 'the boy from County Clare', the outsider who wouldn't play their game, who wouldn't give them neat sound bites, who wouldn't chat to them outside the weighing room, who wouldn't smile for their cameras, who wouldn't jump off horses in the parade ring and bow politely to the stewards. I had won four jockeys' titles and still they were saying my 'rough edges could not be ironed out'. It made me laugh.

I won the jockeys' championship again in 2002. It was an unusual year for me in that I didn't win any of the Classics, but at Royal Ascot I won the Ascot Stakes on Riyadh and the Queen Alexandra Stakes on Cover Up. I teamed up with Golan again to win the King George VI and Queen Elizabeth Stakes at Ascot in July and I won the Nassau Stakes at Goodwood and the Yorkshire Oaks at York, both on Islington. Not bad for a boy from County Clare having an average season.

I rode only 149 winners that season, so it wasn't a vintage year compared to my previous championship seasons, but I beat Richard Hughes into second place and I had plenty of big winners. But I was not totally blind to what was happening. My numbers were down a bit. The bare statistics told you that and I accepted that some of the criticism was fair. I wasn't enjoying my riding quite as much. I realised that I needed to do something about my lifestyle. I was as keen as ever to be the best I could be and I wasn't helping myself, particularly with my drinking habits.

Nor was it an ideal end to my season when I was dragged into a *Panorama* exposé called 'The Corruption of Racing'. It was broadcast on 6 October 2002, and claimed that British horseracing was institutionally corrupt. The Jockey Club came out of the documentary particularly badly and was made to look outmoded and ineffectual.

The programme was full of allegations about race-fixing, betting scams, no-lose betting accounts and jockeys consorting with criminals. *Panorama* based its programme around information from Roger Buffham, the Jockey Club's former head of security, who accused his ex-employers of lacking 'the moral courage and resolve' to deal with corruption.

Buffham was an interesting character himself. His tenure at the Jockey Club, from 1992-2001, had been controversial and he had quit with a pay-off over a contested incident of sexual harassment involving a female colleague, which he denied. As he thrashed around in the wreckage, I was one of those caught in the crossfire.

In a review of the *Panorama* programme for the *Guardian*, racing journalist Greg Wood attempted to put Buffham's evidence and his departure from the Jockey Club into some context. 'By the time of his departure,' Wood wrote, 'Buffham had lost the confidence of much of the racing community. He was, perhaps unfairly, blamed for the very public collapse of a trial at Southwark crown court, the product of a long, and ultimately fruitless, investigation into alleged doping and race-fixing.

'There was also unease at the club's Portman Square headquarters when evidence emerged of business links between Buffham and Wouter Basson, who was acquitted after a controversial trial in his native South Africa for hundreds of alleged offences including murder and fraud ... Though Buffham's integrity was not questioned, his judgment in his choice of business associates certainly was.'

Panorama set up a sting on Jeremy Phipps, Buffham's successor at the Jockey Club. The two men went out for lunch at the Tapster wine bar in Victoria, Buffham was fitted with a wire and Phipps was caught on tape saying of Jockey Club members: 'The backbone is not terribly strong. You've got to think about the members – they are fucking ignorant.'

Phipps only lasted a few days before he had to resign. The Jockey Club was in chaos and was forced into a series of reforms. Not long after, it formally ended its link with the regulation of the sport and its responsibilities in that area were eventually passed on to a new organisation, the British Horseracing Authority.

I was very much on the periphery of the programme's claims and allegations but because I was the reigning champion jockey and because I already had a controversial reputation, I was a useful marketing tool to sell the documentary. I suppose I was a more interesting target than a man in a suit.

My part in that *Panorama* centred on the false accusation that I had been consorting with Triads while I had been racing in Hong Kong in the 1998-99 and 1999-2000 seasons. The only part of it that was true was that I did race in Hong Kong during those two English winters. I loved it there, actually.

The first time I went was in February 1999 and I didn't have a great month on the track. I rode for a series of owners and trainers at Happy Valley and Sha Tin and had a few big-price seconds and thirds but I couldn't ride a winner. My last ride on my last day there that year was on a 33/1 shot, so it wasn't thought it had much of a chance. The horse was owned by a big syndicate of some sort, which is very common in Hong Kong, and there were about twenty members of this syndicate in the parade ring before the race.

I was trying to make conversation with the guy who ran the syndicate and was doing most of the talking and I admired his watch. I love watches. I can't wear rings or have anything on my hands, but I'm fascinated by emeralds and diamonds and I love looking at precious things. This was a gold Audemars Piguet watch and I told the guy how much I liked it.

'You win on this horse,' the guy said, 'I give you watch.'

He was laughing and joking with the rest of the syndicate members, showing off a bit. He obviously thought the horse didn't have a chance. As it happened, the rest of the field went off too quickly, started to struggle in the final furlong and I came down the outside and got up to win by a short head.

I came back in and there was no mention of the watch. All of the syndicate members were hanging onto the rope, leading the horse back in, but the main guy wasn't looking at me and he certainly wasn't taking his watch off. In the end, I caught his eye and tapped my wrist. The other guys started laughing and he had no choice. He had to give me his watch. The watch aside, it was a great way to finish my stint there. It was a win and it helped get me a three-month contract with the Hong Kong Jockey Club the following winter. When I went back, I couldn't do any wrong.

At the time, I think Gary Stevens held the record for the Hong Kong Jockey Club jockey with 24 winners. In the three months I was there, I rode 27. It was a golden run and I thoroughly enjoyed my time out there.

I've heard other jockeys say it's a nightmare out in Hong Kong, with owners ringing you in the middle of the night and trainers refusing to leave you alone and syndicates insisting on you being available to talk to them, but that wasn't my experience. The owners over there are lovely. All they want to do is entertain you. They take you out and look after you really well. It's an unbelievable city. I had a few big nights in Lan Kwai Fong, where all the bars and pubs are open from dusk till dawn. I came out at 6am a few mornings. I didn't go in the Dentist's Chair like Gazza, though, and have neat spirits poured down my throat. I'm not that crazy.

I got friendly with a guy called Eddie Lo while I was out there. He introduced me to an important owner that I got a lot of rides from. Eddie was obviously well connected and he had shares in horses and syndicates. He was someone who helped me get on the ladder and I enjoyed his company. He was a lovely guy. He never asked me for a single thing.

But the Hong Kong authorities didn't like him. I don't know why but they were suspicious of him and the Hong Kong Jockey Club told me to stay away from him. I was just going out and meeting owners but in Hong Kong, apparently, Eddie was regarded as an 'undesirable'. He was on their radar and because I'd been out for drinks with him, I was on their radar, too.

I couldn't go back in the winter of 2000–01 anyway because of my shoulder injury but I was told I might have problems getting relicensed and so my experiences in Hong Kong were short-lived. It was a shame because I had a brilliant time there.

Through Buffham, *Panorama* got hold of some documents about my time in Hong Kong. Unbelievably, the British racing authorities had not prevented Buffham from removing these and other security documents from the BHA headquarters when he left their employment. The programme said that I had been warned about associating with Chinese gangsters. They quoted a report from the Hong Kong Jockey Club that said: 'Kieren Fallon is either unwittingly or knowingly being used. The risk of damage to Hong Kong racing is high if he continues his relationship.'

Some of these allegations had already been aired by my old friends at the *News of the World* and I was in the process of taking legal action against them because of it. The allegations were absolutely groundless. I never made any secret of meeting with Eddie Lo and having the odd drink with him. I did it openly. Like I said, I enjoyed his company. I never saw or heard anything that suggested he might be a gangster or that he might be involved with Triads. I was never asked to do anything for him that might compromise me or racing in any way. He was a restaurant owner, with no criminal record.

When my lawyers heard about the *Panorama* programme before it was aired, we began legal proceedings against them, too. But *Panorama* still saw fit to put Buffham on camera and ask him whether, on the basis of the Hong Kong report, I should be allowed to ride in the UK. Buffham said I should not.

Near the end of the programme, footage showed the *Panorama* reporter Andy Davies trying to interview me as I walked back to the weighing room after I had ridden the Queen's horse, Right Approach, in the Dante Stakes at York a few months earlier.

'You are a disgrace to those colours you are wearing,' Davies said after he had introduced himself. It was quite an opening line.

It takes a lot to wind me up but that did it. I was holding my whip, and you can see in the footage that I jerk it at him. I hate bullies and I thought he was acting like a bully. He had me at a vulnerable moment because I had just come off the course, I've still got adrenaline surging through me after the race and he is standing there surrounded by his team and his cameraman, pressing his microphone into my face.

He was lucky – and I was lucky – that I was carrying my tack because I wanted to rip his throat out. Many people made a lot of the stare that I gave him as he was walking along beside me and they were right to. But we are not allowed to touch anyone on a racecourse or we are in trouble for bringing the sport into disrepute, so there was really nothing I could do but stare at him.

He kept on at me about associating with Triads and in the end I had to tell the security guys at York to get him out of my face. I might still have gone back and confronted him because I was so angry, but Kevin Darley was walking alongside me and he shepherded me away. 'He's not worth it, Kieren,' he said, and he was right.

The programme's allegations against me were flimsy and groundless and I successfully sued Roger Buffham over them. A couple of years later, Buffham made a fulsome apology in the High Court for having said that I should not be riding on the basis of the contents of the Hong Kong Jockey Club report. Andrew Monson, my counsel, said Buffham now accepted my assurances that I had never knowingly associated with Triads while in Hong Kong during the 1998–99 and 1999–2000 seasons.

Even though I was peripheral to the documentary, that *Panorama* sent a wave of change through racing that was to affect my career profoundly. It made the Jockey Club, and later the BHA, desperately keen to be seen to be doing the right thing when it came to corruption in racing. It was the genesis of change in the way that racing was regulated. The Bufton Tuftons of the Jockey Club were moved aside and a new generation of Blairite officials were brought in with the brief of cleaning up the sport in the shape of the BHA.

One of these was a former chief superintendent with the Metropolitan Police called Paul Scotney, who joined the Jockey Club in November 2003 as director of security and later assumed the title of Director of Integrity Services, Compliance and Licensing at the BHA.

Scotney was interviewed by the *Guardian* a couple of months after he took the job. 'It was such an easy decision,' he said. 'I knew the job was coming up and as soon as it was advertised, I put in for it. I'd been a detective for almost twenty years, but I'm a sports fanatic and particularly into racing, so it was a fantastic opportunity to combine the two.

'I disagree with any idea that racing is institutionally corrupt, because it's not. What we have is a few people out there pulling strokes because money's involved, and one measure of how well I'm doing my job will be how many of the wrongdoers we catch.

'But it's not just about catching them. It's about creating a perceived level of threat of people being caught that they won't do it in the first place. What we're going to do is get off the back foot, and move onto the front foot.'

Not long after Scotney arrived at the Jockey Club, the City of London Police began to get involved in a race-fixing investigation, even though the Metropolitan Police had already decided not to pursue it. I don't know how much Scotney knew about racing, but it looked like the Jockey Club were desperate to claim high-profile scalps in the war against corruption so that they could show the government they were getting to grips with some of the things that *Panorama* had alleged.

To begin with, that meant restrictions on jockeys' use of mobile phones on racecourses, rules banning trainers and owners from laying horses on betting exchanges, improved CCTV security in racecourse stables and tightening up security and restricting access to the weighing room.

Later, it became something very like a witch-hunt.

CHAPTER 18

Aiséirí

In January 2003, I took a radical step. I checked myself into an addiction treatment centre called Aiséirí in Cahir, County Tipperary, and admitted that I had a problem. Aiséirí is Gaelic for 'resurrection'. I had reached a point in my life and my career where I knew something had to change.

It sounds very simple but part of the reason for checking myself in was just to get away from everything. I had started to get sucked into a cycle in horseracing where everything revolved around alcohol. If you were celebrating with each other, you had a drink. If you were commiserating with each other, you had a drink. I realised that I was the one who was choosing which Newmarket pub we would drink at if there was a night out with some of the other jockeys. Even if I went away somewhere on holiday with Julie and the kids, the way I relaxed was by having a drink. I wanted some time away from that kind of social pressure.

I wasn't sure I was an alcoholic. I gave an interview to David Walsh of the *Sunday Times*, who was someone I trusted, around that time which shocked a lot of people because I was open about the way I felt about alcohol. David had said to me that he thought I could be an ever better jockey if I didn't drink and it had made me think.

'How do you define an alcoholic?' I asked him as part of that interview. 'We imagine the alcoholic as the guy with the wine bottle in a brown paper bag, sleeping on the bench. You can drink once a month and be an alcoholic, you can be a binge alcoholic or a social alcoholic, many different kinds.

'I was a serious social drinker, a few drinks after racing, a few in the house that night, and eventually it started to tell on me. But I've never had a craving for a drink. Does that make me an alcoholic? I don't know. I do know I have a problem with alcohol.'

This was the kind of thing I'd do: if I got to a pub and the bar was busy, I'd have a couple of double vodkas straight away just so that if I did have to wait to get served the next time I came to the bar, it wouldn't matter. If I got a couple of quick doubles in, I wouldn't resent a little bit of time without a drink in my hand.

I also knew I had a problem with food. We all did, didn't we? Flipping was just a way of life for a jockey, but the battle with weight took its toll, too. Being sick, taking diuretics, pills for appetite suppressants, pills for everything. In lucid moments, I realised I had lost track of what was healthy and what was not.

My life had become a whirlwind. It was a hurricane. I had no time for anything except racing. It was Lingfield, Ascot, Kempton, York, Epsom, Newmarket, Sandown, Mumbai, Kolkata, Hong Kong, Dubai, Santa Anita, Japan, Thirsk,

Ayr, Catterick and on and on and on, never stopping, never getting off the treadmill, never breathing.

I never really saw Julie and I never really saw the kids. I knew I was missing them growing up, but I felt trapped in the cycle of riding and work. Riding was the thing that made me happiest. I had to ride the horses. I had to ride the winners. Nothing else would do.

You didn't have to delve too deeply into my psyche to realise that that was also an excuse to stop me having to interact with people too much. I still didn't feel comfortable with people. Just with horses. I didn't need alcohol to ease myself into a conversation with a horse, but I needed a drink to get on with people. That was still the way I was.

I spoke to Sir Michael about going to Aiséirí and he was very supportive about it. He was still the guy I rode for the most and I valued his opinion. I think he was probably pleased that I was doing something about my lifestyle. One of our recurring conversations involved him telling me that I had to slow down, and now, off the track at least, that was what I intended to do.

So I went out to Ireland and an old friend of mine, Father Pat Cotter, picked me up at Limerick and took me over to Aiséirí. He had been a patient there a long time before and I think he wanted to make sure I didn't have any last-minute change of heart. He knew it was a big step for me to take. When I arrived, they went through my bag and took away my phone. They took everything, everything that was a connection to the outside world anyway. And they asked me what my problems and my addictions were. I still didn't really think I had any addictions. I liked a social drink but I wasn't addicted.

They asked me about alcohol. I said I liked alcohol but I

wasn't an alcoholic. They asked me about drugs and I said 'no'. They asked me about gambling and I said 'no'. I mean, I knew gamblers and the world in which I lived revolved around gambling in many ways, but I didn't gamble myself. Then they asked me about sex. I didn't even realise that could be one of the addictions.

It was daunting being at Aiséirí but it was amazing, too. That first day I was there, I ate properly. I hadn't eaten properly for a while. I hadn't been to bed early for a long time. It was the first night I hadn't had a drink for years and years. It actually felt like a relief. It was a revelation.

It strips everything away from you, being in a place like Aiséirí. I was up at 7am, tidying up my room, showering and going down for breakfast. I was someone who was important in my world, someone who chatted with the Queen, and now I was walking into a breakfast room with twenty or thirty people I didn't know, and I was nobody.

Some of the people there looked awful, as if they had just been brought in off the street, others looked a bit better and some looked great. I gradually realised that the ones who looked great had already been in Aiséirí for a month and they were getting ready to leave. They were doing cartwheels. They had got their lives back. They were probably looking at me and thinking I looked dreadful.

I walked in there as if I were walking into the Old Bailey, facing a murder charge. You don't know what to say or who to sit with. Everyone knows when you are in a place like that that you are all in there for a reason. It might be an accident that you had. It might be a debt you couldn't pay. It might be the pain of your upbringing. There's always a reason. It doesn't just fall off the tree.

After I had been in Aiséirí for a little while, we began to talk in more depth about my issues and my reason for being there. What it boiled down to with me was that I never really got over the death of Ann. I could see that myself because the pain you feel, you don't want to feel it again. As I mentioned earlier, even with my own kids, I found it hard to love them the way normal people did. I found I was pushing them away all the time. Julie's family were a huggy family and we never were. In Aiséirí, they get to the bottom of why we are as weird as we are.

My own kids were very young when Julie's mother died and I knew they would be very sad, but we all went to the church for the funeral. I thought it was wrong. I said to Julie: 'Why make the kids come? They are heartbroken and it's not fair on them.' It wasn't until afterwards that I realised she was right.

The kids were heartbroken for the day and then they were fine. They got it all out, but we never did when Ann died. We kept it all bottled up, all of us. We didn't cry. We weren't allowed to cry. We had been taught that if you cried, you'd get something that would make you cry some more. So the grief was always pushed back in. It was pushed down. It was hidden away. It was something guilty and forbidden. But in Aiséirí, I cried at last. I cried about Ann and the way she had been taken away and how I had never said goodbye and how much I missed her and how cruel it had all felt and how it had changed our family.

It felt like a huge weight being lifted off me. It felt as if it were something that I could finally be honest about. It was something that I didn't need to hide away any more. Suddenly, it felt silly and unnatural to have been suppressing all that grief all this time. It was a great release. My time in there was my time to reflect on my crazy life, all the people I'd hurt, the mistakes I'd made, the switchback roller-coaster ride I had been on.

They asked me to write down the worst moments I had had when I was drinking. That was an eye-opener, too. Just the sheer act of committing it to paper. There were the things that affected my family, driving home from the races with a bottle of vodka, and on and on.

One of the things that made alcohol dangerous for me was that I would never fall around the place when I was drinking. I never let myself get totally out of control. I never did things that made me utterly ashamed of myself. I had a switch that told me when to stop and go home before things got really out of hand. So I suppose I never hit what people call 'rock bottom'. I think both Richard Hughes and Johnny Murtagh have said that they reached that place, but I never did. I wish I had because I might have tried to deal with the issue earlier. But it took me a long time to recognise that there even was an issue and it was only when I had been at Aiséirí for a couple of weeks that I started to deal with it.

I even started to embrace religion again when I was there. There was a little church there and I went to Mass regularly. I prayed and lit candles and felt a sense of well-being flooding over me. It was something else that took me back to my childhood and the only proper family ritual we ever had, going to church in Ballinruan and then running and jumping and chasing back down the mountain with the other families on our way home.

I did the interview with David Walsh around then. 'What I've seen is the misery,' I told him. 'The misery of the life

I've had, the stupid things I was doing. The waste of time, the waste of opportunity: everything should have been so much better. It has been a rude awakening. Since I've come here, I've had time to think. When you get away from the racing world I move in and you look at it from a distance, it looks miserable.'

I enjoyed the experience in Aiséirí so much, I made a habit of going to drying-out clinics at the end of the year. I went to Cottonwood in Arizona and Betty Ford in California. I became a connoisseur of clinics. I was up in the morning with a spring in my step. I enjoyed all the meetings. I enjoyed the retreat from life. I enjoyed the isolation and the solitude. No one could get at me in those places.

I was in Aiséirí for thirty days and when I walked out, I was doing cartwheels. I never felt as well in my life. I thought I would never drink again and I felt fresh and full of living and pumped up with enthusiasm for racing again. It was no coincidence that I rode 221 winners in the season that followed, more than in any other year of my career.

I didn't drink for nearly a year after I left Aiséirí. I went back to the days when I first started riding for Kevin Prendergast, going to the Silken Thomas in Kildare, having a pool tournament or a darts tournament. They were a great laugh and all I drank then was 7Up or lemonade.

After a year or so of not drinking at all, I started to have a glass of wine here and there. I enjoyed it and slowly but surely it crept up. I never went back to the bottle of vodka a day again. I never went back to the crazy times. But there were occasions, particularly when I felt, rightly or wrongly, as if I were being unjustly pursued, when I took refuge in alcohol again.

I never had a problem with drugs. I was never addicted. But sometimes, after a couple of drinks, I'd think I was invincible and one thing leads to another. That was what happened when I was banned for taking cocaine later in my career. It was ironic, really: I was banned for cocaine but alcohol was my poison.

CHAPTER 19

Derby Days

Sir Michael Stoute said that my ride on Kris Kin to win the 2003 Epsom Derby was one of the greatest in the history of the race. My own view is that there was a lot of luck involved as well. There always is in race-riding. But I loved Epsom and I loved the Derby and when you look back over the arc of my career, it is as good a ride as any to examine in fine detail.

It is hard to overstate the position of the Derby in the lore of the racing world. In the words of Federico Tesio, the great breeder of Thoroughbred racehorses, 'the Thoroughbred exists because its selection has depended, not on experts, technicians, or zoologists, but on a piece of wood: the winning post of the Epsom Derby'.

This is the race above all others that will determine the genetic make-up of racehorses for generations to come. Winning it is therefore the pinnacle of the ambitions of every breeder, owner, trainer and jockey. It is a race like no other on a racecourse like no other, and all of the skills of the breeder, owner and trainer depend upon split-second decisions made by the jockey on a day early in June of every year.

I had rushed at the 2003 season with a renewed enthusiasm for riding. Nothing could get in my way. I opened up a commanding lead in the jockeys' championship early on and I knew no one was going to stop me winning my sixth title. My nearest challenger was Darryll Holland but he was so far back he might as well have been riding in a different race.

I won the 1000 Guineas on Russian Rhythm for Sir Michael when no one fancied her at all. I'll never forget the first time I sat on her up on the Limekilns gallops near Newmarket. I knew she was special then. I said it to Sir Michael. I couldn't wait to ride her in a race.

Sometimes a race ride is like putting a jigsaw together and that ride on Russian Rhythm in the Guineas was a good example. We were down the inside, saving ground, two or three back for the first few furlongs. When I watched the race back, I noticed the commentator only mentioned us once before we hit the front with less than a furlong to go.

We were down the inside and then a gap opened up to our right and we surged into that and then another gap opened up and we surged into that, too, and then we were at the front. She hadn't been fancied and she started the race at 12/1, but she had great finishing speed and we won comfortably in the end. I loved Russian Rhythm. She has to be the best filly over a mile I have ever ridden. She won the Coronation Stakes that year, too, and the Nassau Stakes at Goodwood and then the Lockinge at Newbury the following season. She had everything. She was a joy to ride.

I wouldn't necessarily have said the same about Kris Kin. He was one of Sir Michael's, too, and there was a suggestion that he would be a Derby horse, but I wasn't sure about him. He showed nothing on the gallops and when there was a choice between riding him or Big Bad Bob in the Dee Stakes at Chester, one of the Derby trials, I made sure I was on Big Bad Bob.

I barely even knew Kris Kin was in the yard when we had him at Freemason Lodge. He was a terrible work horse. You could run faster than him in your back garden at home. You get that sometimes. When you go racing, you see a different horse. It's like when people say footballers are bad trainers but in a match, they come alive.

Big Bad Bob was the favourite for the Dee Stakes. Sir Michael had said he wouldn't stand in my way if I wanted to ride him because he didn't think that Kris Kin had much of a chance. He wasn't even entered in the Derby at that point. He put Fergal Lynch on Kris Kin and he went off at 20/1, the outsider of the four horses in the race.

I made the running for most of the Dee Stakes on Big Bad Bob and came round the home turn in the lead. Kris Kin was still the backmarker. The next thing I knew, this thing comes past me at 100mph and it's Fergal and Kris Kin and they romp home to win. Fergal got so carried away, he started waving his whip at the crowd and Kris Kin did a little jink fifty yards after the finish and dumped him on his backside.

I took Kris Kin a bit more seriously after the Dee Stakes and so did Sir Michael. He paid the £90,000 supplementary fee that was necessary to enter him late for the Derby. I rode out on him a couple of times, but you still couldn't tell anything from his work.

Even the day before the race, they said he was lame and there was talk he wasn't going to run. But he made it to

Epsom and he seemed fine. There was certainly no problem with him sweating up in the parade ring or anything like that. He would have paraded up and down all day if you had let him. He was so laid back, you couldn't get to the bottom of him. He was a lazy horse. He was sluggish and slow and lazy.

Epsom is not a simple course to ride. It requires thought. The first five furlongs are run up a steep hill with an incline of about 150 feet from the stalls to the seven-furlong marker.

The mile-and-a-half course over which the Derby is run is a horseshoe shape but the first furlong is set off from the horseshoe so that the horses have to take a right-hand bend at the end of the furlong before joining the horseshoe.

They then tack across the course to their left to the rail on the inside of the course. Next, they run alongside that rail all the way to the finish. At the seven-furlong marker the course starts to go downhill sharply for three-and-a-half furlongs into Tattenham Corner, a left-handed bend into the home straight and just over three furlongs from the finish.

Kris Kin had a low draw, 4 in a field of 20 runners, which meant that he was at a disadvantage running to the right-hand bend on to the main course. I knew that we would have to get a prominent position in the field going into that bend. If we were at the back of the field going into that bend, it meant we would be in a very poor position when the field rounded the right-hand bend and started to tack across to the rail on the left. We would be at the back and on the inside.

I knew these things but Kris Kin did not. It was my job to communicate to Kris Kin what I wanted him to do, so as to give him the best chance of being in a position to go and win his race when we got into the finishing straight.

In the early-morning betting, Refuse to Bend, who had

won the first Classic of the season, the 2000 Guineas (over a mile, rather than the mile-and-a-half of the Epsom Derby), was favourite with the Aidan O'Brien entry, Brian Boru, as second favourite. Kris Kin had been 12/1 in the morning but as the day wore on, the bookmakers reported a flood of money for him, which they attributed to the 'Fallon factor'. By mid-morning, Kris Kin was 10/1 and by the off he was 8/1 third favourite.

Because he was such a laid-back horse I knew that I would have to wake Kris Kin up from the start and cajole and push him in the early stages of the race. In the event, he woke me up. As the stalls opened Kris Kin reared up and plunged forward out of the open gate.

Fortunately, I was able to keep my balance and we did not lose any ground on the other horses around us. I was immediately pushing Kris Kin along. I knew there was no chance of reaching the right-hand bend before the front runners drawn near to the right-hand rail, but I knew that in a big field of 20 runners we needed to be in the first ten runners coming out of the right-hand bend.

We got to that bend in about seventh place, which I was happy with. But now the horses in front would start to tack across to their left as would the horses to my inside, in order to go the shortest route to the inside rail, which in turn takes you the shortest route to the winning post. Because we were on the outside around the right-hand bend, it was inevitable that we would find ourselves on the inside once the field reached the left-hand rail and I was very anxious to make sure that we did not lose any ground going up the hill.

Kris Kin started to race lazily and I again started jostling and pushing him to maintain our position. Very few horses win the Derby coming from the back of a large field such as this was and even fewer do it coming from a position at the back and hemmed in on the rails. The Derby is not won in the first five furlongs but it can easily be lost. As we got to the seven-furlong marker, we had lost a few places and were now running in about tenth position. The helter-skelter of the downhill run into Tattenham Corner was in front of us.

Also directly in front of us on the rail was Brian Boru and just to his outside was the favourite, Refuse to Bend. Up to this point, my main focus had been on Kris Kin's overall position but now, as we hurtled down into Tattenham Corner, I started to focus on the runners around me and in front of me. I was particularly watching the manner in which they were being ridden to interpret how well they were going and I was also taking into account things I knew about the horses' characteristics and their previous form.

Although I did not want to be quite as far back as we were coming down towards Tattenham Corner, I was at least behind two horses which I thought were likely to be going forward in Refuse to Bend and Brian Boru, the favourite and second favourite. I was confident enough to start riding Kris Kin and ask him to stretch the moment we entered the home straight. He responded to my urgings immediately, picking up on Refuse to Bend and Brian Boru much more quickly but not as quickly as I had hoped.

Almost at the same time, I noticed that Mick Kinane, on Brian Boru, was starting to ride his horse vigorously. I had in the back of my mind a plan B if I came up behind these horses and could not get past them, which was to switch Kris Kin into the centre of the course.

But because he had not picked up as quickly as I had hoped,

I was reluctant to do this as we would lose valuable ground and impetus. Impetus is everything with a horse like Kris Kin. He did not have a turn of foot, but once he built up a head of steam he was like a machine.

The straight at Epsom has a very marked camber from right to left so that in switching Kris Kin to go round these horses, I would be asking him to move uphill to his right. We were getting dangerously close to these two horses and I was about to switch Kris Kin to our right. A split second before we got to them, I noticed that Refuse to Bend was starting to roll away from Brian Boru and to his right. I knew Refuse to Bend was a doubtful stayer and my instinct was that he was finished and that a sufficient gap for us to go through would open between him and Brian Boru.

Almost exactly as we got to them, the gap appeared and Kris Kin, who was now building up some serious momentum, went in between and past the favourite and second favourite with contempt and we were still on the rail.

Now we had five horses in front of us, all of whom were running close to the rail and we were about two furlongs from the finish. The horse leading the race was another Aidan O'Brien runner, The Great Gatsby, ridden by Pat Eddery, who was taking part in his last Derby.

We were still six lengths behind him and had no clear run to get to him because of the other horses in front of us, who were also on the rail. I knew we had to switch into the centre of the track, but I wanted to do this without Kris Kin losing the momentum he had already built up.

At the same time I could see the Aga Khan's horse, Alamshar, coming down the centre of the track and making ground towards the leaders. We needed to avoid him as he would almost certainly start to come down the camber to his left and obstruct Kris Kin's uninterrupted progress.

At this point, Kris Kin was flying so I angled him gradually up the camber and into the centre of the track at about the two-and-a-half-furlong point. We passed the fourth horse, who had moved off the rail on his inside, just before the two-furlong marker, and now there were three to pass.

Kris Kin was still stretching and giving his all. When we got to the furlong pole, we had got to the outside of the front three and within a length of the third horse. We had 220 yards up the finishing hill to catch them.

First, we passed Dutch Gold but we were still four lengths off The Great Gatsby, with Pat riding for all he was worth. My job of steering Kris Kin was done. It was now up to him.

If you were betting in running, you would have lost your bollocks because you would have had everything on The Great Gatsby. He looked as if he was home and hosed, but in the last 100 yards he just died and my lad wore him down. It was at this point that I heard the roar of the crowd for the first time, so focused had I been up until now. Kris Kin had clear ground in front of him and he had the camber to his left, which gave him added impetus to get to The Great Gatsby.

I found it hard to believe but somehow Kris Kin managed to pick up again for me and we passed Tesio's piece of wood a length clear of The Great Gatsby. After I had dismounted from Kris Kin and walked out of the winner's enclosure I did not look back and we never saw each other again.

Racing can be strange like that. You form a bond with a horse in a few minutes of a race and your names are linked together in racing history for the rest of time but after a race, you move on. Sometimes you ride a horse again. Sometimes you don't. In the horse-racing industry, they never organise teammates' reunions.

My season went from strength to strength after the Derby, and the 221 winners I rode that year had been beaten only by Frankie Dettori and Sir Gordon Richards in the previous 100 years. Sir Michael won his seventh trainers' title and I rode Islington to victory in the Breeders' Cup Filly and Mare Turf at Santa Anita to round my season off at the end of October. It was my first victory in the Breeders' Cup and to do it at Santa Anita, one of my favourite places in the world, made it even more special.

Controversy started to chase me the following season, but I won the Oaks, for the third time, on Ouija Board, and started the 2004 Derby the next day confident of victory on North Light. I was beset by troubles by then, but that ride on North Light was a glorious island of peacefulness and calm. Of all my wins, it was probably the one I enjoyed most.

I always loved North Light. I couldn't see him getting beaten in the Derby. I knew he would stay the trip. He had enough speed to be anywhere in the race. He was big enough that if he got in some hurly burly, he would be okay. I could have made the running. I could have done anything.

He was the best colt I rode around Epsom. With North Light, there was no thinking. I only had to point him. I think that was why I remember that ride with so much fondness: I could just enjoy it. It was nothing like the ride on Kris Kin, nothing like as complicated or as tactical. Or with as much luck.

When you are going for these big races, you are going to

feel some pressure whether you can block most of it out or not, and I used to get cold sores around the time of the Derby. I guess that was because the nerves were building up and I was run down.

At Epsom, you can't make up if you screw up. You have the Oaks, the Coronation Cup and the Derby in quick succession and I always had live chances because of the trainers I rode for so there was no let-up. Except, there was with North Light. On North Light, I could relax.

He was a lovely big individual and I won the Dante at York with him a few weeks before the Derby. Going to York takes more out of them than you think, especially with a big horse like that, because it's four hours there and four hours back in the box and I didn't want to ride him any harder than I needed to.

In the last furlong of the Dante, we were winning fairly comfortably from Frankie Dettori on Rule of Law, but you want to save as much energy as possible for the Derby so you try to win as cosily as you can. I probably overdid it a little bit in the easing up at the end and Frankie nearly got me on the line. And if he had, the Derby would have been gone for me because I wouldn't have been riding him any more.

It was easy to ride North Light because he was a handy horse, he galloped, he stayed, he was easy to ride in every way. He was easy to get to the start. The mile-and-a-half start was a nightmare at Epsom because you had to go all the way around there and all sorts of things can unsettle the horse. But North Light was unflappable. When the race started, he had good gate speed and I tucked in behind the pacemaker, Meath, as we went up the hill. And that was how it stayed. Meath led and North Light stayed on his shoulder, freewheeling all the way down the hill and around Tattenham Corner. It was easy.

I sent him with three furlongs left to go. A few challengers made a show of trying to close on him, but he was never going to be beaten. It was the best feeling I've ever had. I didn't see a danger. I didn't have to worry. I didn't have to do anything.

So many of the other big races I'd ridden seemed to be loaded with issues and worries. If I got it wrong, it killed me. I loved my pieces when I was playing chess and if I lost a piece, I'd be raging. When I was riding, if I made a mistake and lost a race I would have won if I had done something different, that killed me. That was never going to happen on North Light. Coming in after the race, I was actually able to enjoy it, to look around and enjoy the atmosphere and the cheers and the excitement of Epsom on Derby day.

I rode other Classic winners after that, but that was my last victory in the Derby. By then I had been the victim of a sting operation in the *News of the World* that levelled race-fixing allegations against me and it was becoming obvious that the BHA had their binoculars on me.

The controversies started coming thick and fast and even though in many ways I was happier than I had ever been riding for Sir Michael, and as convinced as ever that it was as close to the perfect job as I was ever going to get, I got fed up with the constant negativity that surrounded me. The scrutiny seemed to be for all the wrong reasons.

I loved Epsom. The last horse I ever rode there, for the late Dandy Nicholls, was a winner, but that win on North Light represented a beacon of achievement in a year that was disfigured by scandals, a year where I won the Derby and the Oaks on successive days but people started to talk more about things that were happening to me off the track rather than on it.

But I'll always have Epsom. I'll always have those Derby victories on Oath, Kris Kin and North Light. Those are the times when you test yourself, when you use everything you know, all the homework you have done, all the times you have been a student of human moves as well as a watcher of horseflesh and put it all together.

That's what happened in all my Derby victories. Everything came together beautifully. Oath was my first. He's the horse my parents' old house is named after. North Light was my last. That win was the one I enjoyed the most. Kris Kin was sandwiched between them. That was my best.

CHAPTER 20

Ballinger Ridge

At the end of February 2004, my agent, David Pollington, rang me to talk through some of his recommendations about rides for upcoming races. He said the trainer Andrew Balding wanted me to ride a horse called Ballinger Ridge in the third at Lingfield the following Tuesday afternoon.

Ballinger Ridge. I thought it sounded a bit like a war film. I'd been hoping to have that Tuesday off. It wasn't a great meeting, he wasn't a great horse and it was very early in the season. I wanted to pace myself for the months ahead. I said I wasn't keen. Dave admitted Ballinger Ridge was a horse that ran well but never won. He was being kind. As Andrew Balding's sister, Clare, wrote in an article the following week, he was a horse who had had 'an uninspiring career' to date.

He was a five-year-old gelding and in eighteen previous races, he had never won, had finished second five times, third four times and out of the money on nine occasions. He was not on a hot streak, it would be fair to say. He had a tendency to pull hard in the early stages of the race, so was likely to be leading for some time, perhaps flattering to deceive and getting the hopes of his backers up. But he lacked acceleration, so he often led into the final furlong and then faded.

But David also pointed out that the owners, Hazel and David Barber, who had bred him at home, were big fans of mine and that Andrew had put me up on a lot of good horses and it would be helpful all round to do him a favour. It was a fair point. I thought about it and felt obliged to ride him.

The Sunday before the race, I read an article that quoted trainer Jamie Osborne saying that the best prospect in his yard was a horse called Rye, who was the favourite in the Betdirect.co.uk Median Auction Maiden Stakes, also known as the third at Lingfield on Tuesday. Rye was 16lb well in at the weights and I thought he would win. The bookies did, too.

It was a mile race and there were ten runners. We jumped out and I hoofed Ballinger Ridge down the hill. After a short while, I looked around and thought there must have been a false start. Where was everybody? It seemed like I was about 20 lengths clear. The rest were a dot on the horizon. So I sat up and eased up. The rules now say that you have to push all the way to the line but in those days, you didn't have to. I wanted to let the horse coast in without giving him a hard race. I was also aware of Ballinger Ridge's talent for losing late in the race, so I thought I might as well conserve a bit of energy.

I checked over my shoulder again at about the two-furlong marker to see how far clear I was. There was a low winter sun at our backs, but I could see that the field was still well behind me. It was then that I dropped my hands, intending to coast from there to the winning post and not win too far, as the racing expression goes.

Ballinger Ridge was three or four horse widths off the rail at this point, and what I couldn't see was that to our left and on the rail was my nemesis, Rye, making ground slowly but relentlessly. Shortly after looking over my shoulder, I became aware of a horse much closer to me than I thought was possible.

The low winter sun had caused the shadows of the horses behind me to lengthen, and what I'd seen out of the corner of my eye was the shadow of Rye looming ominously. Rye had now moved off the rail and out into the centre of the course to make his challenge. I thought that perhaps the flickering shadow was an optical illusion, given I'd seen nothing when I'd looked around before, but there, to my horror, was Rye, now within three lengths.

I started to try to re-galvanise Ballinger Ridge, but even with a genuine horse, it's almost impossible to regain impetus once you've signalled to it that it's done enough. And Ballinger Ridge was not a genuine horse. Even so, he and Rye passed the winning post locked together.

As the horses walked back to the winner's enclosure, Rye's jockey and I were speculating as to who'd won. Neither of us was sure. I came in and asked Andrew Balding how bad it looked. He said, 'Bad.' I was so angry with myself. When the result was announced, my heart sank. I knew I'd get a lengthy ban, meaning I'd miss the World Cup in Dubai. Had that nose verdict gone the other way and Ballinger Ridge had won, then the rest of this book would tell a very different story. It would be a litany of my successes on some of the great Coolmore Group One winners in the following years. Rye changed everything.

*

I was devastated. It was a bad misjudgement. I knew straight away I'd really screwed up. I hadn't wanted to win by too far, because it would have affected Ballinger Ridge's handicap for the next race. Instead of getting seven pounds, he would have got a stone.

It's not the first time a jockey has eased up and been beaten. You don't get the same flak for easing up and getting beaten as you would for winning by 15 lengths. Your trainer would kill you for that. You wouldn't just get a bollocking. You would ruin the horse for a year, or two years, in terms of its handicapping. For the sake of one little race worth two grand. And that's all it was: a two-grand race.

I knew it was a screw-up. Of course it was. But it was an honest screw-up. Jockeys are human, too. I was indulging in a bit of brinksmanship and I got it wrong. But straight away, people tried to turn it into something massive. I was made to look like a criminal. I was effectively accused of race-fixing.

This ride featured strongly in the subsequent police investigation into me and in the trial that followed. In order to counter the allegations surrounding it, my legal team showed the jury a number of rides where I had dropped my hands and won. It was explained to the jury that trainers did not like their horses winning by too much as it would mean that they would be allocated more weight for doing so the next time they ran, lessening their chances of winning, and that is why jockeys did it. My lawyers then showed eight races of other jockeys getting caught out in exactly the same way as I had on Ballinger Ridge.

Once again, it was a screw-up. I admit that. I haven't got any choice but to admit that. As I've said, it was a bad misjudgement. But that's all. If it had been a lesser-known jockey, as Clare Balding wrote in that piece, 'the story would have merited little or no coverage, just another cock-up by a jockey who lost his concentration'. But it wasn't a lesser-known jockey. It was me.

John McCririck went nuts on At The Races, the racing TV channel, and called for me to be suspended for six months. The racing authorities also let it be known they had been concerned about what they considered suspicious betting patterns backing Ballinger Ridge to lose. The Jockey Club announced an investigation. It was a perfect storm.

There were some sane voices in the midst of all the wailing. Andrew Balding was one of them. 'It looked worse than it was,' he said after the race. 'Kieren said he was giving our horse a breather and then was asking him to go again. The horse is a maiden after a lot of opportunities and is not the easiest of rides. Everyone realises Kieren made a balls-up, especially him, but it's ridiculous to suggest that there was anything sinister going on. As if the champion jockey is going to risk his career for the sake of a class H regional race. It's just crazy.'

That was absolutely right. It was absurd to think I would have done something like that deliberately. Anybody who thought about it for more than a second would have realised that. Why would I have ridden it into such a commanding lead, for a start? Why would I have done that if I wanted it to lose?

The whole thing did not bear any sensible analysis. It happens in racing sometimes. It happens in life. People make mistakes. I made a mistake. It wasn't my first and it wasn't my last. But none of it changed the fact that the reason I was a jockey was to ride winners. That's what I lived for.

At the stewards' inquiry, I told them my instructions had been to make the running and hang on to win the race. After watching a video, the stewards found me in breach of the rules in that I had failed to ride out for first place. I was banned for twenty-one days and missed the Dubai World Cup.

By the time that penalty was handed down, though, I had other worries.

On 10 February 2004, there was a meeting between the Jockey Club and the police. On 13 February my agent, David Pollington, received a letter on behalf of a company in Sharjah, in the United Arab Emirates. It said the company was looking to invest in British horse racing by sponsoring a world series of Group One races, very similar to what the Qataris are doing now both in Britain and abroad. They knew I was the champion jockey and wanted me to help them get started.

Dave was always on the ball and he looked these guys up to make sure it was all legitimate. It appeared to be, so we made contact with them and swapped telephone numbers with a man called Sean de Silva. Sean was very friendly and super smooth. He was a master of chat. He asked me if there were any horses I fancied that day and I gave him three or four tips.

We arranged to meet at the Dorchester Hotel in Park Lane, in London, for dinner on the night of 23 February. Sean said the main man in his business operation would be present at the dinner. He told me he was a sheikh.

A friend of mine, John Woods, drove me in and we parked up, got our bags out of the car and wandered into the hotel to check in. Before we got to the front desk, Sean came up to us in the lobby. He introduced himself and said he'd already checked us in. He handed me a room key.

He said we'd be meeting his boss, the sheikh, at 7pm for dinner. John and I went upstairs to the room and started chatting away. I had a bit of a look around and noticed that our room had a connecting door to the next room, which I thought was a bit odd. I had another look around and couldn't see anything out of the ordinary, but I just felt something wasn't right.

I rang down to reception and said I wanted to change rooms. They wanted to know why and I said the room number was unlucky for me. They asked me what number it was. I didn't know. I had to get John to run into the corridor to look at the door. It was 19. They must have thought I was mad, but they moved us anyway.

I went down to dinner at the arranged time and met up with all these potential investors in racing. I was introduced to the sheikh, but Sean seemed a bit edgy and he pulled me aside and wanted to know why I had changed rooms. He said it had messed things up because he had been planning to get some of his friends over and they were going to use both the connecting rooms for a big party for us before John and I left the next day.

I had a decent chat with the sheikh. It was a conversation of glorified pleasantries, really. He was friendly enough. He said this was just the start for them and they wanted to buy horses and invest in the industry. They rang me a few times during the next week, and on the day of the race at Lingfield, one of them rang me again to ask if I had any more tips. I gave them a couple. I'd read Jamie Osborne's bit about Rye by then. I said I wasn't very optimistic about my ride on Ballinger Ridge and I thought Rye would win.

Several days later, I flew to Mijas in Spain with a few other jockeys, including John Egan, to ride in a meeting there. It was a little holiday weekend away effectively and Sean said the sheikh wanted to take the business talks further and would join us there with his investors and discuss things over a meal. We went out to a big restaurant and there were seven or eight of us around the table. The bill came to about £700 and they paid for it. The conversation turned to various issues associated with my contacts in horseracing.

The sheikh began to talk about black jockeys, asking why there were far fewer of them than white jockeys. He made some disparaging remarks with which I disagreed. I told him about Patrick Husbands, the Bajan rider, who was a close friend of mine, and a brilliant jockey. I told them about America, where Mike Smith, one of the most successful jockeys of all time, is one of several with non-white ancestry. So the sheikh moved onto other topics.

He quizzed me about the Queen. He said she seemed like a bit of a doddery old dear. He was inviting me to criticise her, but I told him the truth and said how sharp and knowledgeable she was about horse racing. I'd ridden for her. She knew a lot more about the sport than most punters, and possibly even than her own racing manager.

So then the sheikh got down to the nitty-gritty. He said they had made a lot of money that week from the tips I had given them and they wanted to repay me. I said I couldn't take any money, so they said they would buy a car for me. I said I couldn't take a car. At that point, Sean caught my eye and gestured that I should leave the room with him. We went into a hallway where it was quiet and Sean said that the sheikh wanted to give me something. He said I was embarrassing the sheikh by refusing his offers of generosity. He pressed me but I didn't want to know. I said: 'I have never done it and I never will.'

The sheikh never tried to get me to say I would stop horses for money, even in the aftermath of Ballinger Ridge. He and his associates only tried to get me to give information for reward. That is not a criminal offence, but it is a BHA offence and I was later to be charged with it by the BHA.

We went back into the main room of the restaurant and I said I ought to go back and meet the rest of the lads. Sean asked me if I needed any cocaine. I said I didn't and that I wanted to go.

They invited us back to their hotel and on the way, they said we were going to stop off somewhere for one last drink. It was a brothel, basically. It was one of those nightclubs where girls suddenly appear at your table and they have rooms upstairs. I wanted an early night as I was aware that we were racing the next day and I wanted to have a chat with a couple of my owners, so we all left after a couple of drinks.

Not long after I'd got back to my room, Sean rang and said we needed to meet up again later. I said I was busy. We were watching the Ireland vs England rugby match on the television. Sean told me to wait while he put someone else on the line. I heard another voice then. It was the sheikh.

'This is Mazher Mahmood,' he said, 'and we are going to run a story in the *News of the World* on Sunday about you race fixing. So we need to meet up.' He told me to come to his hotel room and he'd discuss a deal with me.

I was in shock. I don't think of myself as particularly gullible. In fact, I'd checked that hotel room from top to bottom for hidden cameras and things. I am cautious by nature but I just didn't see it with the sheikh. I never smelled a rat. Later, of course, Mahzer Mahmood was to become notorious as the 'Fake Sheikh' and a number of high-profile sportsmen and public figures would be caught up in his entrapment. He was eventually jailed for 15 months in October 2016 for conspiring to pervert the course of justice by falsifying a police statement. But Mahmood and his crew were very convincing.

John Egan and I went along and when we got there, Mahmood had this huge minder with him. He had a mouth full of gold fillings and he went by the name of Jaws and, as other victims of the Fake Sheikh have said, he looked as though he had walked straight off the set of a James Bond film. Mahmood said that the deal he was proposing was that if I admitted stopping horses then he wouldn't mention anything about the prostitutes.

'You know I wasn't with prostitutes,' I said.

Mahmood stuck to the line that they would mention the prostitutes and I could feel myself panicking. My marriage to Julie was on the rocks by then and I had three young kids. I hadn't done anything wrong, but I couldn't bear the idea of the shame it would bring on my family.

I stuck to my guns. 'You know you won't be able to stand up a story saying I went with prostitutes,' I said, 'because I was with you all evening. Besides, it doesn't make any difference. I don't stop horses and I never have and I never will.'

I rang Christopher Stewart-Moore at that point and told him I was in a bit of a tight spot. I asked him if he had heard of Mazher Mahmood and Christopher asked me to pass the phone to Mahmood. I heard Mahmood saying that I had admitted to this and I had admitted to that. Christopher gave him short shrift. 'Mr Fallon admits to absolutely nothing,' he told Mahmood. 'He was just being polite to you in accepting your hospitality.'

Mahmood looked a bit rattled. 'I am a force for good,' he told Christopher. 'I have obtained a number of convictions against people and helped the police in numerous cases. I have put paedophiles behind bars.'

'You should be behind bars with them,' Christopher told him. 'And you are certainly not a force for good.'

I couldn't hear Christopher's end of the conversation, but I did see Mahmood's reaction to that. He looked outraged. He held out the phone at arm's length as if it were radioactive and then flung it on the bed.

'That's it,' he said, turning to me. 'You're fucked.'

The next day, Sunday 7 March, my picture was splashed across the front page of the *News of the World* beneath the headline, 'The Fixer'. The paper accused me of illegally giving inside information to undercover reporters for betting purposes and suggested that I had deliberately stopped Ballinger Ridge from winning. It was garbage. The *Daily Telegraph* noted succinctly a day later: 'There was no evidence of race-fixing in the *News of the World* report.'

On Monday, the Jockey Club contacted Christopher and said they were charging me with giving tips for reward and for bringing racing into disrepute in relation to some of the things that the *News of the World* alleged I had said. Within a very short space of time, they had to withdraw the 'information for reward' charge as they had to concede that there had been no reward.

The Jockey Club appeared to be relying solely on the *News of the World* tapes, which the paper had already handed over to them, for their evidence. I now know that in February 2004, Andy Coulson, who was then the editor of the *News of the World* and was later jailed for conspiracy to hack phones, was told by someone at the Jockey Club or the police that I might be a person of interest for him. Whoever it was who set Coulson on my scent, he had then put the sting in place.

The level of contact between the police and the *News of the World*, in particular, is a matter of record now anyway and formed part of Lord Justice Leveson's report into the phone-hacking scandal in 2012. 'For some time before January 2011,' Leveson's report found, 'there was a concern that a number of senior officers within the Metropolitan Police Service had become too close to News International and its staff.'

I sued the *News of the World* for libel and when my legal team began to look into what had happened more closely, they uncovered a disturbing picture. Mahmood, Sean de Silva and the rest of the undercover reporters were all fitted with wires, obviously, and so there was more than just one master tape recording of the conversation. There were several different tapes. I wondered if the reason they had initially booked me into a room with another one adjoining is that, while it is illegal to bug someone in their own room, it's not illegal to have one in a separate room which you yourself are in.

In the open conversation with Mahmood in the restaurant, I had made it clear I didn't stop horses. In part of the recording, Mahmood and his cohorts started talking about how they fixed games of cricket in Sharjah. It made Christopher laugh when he heard that because it was clear I had absolutely no idea about anything to do with cricket.

My lawyers said their tactics were obvious and familiar. They were trying to achieve a kind of consensus. They say they're crooks and the idea is that that will put you at your ease and so you'll say you're a crook, too. That bit of the tape will never appear in their evidence, though, because they'll edit it.

By a fortunate coincidence, Christopher had happened to be watching Sky News on the night before the *News of the World* story broke. They were running an item about it, saying it was coming, which included some footage of the meeting in the restaurant that showed me leaving with Sean.

Some time later, when Christopher was going through the tapes which the Jockey Club had acquired from the *News of the World* and which, as my solicitor, he was entitled to see, he realised that the footage he had seen on Sky was not among them, and that there must be a tape missing from the evidence they had provided. He asked them to look into it and eventually they sent him the tapes and film footage as well as the transcript of the conversations that had taken place in Mahmood's hotel room.

Christopher was listening to the tape and checking it against the transcript when the tape appeared to come to an end. It started to make a fuzzy noise, so Christopher got up to turn it off and as he did so, he heard the recording of the conversation between me and Sean start again. He heard someone offering me a Mercedes and me saying that I'd never done anything like that in my life and I never would. I had told Christopher about that conversation but there was no record of it in the transcripts. He had found it by accident. It appeared to us as though the *News of the World* had tried to obliterate that part of the tape but had botched the job.

Things started to become a little clearer. When Sean had taken me out of the room, any tape recording of that conversation, which was on his own separate wire, could be ignored if I didn't say anything useful.

Christopher gave the transcript of the missing tape to a journalist and it was subsequently published in the *Sunday People*. The *News of the World* threatened to sue Christopher for breach of their copyright in the tape they had failed to disclose and which showed I was innocent.

The Jockey Club then immediately withdrew the case against me and John Egan. As well as withdrawing the 'information for reward' charge, they had to withdraw the other charge of bringing racing into disrepute when it emerged that much of the transcript provided by the *News of the World* was not a true record of what was said and most of the alleged incriminating material was inaccurate.

But although I had been completely exonerated, some of all this mud stuck.

CHAPTER 21

Duel

The media called the battle for the 2004 jockeys' championship between Frankie Dettori and me a duel. It was no duel. It was a sham of a fight where one man was swinging freely and the other man's hands were tied behind his back. If they had clapped me in chains, they could barely have tipped the scales more in Frankie's favour. So it wasn't a duel at all where I was concerned. It was a nightmare.

At the end of August, the dash for the championship wasn't even a race. I was miles clear. I was home and hosed. I was 17 winners clear of Frankie and even more ahead of Seb Sanders, who was in third place. My seventh title was within touching distance. Everyone knew it.

On 1 September, I was supposed to be travelling up to York to ride Red Bloom for Sir Michael Stoute in the feature race of the day at York, the Strensall Stakes. Red Bloom won all right. In fact, she beat a horse ridden by Frankie into second place. But I wasn't on her back. I was otherwise detained.

I had split from Julie by then and I was living with a

friend of mine, Paul Thomas, a builder, in a village out-side Newmarket called Kentford. Just before 4am, there was this almighty hammering at the front door. It was the police trying to smash their way in. There were eight detectives and they were trying to break the door down. By happy coincidence, there was a photographer from the *Sun* there, too.

Paul got downstairs before they smashed the door and opened it for them himself. They might as well have rung the bell. They brought a female detective, too. They had been watching the house for a while, apparently, and I think they were hoping they might catch me with a female friend to add to my discomfort. They didn't.

They came running up to the room I was sleeping in and burst in before I had got out of bed. They said they were arresting me for conspiracy to defraud the public. I didn't have a clue what they were talking about but they seemed very hyped up about it all.

They asked if there were any drugs in the room. I said there weren't. They asked if I had any money in the room. I pointed them to my rucksack, which had a brown paper bag in it with some cash that had been given to me by an owner as a thank-you present when I won a race on one of his horses the weekend before. The police looked like all their Christmases had come at once.

I told them I needed to go to the toilet so they came and stood over me while I was in the bathroom. A couple of the others ripped open the paper bag and I think there was a few grand in it. I couldn't say for sure because I hadn't looked to find out. Maybe that sounds blasé, but it was a reasonably common occurrence for an owner to give his jockey a few quid for winning a race. It was an exaggerated version of giving a waiter a tip.

It turned out they had arrested fifteen other people that morning as well. Two other jockeys, Fergal Lynch and Darren Williams, and the trainer Karl Burke were among the others detained. So was a gambler called Miles Rodgers, who was the founder and former director of a syndicate called the Platinum Racing Club. The police had been following him for a year and had bugged his car.

It was suggested that the arrests had taken place as a result of an investigation into eighty suspicious races, with 130 officers from four police forces, headed by the City of London Police, raiding nineteen addresses across three counties. The police, the Jockey Club and Betfair all rushed to trumpet their part in developments.

The police also raided the house I had shared with Julie in Cowlinge. They left with binbags full of stuff and confiscated a tower computer and a laptop which Julie and the kids used and which were full of computer games. They wouldn't have got much joy out of the PC, because I've never even known how to switch one on.

They drove me the twelve miles to the police station in Bury St Edmunds and threw me in a cell. I fell asleep. They came down to get me when Christopher Stewart-Moore arrived and they couldn't wake me to begin with. They seemed a bit put out. Maybe they thought I'd be down there quaking with fear.

The detectives put their tapes on and Christopher told me I didn't have to answer any of their questions and could just say 'no comment'. I told them I was happy to talk. 'I've nothing to hide,' I told them. 'I'll answer any of your questions. I have done nothing wrong.'

One of them pulled out a copy of the *News of the World* with the 'Fixer' article from February 2004 and left it on the table. Christopher asked them if they normally used newspaper articles as evidence, particularly articles from the *News of the World*. They asked me if I knew Miles Rodgers and I said I didn't. They seemed very interested in Rodgers, right from the start. He had been warned off racetracks by the Jockey Club earlier in the year for laying his own horses to lose. Karl Burke had trained three of the Platinum Club's sixteen horses and Darren Williams had been Karl's stable jockey.

The police in Bury seemed very keen to put me and Miles Rodgers together. It became clear later that their case was heavily dependent on the idea that he and I were in league. They asked me if I had ever met him and I said I hadn't. So, with great triumph, they pulled out a little picture of me at a race meeting at Doncaster in the parade ring. I was standing there with about twenty members of a racing syndicate who owned the horse I was riding and, apparently, Miles Rodgers was one of them.

So the police produced this picture and said: 'You have met him. Here you are in the picture with him.' I told them I didn't have a clue who any of these people were and they pointed to one man and said: 'This is Miles Rodgers.' That counted as me meeting him, as far as they were concerned. Christopher asked when the picture was taken and they said it was three or four years earlier.

They then told me with renewed triumph that I had once shared a car with Rodgers. I had no recollection at all of that, but they mentioned that they had evidence I had been in a car driven away from Leicester racecourse by Rodgers. Then the penny dropped.

I'd flown up to Leicester from Newmarket with Seb Sanders and Darryll Holland to ride in a meeting there. We had got a taxi from the airstrip to the course and asked the driver to meet us back at the main gate straight after our last race. We were going to head back to the airstrip so the plane could fly us to an evening meeting at Windsor.

I saw a friend of mine, Shaun Lynch, Fergal's brother, at Leicester racecourse, had a brief chat with him and then went to the weighing room. Afterwards, when we got to the gate, there was no sign of our taxi driver, the traffic was starting to build up and we were all getting a bit panicky about making it to Windsor in time. I phoned Shaun and asked him if there was any chance he could give us a lift to the airstrip. He said he wasn't driving and he was in his mate's car. I asked him if his mate would give us a lift. I didn't care who was driving, to be honest. I would have hopped in a car with Genghis Khan if he could have got us to the airstrip in time.

After a couple of minutes, a big car pulled up outside the front gate, we slung our bags in the boot, hopped in and drove to the airport. There wasn't a conversation. I didn't even see the guy who was driving, who turned out to be Miles Rodgers. I was talking to Seb and Darryll in the back. When we got to the airstrip, we leapt out of the car and got on the plane and away we went.

The police moved on then. They asked me if I knew Fergal Lynch and I said of course I knew him. They asked me if I knew Darren Williams and I told them I knew him, too. Then one of the detectives said: 'Is it true you can make a horse go slower by pulling on the reins?'

Christopher started to laugh. 'Oh come on,' he said. 'You can't be serious.'

They released me that evening and helped me avoid the media scrum outside the police station by letting me get in the back of a police car. They then drove me back to Newmarket, and Christopher released a statement through the Press Association: 'Kieren Fallon has not been charged with any offence,' he said. 'Following an interview with the police in Bury St Edmunds, he has been released without charge.

'The circumstances that relate to his arrest involve an individual whom Kieren Fallon has met on one occasion and whose name he did not even know at the time the meeting happened. This was during the course of a ten-minute car journey from Leicester races to the airport at Leicester where he then flew on to an evening meeting at Windsor.

'During this car journey Kieren Fallon did not speak to the individual concerned. In the circumstances we do not anticipate that this matter will be taken any further by the police.'

The Jockey Club was quick to draw attention to the role of its security department in the investigation that had led to the arrests and in particular to the presence of former senior police officers that had been added to its ranks to replace the army types it had used before.

'The City of London Police investigation was initiated following investigative work by the Jockey Club's security department, headed by Paul Scotney, a former detective chief superintendent,' the Jockey Club statement said.

'The decision to refer the matter to the police was taken following consultation with the chairman of the Jockey Club's security and investigations committee, Ben Gunn, a former chief constable.' The Jockey Club thought they had entered some brave new world. Its tone, too, was one of triumphalism and self-congratulation.

Richard Hughes on Tamburlaine is left trailing as Golan wins the 2000 Guineas in May 2001 – the win lifted the pressure off me following my long injury lay-off. *(Getty Images)*

My time in Hong Kong caused me to be dragged into a *Panorama* documentary in 2002 when I was falsely accused of consorting with Triads. *(George Selwyn)*

Suddenly a gap opened and Russian Rhythm surged to the front to win the 1000 Guineas in 2003. *(PA)*

Kris Kin leads the way home in the 2003 Derby. Sir Michael Stoute called my ride one of the greatest in the history of the race. *(PA)*

Having had one of the best moments of my career on Kris Kin, after I left him in the winner's enclosure we never saw each other again. *(PA)*

Islington (partially obscured on the inside) sets off on his way to victory in the Breeders' Cup in 2003 at Santa Anita, one of my favourite places in the world. *(George Selwyn)*

North Light gave me the best feeling I've ever had on a horse as he sped home to win the 2004 Derby. *(Getty Images)*

After the turmoil at the end of 2004, the approach to join Aidan O'Brien at Ballydoyle came at the right time for me.

Footstepsinthesand (No 7) wins the 2000 Guineas in 2005 – I knew from the moment I first rode him that he was a special horse. *(Getty Images)*

While most of the horses I rode at Ballydoyle were a joy, Scorpion was not easy, though Aidan had a brilliant way of calming him down. *(Caroline Norris)*

On a wet day at Longchamp, Hurricane Run surges home to win the 2005 Prix de l'Arc de Triomphe. *(George Selwyn)*

I may be flying the flag after my win on Dylan Thomas in the 2007 Prix de l'Arc de Triomphe, but he had veered across the track and I felt sure we were about to be disqualified. *(Getty Images)*

Discussing the case with my brilliant lawyer, John Kelsey-Fry. *(Getty Images)*

'You would have to . . . ask the individual horse.' *(Getty Images)*

My last Classic win: Night of Thunder secured the 2000 Guineas in 2014. *(PA)*

With trainer Saeed bin Suroor at Epsom. Now I've retired, I still ride out for him. *(PA)*

My last ride in public at the Curragh on 26 June 2016. There was no fairytale ending and I knew the time was right to go.

(George Selwyn)

Relaxing with Brittany, Cieren and Natalie.

Me and my girlfriend, Jemma Shakespeare.

Betfair, the leading betting exchange, was also anxious to claim credit for its part in the investigation. 'Betfair has played a key role in helping the police with their investigations into corruption in horse-racing,' a statement said.

'Sophisticated technology now available enables all bets to be tracked, and all transactions linked to an end customer. Betfair has long maintained that the transparency of its exchange model, with the audit trail it provides, is a tremendously powerful weapon in keeping sport clean. The capability of tracking every mouse click is an important asset for investigations of this nature.'

At least I was still allowed to ride. The decision not to suspend the arrested jockeys marked a change of policy from the last time the police became involved in racing, when the jockey Graham Bradley had his licence to ride suspended for two months in 1999 after being arrested. Bradley was allowed to reapply for his licence after charges against him were dropped by the Crown Prosecution Service.

I was allowed to ride but it was a fairly hollow privilege. I was allowed to ride but I had also been totally screwed by the Jockey Club and the police. My head was fried. I felt everybody was looking at me, everybody was doubting me. At racecourses, all I wanted to do was hide.

How do you think Tiger Woods felt when his wife put that five-iron through his car window? Everything fell apart for him. It was the same for me. Sure, you can blot some things out when you are riding and you can take refuge in your job up to a point, but this went beyond that. Where do you turn? There are people taking your picture at the track, photographers chasing you everywhere you go, their shutters clicking and whirring as soon as you stick your head out of the weighing room. I didn't like being photographed at the best of times. This was the worst of times.

Then there was the abuse from the punters. Innocent until proven guilty doesn't exist for a lot of people who frequent racetracks. I could hear them shouting at me. I could see them pointing and gesticulating and their mouths forming into ugly yells. What they don't know, they make up.

I rode on for a long time after I was arrested that day in Kentford, but I was never really the same. I still had my moments but my confidence started to seep away and I never got it back. The jockeys' championship began to slip away from me and I never won another. Frankie just wore me down in the last few weeks of that 2004 season. I was riding with no confidence and I wasn't being given the same quality of rides. People were pulling away from me. One trainer wanted to give me a ride on one of his best horses, but he told me the owner had objected. 'Oh, no,' she had said, 'he's a crooked jockey.'

So the smaller owners, the bread-and-butter ones that needed the winners, they wanted me even less and so when I was arrested, effectively that was the end of it for me. They let me continue riding but they knew they had screwed me anyway.

Frankie and I were more or less dominating flat racing in those years and we got on great. We never really socialised or anything but we would have a drink, we travelled together and we flew together. We had a rivalry but there was never any edge to it. I respected him and he respected me.

If I sensed I wasn't going to be in contention, I wasn't going to spoil a race for him and he wouldn't spoil one for me. You do get jockeys who are bitter towards each other but it wasn't like that with us. Racing was like a goldfish bowl and we were all going round and round and round, so it made sense to try to get on with each other as much as you could. You have to work with each other, as competitive as it is. If you don't have respect for each other, you don't have respect for yourself, and Frankie and I never had an argument or a cross word.

We were opposites in many ways. Frankie was sociable. I wasn't. Frankie was confident. I was withdrawn. Frankie was extravagant. I was understated. Frankie was the man racing wanted as its figurehead, whereas I was expendable as far as the BHA was concerned. I was the acceptable collateral damage in the BHA's public relations drive to re-establish its image as an effective regulator following the disaster of the *Panorama* programme.

Frankie's riding style was easier on the eye than mine. His was heavily influenced by his time in America where he studied the way heroes like Angel Cordero and Willie Shoemaker rode and developed a low, crouching style. I loved my time in America, too, and I learned about the clock and switching a horse's leading leg, but I never changed my riding style. It worked for me and that was enough.

If Frankie hadn't had the ability, he wouldn't have got to where he was but I wouldn't have swapped my style with his. I loved the old-fashioned way I was brought up in racing. Jimmy FitzGerald, in particular, was old school and that was the way I liked it. Jimmy's death that autumn was another savage blow to my morale.

As the days wore on that season, Frankie kept on grinding. For him, it was like you're running a race and you're into the home straight and you see the guy in front of you is slowing down. And then you see the guy in front is carrying a back-pack and wearing lead boots and you are sprinting with your little T-shirt on and your trainers. You are going to run even faster because you know you are going to catch him. And that is what Frankie did.

By the end of September, my lead over Frankie had disappeared. My winners had dried up. In the last week of the month, I had gone 20 rides without a win. I'd only ridden three winners in my last 48 outings. It was a dramatic change-around. I had been 19 ahead of Frankie at the start of the month but now I was six behind.

On Monday 12 October, we both went to Leicester for what turned out to be a critical day in the championship. Frankie was ten ahead at the start of the meeting and 12 ahead by the time I was riding a filly called Maritima, one of Sir Michael's. A horse stumbled next to me and Maritima was barged into the rails. She almost fell and I was flung on to the turf.

There was only one horse behind me, Bowled Out, and she trampled on me as I lay in a foetal position on the floor. I was carried off the course on a stretcher to a waiting ambulance and taken to Leicester Royal Infirmary. I was still conscious but in a lot of pain. Not long after I got to the hospital, Frankie rode another winner to complete a treble. I was released from hospital that night with heavy bruising to my back and shoulders and drove to the course the following day. I had six rides booked but the course doctor said I wasn't fit to race.

It was a bitter feeling, that feeling of the title ebbing away. It killed me. In 2000, when I had the fall at Royal Ascot and I lost a title that would have been mine, I could accept it because it was an accident at the racecourse that was not anybody's fault. This was different. My arrest was no accident. I thought it was malicious and it was groundless. That was why I couldn't accept losing the title that season and why I never have and I never will.

I never got the championship back. I got close in 2011, when I had a decent ding-dong with Paul Hanagan and Silvestre de Sousa, but I couldn't quite make it and Paul got over the line. If I had not become embroiled in legal issues, I believe I would have been champion jockey every year, for at least a few years after 2004. And including 2004.

I was riding with that much confidence before my arrest that it was near impossible for anyone to beat me in the championship. I rode, without killing myself, over 200 winners in four different seasons, which few people have done. Before everything that happened, I felt I was unstoppable. It was a goal of mine to beat Pat Eddery's record of eleven titles. I won only six in the end. It would have been seven if I hadn't got injured in 2000 and eight if I hadn't been arrested in 2004. The rest would have taken care of themselves.

CHAPTER 22

The God of Horses

I loved working for Sir Michael Stoute. Nothing will ever come close to the partnership I had with him and the big races we won. I always said it was my dream job and that he was the trainer I most wanted to ride for. The years I had with him were everything that I hoped they would be. I always felt incredibly fortunate to be working with him and for him.

But by the end of 2004, I was at a low ebb. It wasn't anything to do with my relationship with Sir Michael. It was the Fake Sheikh stuff, it was being arrested, it was meetings with lawyers, it was the threat of a court case hanging over me, it was all of that. So when I got an offer to go home, to go back to Ireland, I thought: 'Fuck it, why not.'

Circumstances pulled me back to Ireland, too. Jamie Spencer, the stable jockey employed by the great Irish trainer Aidan O'Brien at Coolmore's Ballydoyle operation in County Tipperary, was a talented rider but he was struggling to cope with the pressure of riding for an outfit that had such high expectations. He had only been there for a year but his confidence was shot.

The bookmakers made Johnny Murtagh the hot favourite to replace Jamie when it became obvious he was leaving, but then Michael Tabor, one of the Coolmore partners, touched base with me when I was riding at Gulfstream Park, the racecourse at the north end of Miami Beach, some time early in February 2005. He sounded me out about going to ride for them. I was flattered, obviously. I had never been to Ballydoyle, the training arm of the Coolmore Stud, but if you are Irish and you love horses, it is your idea of heaven.

I knew the countryside around there, the lush land of Tipperary, and I knew of the reputation of O'Brien, the brilliant young trainer who ran Ballydoyle. At that point of my life, it felt as if it might provide me with a sanctuary.

I just felt so ashamed going out in public onto racecourses in England knowing, or at least feeling, what people were thinking about me. I was really proud of how I had overcome so much to get to where I was, even though I might not have expressed this openly, and I now felt like an unwelcome guest at a party.

I had been robbed of my good name in respect of the part of me that I had the highest regard for – that of a highly skilled professional jockey who was dedicated to my profession and who was always trying to win. I didn't feel good about many other aspects of myself and now the one part where I did feel I had achieved something had been publicly humiliated.

I didn't tell Sir Michael about the informal contact with Coolmore at that stage. I probably should have done, but even though I wanted to get away from England and I was open to the idea, I didn't really think anything would come of it. It's like that in any walk of life: you don't start blabbing about a job offer until it is official. Racing's a village, though, and rumours began to circulate. I was at a party at Gulfstream not long afterwards when Michael Holding, the great West Indies fast bowler, came up and started chatting to me.

I knew that Michael was a great friend of Sir Michael's and he asked me whether there was any substance in the rumours about Ballydoyle. I told him they had approached me. Again, that was probably not the smartest move. He told Sir Michael straight away, so he heard it from Michael before he heard it from me.

Soon after that, John and Sue Magnier invited me to Barbados to talk in more depth about the job. Sue is the daughter of the legendary trainer, Vincent O'Brien (no relation to Aidan), who ran Ballydoyle before Aidan. Sue married John Magnier and John became the boss of Coolmore and turned it into an incredibly successful and universally admired stud and training operation.

Sue names the horses and John is the boss, but there are other important partners. Michael Tabor is a bookmaker turned currency dealer and Derrick Smith is a former Ladbrokes trading director, now based in Barbados with his wife, Gay. They all feature prominently on the *Sunday Times* Rich List.

So John and Sue Magnier invited me to Sandy Lane, the hotel they co-own in Barbados, to speak to them in the last week in February. They live on one side of the hotel, J.P.McManus, another associate of John's, lives on the other side. Michael Tabor lives a hundred yards down the road and Derrick Smith lives across the road. They've got Sandy Lane surrounded.

I went for tea there with John and Sue one evening and we discussed what the terms would be and how the job would work. I have never been money-orientated but, even though Coolmore had struggled the year before, I did know they had the best horses in the world. An operation like that might have one bad year but the lean spell never lasts. I decided to take the job.

That was when I rang Sir Michael. As great as the offer from Coolmore was, I still found it very hard to tell him I was leaving. He had stood by me through all my troubles and even though I had ridden for him as a freelance for the last few years, we still had a very close bond. He wasn't pleased. He said he already knew I was going and he was disappointed he hadn't heard it from me. That was fair enough. It wasn't an easy situation and, with hindsight, I didn't manage it well. I think he felt he was the last to know.

It wasn't just Sir Michael, either. I was very friendly with Mrs Thompson, who was the head of Cheveley Park Stud, which is one of the biggest breeding operations in the world. Sir Michael is a director there, too, and Cheveley Park supplied a lot of horses to Freemason Lodge. Mrs Thompson is a lovely woman and I always had a lot of respect for her.

Not long after I had left to go to Ballydoyle, I was standing with some of the Coolmore people in the ring at Newmarket when I saw her. She saw me, too, and she just turned away. She didn't say anything. She didn't need to. I found that hard to take. I rode for them again eventually but she was disappointed in me. When you have had a successful partnership, it is difficult when it comes to an end.

*

When I was spotted at Sandy Lane, it became an open secret that I had been offered the Coolmore job and when I accepted, they put out a statement. 'Owners John Magnier, Michael Tabor and Derrick Smith are delighted to announce that Kieren Fallon will be the retained jockey for the horses at Ballydoyle and elsewhere for the 2005 season,' the statement said. It was a relief that it was finally official.

And when I got to Ballydoyle, I loved it. As soon as I got back from my meeting with John and Sue Magnier in Barbados, I went straight there so that I could get used to the horses and the way the yard worked. I sat on Footstepsinthesand and he felt as good as any of the best horses I had ever ridden. I felt straight away we had a special horse.

It was very early March by then and I thought that Footstepsinthesand would win the Guineas. Getting on his back was like easing yourself in behind the wheel of a top-of-the-range Mercedes. It's a machine. It's the way they move. It's the way they feel. It's the speed. It's the smooth, smooth ride. Riding Footstepsinthesand was like getting into a nice big car and floating along. Riding a lesser horse can be like climbing into a clapped-out old Volkswagen and rattling around all the way to your destination.

Aidan's operation at Ballydoyle was hugely impressive. Everyone who worked there was really professional and very able at what they were doing. In most yards, the head lad might wear some sign of seniority, as if he were a traffic warden or a supervisor in an office, but it wasn't like that at Ballydoyle.

Aidan, who had been in charge at Ballydoyle since 1996 and had been England's champion trainer in 2001 and 2002, treated every one of them exactly the same, from the grooms to the maids to the housekeeper. That's the way he treated them, so he expected everyone who worked for him to treat each of their colleagues with the same sort of respect that he showed.

When John Magnier turned up to watch the horses work, he wasn't treated any differently from Eileen, who did the cooking for us. We were all striving for the same goal: to be successful. I loved working for the team Aidan had built there because a team like that creates energy.

When you have that, horses sense it, too, and there is a great atmosphere in the yard. There's an old saying in racing that goes like this: 'We're on such a good run, if we entered the yard cat, it'd win.' That's the energy. That's what it's like at Ballydoyle. You didn't see the lads fighting. You didn't see them arguing. You didn't see anybody falling out. Everyone was genuinely pleased for each other when successes started to come.

They didn't leave any stone unturned in the quest for success, either. If they haven't got the best, they'll get the best. Horses, staff, gallops, gallops men: they go after the best and they build the best. It's 24/7 at Ballydoyle. Aidan hates being away. He doesn't take holidays. His holidays are going racing. I had had the best team in England and now I had the best in Ireland and I felt thoroughly at home. In the context of everything that was going on with my life outside racing in England, I felt like I had made the right choice.

There is a little cottage just inside the main gates at Ballydoyle and that was where I lived. I became close friends with a couple of the boys there straight away. There was a handyman and good amateur rider called Diddly and the travelling head lad, T.J. Comerford, was a real horseman and we'd hang out together.

We had an open fire in the cottage and we went out into the grounds to cut down trees and chop wood for it. We stacked it and ordered it and carried it in. I found the whole process very therapeutic and restful. It was as good as anything at clearing my troubled mind. I felt like I was in heaven there. Or as close to heaven as you are going to get. All the irksome travelling that I had in England was gone because all the courses were pretty handy and I loved being back in Ireland.

I'd always loved hurling and if we weren't racing, we would sometimes go to see Clare playing at Cusack Park in Ennis or Tipperary at their stadium in Thurles, which wasn't far away. Before I knew what a horse was, I knew what a hurley was. It felt like being home.

I got friendly with Willie Crowe, who owned the Dundrum House Hotel, a hotel and golf course that was nearby, and we played a few times a week. We could just turn up and play, and there were competitions and there was always something going on. It was a great part of my life and my work.

And it was great working with Aidan, too. Aidan was a god around horses and he is also a stickler for routine. Every morning, everybody has to be ready at the riding school at Ballydoyle at 8.05am. You wouldn't want to be walking in there at 8.06am, believe me. Aidan always drove in on the dot of 8.05 and said good morning to everybody. Everybody was on first-name terms, by the way.

You jogged away on the horses and warmed up, noted how the horses sounded. Then, they would be split up into groups, some of the horses working six furlongs, some of them working seven and some of them a mile. All the work riders had an earpiece so Aidan could relay instructions to them and tell them when to jump off and how quickly to go and that sort of thing. Aidan's voice was always in my ear, saying 'steady lads' or 'go on Kieren'. It was simple. Aidan would fly around in the jeep, keeping an eye on everything, watching how the horses were working.

As a jockey, everything was ready for you to go. It all worked like clockwork. Everything slotted in. There were various gallops and some of them had been built to replicate the undulations of Ascot or Epsom. The attention to detail was breathtakingly impressive.

I hadn't been there very long when Michael Tabor rang me and said that he was concerned because our horses kept missing the gate in races in America. We weren't as quickly away from the stalls as we should have been, he said. We keep getting left. It was clear it was irritating him. I told him it was probably because our horses weren't used to the bell. He wasn't sure what I meant so I went down to his house, we put on a video of his horse, Thunder Gulch, going to the start of a race and we switched up the volume.

We heard the commentator saying they were in the gate and then we heard the bell ringing just before the gates opened. It's a feature of American racecourses that we don't have here. The problem with our horses was that they weren't used to the bell so it scared them in the split second before the gates opened and they weren't ready to go. So they missed the start. Within a week of my conversation with Michael Tabor, we had the bell and the American stalls installed at Ballydoyle. Now they do that as a matter of routine in preparation and it made a big difference.

*

I had never seen anybody like Aidan around horses. It is the energy he carries. He just has to put his hand on them to quieten them. I know horses and I pride myself in being able to switch them off and calm them down but Aidan is on another level. He would never admit that himself, of course. He is famously reluctant to talk about himself or say anything at all that could ever be construed as boastfulness. For a man who is a genius, he is also one of the most modest men I have ever met.

I know that a journalist from the *Mail on Sunday* went to see him at Ballydoyle recently, partly to talk about me and partly to talk about him. Aidan was very generous in what he said about me but when the conversation turned to him, he deflected anything that seemed like praise and said the success of Ballydoyle was down to the people he worked with.

'We are very lucky here,' O'Brien told the interviewer. 'We always try and employ the very best special people and Kieren was one of those. Those kinds of people have a sixth sense with horses.'

'Do you have that?' the interviewer asked him.

'They're the kind of people who have that,' he said. 'It's a total team thing and a lot of people here have it. We really appreciate those people working here together with everybody and they're the people that make it happen.'

'Do you recognise that in yourself, though?' the journalist said, trying to press him.

'I would say that the likes of Kieren had it and other people had it. For me, I can see it in Kieren and other people here but not a lot of people have that. Do you know what I mean? I would know by watching those people working with the horses. They're the ones that the horses really respond to.

'Kieren was a very sensitive person and horses are very sensitive as well. That's why they responded to him so well. We have a lot of those people. Those people have people around them that are very sensitive. It's all about those people collectively that make it happen.'

When it was put to him that he had a gift, he said it was people like me who had a gift. He was very generous about me, altogether, actually, which meant a lot to me. He is one of the greatest men in racing.

'I didn't have a big part in Kieren's arrival,' he said during the interview, 'but we were over the moon when he arrived. Kieren was an unbelievable rider and we would never have expected him to come here. People that weren't around when he was at the height of his powers don't really understand how good he was.

'He could do things on horses that were incredible. It was what he could get them to do. He had a different sense, you know. His feel of a horse and his balance and his power and what he was able to get a horse to do without even catching hold of its head was unbelievable.

'He was able to guide a horse more than steer it, which was very unusual. When he put a horse into full flow, he used to do it without touching their heads and he nearly used to carry them. He was incredible.'

It was a lovely thing to say and it is always going to be up to others to say how awe-inspiring it was to be around him. Aidan will never even begin to talk about himself and his wider place in racing. To listen to him, you would think he was a stable lad and nothing more.

You can tell a lot about a parent by his kids and you can tell a lot about a trainer by his horses. Some parents have unruly kids and you will see them kicking and screaming. In some yards, we have got kickers and screamers and if you let a horse get away with being unruly and not going in the gate, then that kind of behaviour will multiply with your horses, too.

You will never see one of Aidan's horses not wanting to go in the gates and if you look at Aidan's kids, they are great kids, too. It sounds simplistic, I know, but a lot of the same rules that apply to raising kids apply to raising horses, too. Aidan's kids are great. I worked with his son, Joseph, for a long time. He wasn't just a fine jockey: he was polite, he had good manners and he always wanted to learn. The girls are the same. His horses are the same as his kids. You will never hear anybody saying anything bad about them.

The only two difficult horses I came across when I worked at Ballydoyle were Scorpion and George Washington. George wouldn't come back into the paddock after he won the Guineas in May 2006. I don't think Aidan would have been too happy about that. George was a beautiful horse with a mind of his own and a strong independent streak, but that was like your kid kicking you on the shin on the way into school.

I had trouble with Scorpion, too. Once, in particular, I was in a stall with him and I thought he was going to hurt me. He was snorting and plunging and rearing. I asked Aidan to come over and Aidan put his hand on him and he went quiet straight away. I had never seen anything like that.

There was another occasion where Aidan led him out of the parade ring with me on his back on the way to the track before a race. Aidan likes to do everything himself. He was fine while Aidan was with him but as soon as he let him go and I jogged out on to the course with him, he reared right up. He walked out like a mouse when Aidan had him and then as soon as Aidan walked away, he was back to his old tricks.

But the funny thing about Scorpion is that he was afraid of Yeats, who would go on to rewrite history by winning four Ascot Gold Cups. For all his macho posturing, Scorpion always gave way to Yeats. He knew who was the boss.

CHAPTER 23

In Paris and London

Aidan O'Brien liked to walk the course before every race meeting. He said it was useful and, sure, we got to talk about the race and test the ground a bit and discuss tactics. But, it used to frustrate me a bit. I always got my feet wet for a start, with the dew. I should have learned to bring my welly boots with me, I suppose, but I never did.

I didn't really see the point of doing it. I had been up and down and up and down every course in Britain and Ireland hundreds of times. It felt like that anyway. I knew them all like the back of my hand. It was like a superstition for Aidan, though. It was like going to Mass on Sunday: if you don't go, you feel you've done something wrong. You think you're going to get punished.

So we walked the Rowley Mile before the 2000 Guineas at Newmarket on 30 April 2005. It was a new routine for me but I went along with it. We had a decent chat, we satisfied the superstition, we made sure we weren't going to get punished for not doing it and then we got ready to go racing. It turned out to be a pretty good start to our partnership.

Footstepsinthesand did not start as the favourite. That was Dubawi, who had already been touted as the horse that would provide Frankie Dettori with his first Derby winner later that year. Judges as good as Sir Michael Stoute thought Dubawi was pretty much a certainty for the Guineas. The rest of us were just there to make up the numbers.

But Dubawi struggled on the firm ground and guiding Footstepsinthesand home was actually one of my more straightforward Classic wins. I had taken him down to the post early and when the race began, I always felt we were in control. Kandidate, Tony James and Party Boss set the early pace, but I always knew they would fall back and when I asked Footstepsinthesand to quicken, no one had an answer. We won by one-and-a-half lengths. It was comfortable.

When I won the 1000 Guineas the next day on Virginia Waters, a good start to my relationship with Coolmore turned into a perfect start. It was the first time for nearly forty years that the same trainer-jockey combination had completed a Guineas double. The last pair to do it was Noel Murless and George Moore in 1967. The win also completed a career clean sweep of Classic victories for Aidan.

Riding winners in big races like that wasn't new to me but I was hoping I would get even more of them now I was riding for Coolmore. I knew that competing for the British jockeys' championship while being based in Ireland was unrealistic and I was content to concentrate on quality more than quantity for once in my life.

In many ways, I would have loved to have been following the same old pattern in England, running around and jumping on horses at two meetings a day. It was in my blood. But my arrest had cast a shadow over my life in England that had still not been lifted and the greater peace that I found in Ireland offset the regret I felt at surrendering my title.

I had won six titles by then and I wanted more big-race successes. I knew that by riding for Ballydoyle, those successes were going to come. I knew there would be pressure, but once I won that Guineas double on the last day of April and the first day of May, it was going to take a lot to disrupt the party.

We soon unearthed another fine horse at Ballydoyle, too. Oratorio had had a few uneven runs but Aidan and I could both see his potential. I rode him in the Eclipse at Sandown against Motivator, that year's Derby winner, who was still unbeaten. Many thought Motivator could not be beaten that day and he was a prohibitively short-priced favourite, but we beat him by half a length. When that summer had turned to autumn, Oratorio and I won the Irish Champion Stakes at Leopardstown, too.

That autumn also brought me one of the greatest days of my career. That day at Longchamp, 2 October 2005, the day of the Prix de l'Arc de Triomphe, one of racing's greatest prizes, was also the day that John Magnier said was the best day's racing of his life. And he has had a few good days, trust me.

We were second on Mona Lisa in the Prix de l'Opéra and then won the Prix Marcel Boussac on Rumplestiltskin, who was also trained by Aidan. I won again for Ballydoyle on Horatio Nelson in the Prix Jean-Luc Lagardère and then rode Hurricane Run in the Arc. Hurricane Run was trained by the great Frenchman André Fabre, but raced in the colours of Michael Tabor, and was close to the hearts of the men in charge of Coolmore.

The day of the Arc in Paris is special. On that day, Longchamp, moulded between the Bois de Boulogne and the River Seine and one of the most beautiful racecourses in the world, is loud and intense and fierce in a way it never is for the rest of the year, when it is more characterised by French reserve.

I had never won the Arc before, but I knew I had a good chance on Hurricane Run. I had won on him in the Irish Derby at the Curragh in the summer of 2005 and then again at Longchamp in the Prix Niel a few weeks before the Arc. I knew what a brilliant horse he was.

And Fabre was a genius. He is a god in France. When you ride for guys like him and Aidan, you are like a child at Christmas. I was getting on a bit by now, but the chance to ride for André Fabre on a horse like Hurricane Run was the kind of thing that kept me as driven as ever. It was an honour, really. Fabre just has an air about him. He never really gave me instructions. The best trainers don't.

Hurricane Run caught a bump leaving the stalls and was not quite in the position I would have liked in the early stages. We were one ahead of the backmarker for a lot of the race. Horses like Motivator and the filly Shawanda, winner of the Irish Oaks and the Prix Vermeille, cruised along much closer to the pace but it was a fast-run race and you're never too worried about being at the back when you know that they're going a real good pace up front.

I didn't panic. I was too old and too experienced to panic by this stage of my career. I knew Hurricane Run had good acceleration and so I stayed close to the rails and saved ground as the field turned for home and moved out wide. I made up some distance there immediately.

Johnny Murtagh had kicked on on Motivator and I thought he might stretch away, but he tied up a furlong from home and rolled away from the rail. He almost baulked me, but I switched back inside him and got a clear run up the rail. We surged clear and held off the late challenge of Olivier Peslier and Westerner by two lengths.

Yeah, I had been further back than I wanted to be, but I knew that I had the horse to take me through the race if I got the gaps, which I did. Sticking to the rail is the only way to ride a race on a track like Longchamp. You're never going to win there by going around the field, at least not before the final straight, because the course is so much on the turn and you'll lose too much ground.

You take risks when you go around the inside, but eight times out of ten it will win you races. It was a big day for me when I won my first Breeders' Cup race on Islington at Santa Anita, it was a big day for me when I won each of my Derbies, it was a big day for me each time I won the jockeys' title, but it really didn't get any better than this.

Fabre had an interesting slant on it. He said that Hurricane Run and I shared some of the same characteristics. 'Kieren found something in the horse no one else did,' he said. 'But this is a talent possessed by all great jockeys. Hurricane Run was a very powerful horse with a very generous nature. He wanted to be respected and, if he was, he gave that respect back. I think that was why he got on so well with Kieren. They had the same attitude.'

*

I had just won three Group One races in a row and the last of them was the Arc. People were calling me the best jockey in Europe and saying that I was at the peak of my powers and it felt like that to me, too. But I also knew there was a dark side to my life. I knew that later that week, I had to report to a police station in London to answer bail, as I regularly did, as a consequence of my arrest in September 2004. I loved everything about riding for Coolmore, but the stress of the legal battle I was engaged in was never far from my mind.

I still thought I had a chance of riding more Group One winners in 2006 than I had during any previous year of my career. I really thought we had the horses for it at Ballydoyle. And there were none that I was more excited by than George Washington. George was a fine big horse, imperious and grand and proud. The press dubbed him Gorgeous George and he could be headstrong and difficult but he was also absolutely brilliant. I rode him in the 2000 Guineas at the start of the 2006 season and he blew the field away.

I had an injured foot going into the weekend at Newmarket. I had gashed it and it needed stitches, so I had rationed my races and was only riding the Guineas double. I didn't need to be at my best with George Washington anyway. I had already ridden him to a series of victories in Ireland as a two-year-old, and he was too good for the rest in the Guineas as well. I went for home a bit earlier than I wanted to but I couldn't sit on him any longer. He had an electrifying turn of foot and he just did everything right. He won very easily from Sir Percy, who went on to win the Derby that year.

On the Tuesday before the Derby, I rode all four of Ballydoyle's possible entries over the gallops. My inclination had always been to ride Dylan Thomas. Dylan Thomas was a favourite of mine because he was a gentle giant. I loved that horse. I barely knew he was in the yard until the day I rode him in a maiden at Tipperary in June 2005. I got on him in the paddock and he went around like an old shire horse and then pottered down to the stalls. Then he jumped out of the gate and he won easily.

I won on him again at Leopardstown a few months later, but I didn't think he would win the 2006 Derby because he didn't have the zip. I wanted to ride him because I loved him, but that morning when I rode out on our four candidates at Ballydoyle, Horatio Nelson was the best performer by a distance.

I won the Oaks on Alexandrova and then rode Horatio Nelson the next day in the Derby. I believed we had a good chance going into the race, but something felt a little wrong about his action when we were going to the start and I summoned the vet to get another opinion. The vet gave him the all-clear.

Poor Horatio Nelson ran a fine race and was beginning a final challenge around two furlongs out when he snapped a leg. It was a sickening feeling as he buckled underneath me, that majestic animal throwing up dust and turf as his body crashed to the floor. He had broken a cannon bone and dislocated a joint in his fetlock. There was no alternative but to put him down.

I was devastated. Inevitably, I asked myself questions about whether I should have started the race on him, but I still felt I had made the right decision in the circumstances. The vet had said Horatio Nelson was okay and I abided by that decision. He was one of the best little horses I have been around. He wanted to do everything for you and those are the horses you want to be associated with. If I wasn't happy with him, I wouldn't have gone around there on him, especially down that hill at Epsom. After he had been put down, I gave up my ride on Indian Trail in the last and went home.

Sir Percy won that Derby but Dylan Thomas should have won it. It was a thrilling race but Johnny Murtagh hit the front and kicked too early on him. He had nothing left and Sir Percy caught him in a four-way photo with Dragon Dancer and Hala Bek. It is easy to say when you're not riding it, but Dylan Thomas was in a different class to Sir Percy. He just used up his energy too soon.

A month later, I rode Dylan Thomas in the Irish Derby at the Curragh and he won by three-and-a-half lengths. Again, he was brilliant that day. All heart and class. It was a half-decent ride, too. John Magnier liked it. 'If Ireland were in the World Cup and in a penalty shoot-out, the man I would pick to take the fifth penalty would be Kieren Fallon,' he said.

The next day, Monday 3 July, I answered bail at Bishopsgate police station in London. There were a lot of reporters outside, as there often were on those occasions. I was getting used to it. I was one of twenty-eight people answering bail that day as part of the City of London police investigation into racing.

I thought it was another routine visit and I turned up in a black T-shirt and jeans with my criminal solicitor, Ian Burton. But when I got to the front desk, I was told that I was being charged with conspiring to defraud customers of the online betting exchange Betfair. That was it. I couldn't believe it. Everyone in my legal team had been telling me there was no way I would be charged and that it was only a matter of time before the police dropped the case. It was obvious there was no evidence and I had got to the point where I thought the next call was to tell me I had been cleared of all suspicion.

I was stunned, I was furious, but most of all I was shocked. I began to think about the effects it was going to have on my racing. As I walked out, trying to avoid the photographers, ducking into a waiting car and being driven away, I wondered if my career had just been dealt a fatal blow.

Miles Rodgers, Fergal Lynch and Darren Williams were also charged and we were all due to appear in court a couple of weeks later. Eleven people were charged in total. Early estimates said that a trial was unlikely to take place for at least a year. That turned out to be conservative.

A short while before I was charged, the Horseracing Regulatory Authority, who were aware of all the developments happening in my case, had changed their rules so that a jockey riding under a foreign licence in Great Britain, who had been charged with a criminal offence, would automatically be suspended from riding in Britain. I wonder who they had in mind? I suppose I should have anticipated what was coming towards me, given the close relationship between the BHA and the City of London Police in this investigation.

Just how close was highlighted when Michael Bowron, the commissioner of the City of London police, made a written statement: 'I was subsequently advised by Dr James Hart [the previous commissioner of City of London police] that a verbal agreement had been reached with Ben Gunn of the BHA undertaking for them in due course to meet the additional costs incurred by the force in investigating this matter.' The BHA, through Ben Gunn, denied that there was any agreement by BHA to pay police costs, but conceded that there had been discussions about the BHA making payments. The point is that such payments are not permitted and are an abuse of process.

I had an Irish licence but even though the BHA knew what the evidence against me was, even though they knew that Miles Rodgers, the man who was supposedly profiting from information I had given him, had actually lost more than £300,000 on those bets, I had to go before an HRA panel in London to plead to be allowed to keep it.

It worked like this: as soon as I was charged, my licence to ride in Britain was automatically suspended. My racing licence had been issued by the racing authorities in Ireland and they made it clear that they regarded me as innocent until proven guilty and that I would be free to continue riding in the land of my birth. But I had to appeal to a three-man panel to retain the same rights in Britain where the principle of innocent until proven guilty was not regarded, apparently, with quite the same respect as it was in Ireland.

The hearing took place at the HRA headquarters on Shaftesbury Avenue in London on the Friday after I was charged. Even then, I was hopeful that there would be a just outcome because the trainer Alan Berry, who had also been charged as part of the investigation, had been allowed to keep his licence at another hearing earlier in the week. On that occasion, the panel had decided that a ban would be 'disproportionate' for Berry because the trial was unlikely to start for so long. They decided on a different outcome for Fergal Lynch, Darren Williams and me, though.

The panel, chaired by HRA board director Sir Michael Connell, ruled that I should be prohibited from riding in Britain on my Irish licence 'until the conclusion of the trial or further orders'. I was devastated. This was the stuff of my worst nightmares. In the short term, the panel's decision meant I would miss out on my ride in the next day's Eclipse at Sandown, where I would have partnered Aussie Rules, one of Ballydoyle's new stars. In the long term, it destroyed my ability to do my job.

My solicitors, BCL Burton Copeland, issued my statement. It was reported widely in the press the next day, beneath a variety of newspaper headlines such as: 'Royal jockey is charged with throwing races' and 'Fallon charged in £10m race-fixing scandal'.

'I am obviously devastated by the HRA decision,' my statement said. 'I always thought that a man was innocent until proved guilty. I cannot understand this decision as I am confident that I have done nothing wrong, and my lawyers are confident that the case against me has no validity whatsoever.

'In fact I am utterly amazed the police were able to charge me based on the evidence I have seen and the questions that they have been asking me this year. My livelihood is dependent upon racing and I will be appealing against this decision as it is extremely harsh and inconsistent given the HRA panel's verdict on Alan Berry published earlier this week.

'I am grateful for the support I have received from many trainers and owners around the world. However, unless my suspension is lifted, my career is in ruins.'

My suspension wasn't lifted. My trial did not begin until October 2007. I had ridden four Classic winners in my first fourteen months with Aidan O'Brien. My ban meant I only rode one more throughout the rest of my career.

CHAPTER 24

Nought Plus Nought

I appealed against the suspension of my licence in the UK, but the appeal failed. On the day it was dismissed, Aidan O'Brien spoke out on my behalf when the press cornered him at the July meeting at Newmarket. Aidan goes out of his way not to be controversial but he was forthright in his support for me, which was a huge fillip.

'Kieren is the most unbelievable jockey that we have ever dealt with,' Aidan said. 'He is an absolute master of his craft. We go back and look over the records – we keep records – and he senses things other people don't. So instead of condemning him, we should be celebrating him, not, like a lot of geniuses are, when they have been dead and gone for twenty years.'

Aidan gave short shrift to the idea that I would be sacked. He said losing my services in the UK was 'like taking the wheel off a car', but he insisted that I would still be Ballydoyle's stable jockey and ride their horses in territories where I was allowed to ride, mainly Ireland and France.

'Kieren would die for horses,' Aidan said. 'He wouldn't come back from the injury like he has unless he loved it like nothing else. Kieren is going to get better, if racing allows him. I just hope that the most unbelievable talent that we have had doesn't get destroyed.'

To say it was good to hear was an understatement. I hadn't known where to turn, but Aidan's words were very reassuring. I didn't think Ballydoyle would cut me loose because I could still ride in Ireland and France and contribute to the development of their horses, and we had had so much success. Others expected them to fire me but I didn't.

On the evening my appeal failed, I rode a treble at Naas. A few days after that, I won the Irish Oaks on Alexandrova for Coolmore. The support I got when I rode back into the winner's enclosure at the Curragh that day was unforgettable. I think they were the loudest cheers I'd ever had.

It was typical of the kind of surreal rhythm that my life was now settling into that, the next day, I appeared at City of London Magistrates Court to hear the charges against me and was remanded on unconditional bail for a trial date yet to be fixed.

I stood behind a glass panel with ten others, who were also to be tried, and listened as they said I was accused of conspiring to throw races and defraud online bookmakers Betfair over a two-year period. The two-women-and-one-man magistrates' bench remanded us all to Southwark Crown Court, but both the prosecution and the defence gave notice they would apply to have the case heard at the Old Bailey because it had better facilities for viewing race videos and computer presentations.

It was a sobering day. Maybe you will think it ridiculous

that the reality of the situation was only just starting to dawn on me. Maybe it was ridiculous. I found it hard to accept what was happening to me, but I didn't really have much choice any more. I was in for a hell of a fight to clear my name.

I kept trying to resurrect my career in the UK. At the end of July, I was hoping the High Court would overturn the HRA's ban and allow me to ride Hurricane Run in the King George VI and Queen Elizabeth Diamond Stakes at Ascot, but Mr Justice Davis took seventy minutes to dismiss the appeal. The die was cast.

It felt tantalising. I was still available to do my job. It wasn't as if I were injured. It wasn't as if I had been found guilty of anything. I hadn't been sacked. I hadn't hurt anyone. And trainers still wanted me to ride for them. But so much was out of reach.

And so I watched as other jockeys rode horses I would have been riding and won races I would have been winning. And I rode out in the morning at Ballydoyle and I raced around the racecourses of Ireland, and sometimes France, in the afternoons.

I didn't mind watching people win on horses I should have been riding. In a curious way, it wasn't that that bothered me about my enforced absence from UK racetracks. What hurt me was that I had nursed some of those horses through to the point where they were racing and contending, and I wasn't there to look after them.

This is not meant as any criticism of the jockeys who were riding them instead, but I knew they wouldn't care about those horses in the same way that I would have done in those races. It was that jockey's big day, his D-Day, and he would ride the horse for that day only and not with an eye for its future. Whereas if I knew that if they weren't likely to be placed, say, I'd be looking after them because I'd know they'd be racing again in a couple of weeks.

I found it very hard when the American authorities said they had to follow the example of their UK counterparts and suspend my licence, too. That killed me. I love America and it was nearly my second home, but now I was prevented from riding in the Arlington Million in Chicago and the Breeders' Cup in New York. The net was spreading.

I went to Australia to ride Yeats in the Melbourne Cup and we finished seventh. I felt thoroughly dispirited while I was out there. Like a million defendants before me, I just wanted the trial to start. The waiting was almost unbearable.

At the end of November, there was a further blow. This time, I definitely had only myself to blame. After I was charged at Bishopsgate police station that morning in early July, I had gone to Newmarket and drowned my sorrows in a pub there. The old foolishness came out in me then and I got to feeling invincible and one thing led to another.

When I was subjected to a routine drugs test at Chantilly eight days later, I tested positive for cocaine. It was stupid and I still regret it bitterly. And so on 29 November, France Galop announced I was suspended for six months and banned from race-riding anywhere until early June 2007.

I did my best to keep busy. Aidan and the Coolmore boys stood by me and so I kept my job. I rode out every morning and I started playing a lot of squash. I was back and forth to England all the time for meetings with solicitors about the court case, which had been scheduled for 24 September 2007.

I kept telling myself that I could still come back better if I could just get the court case resolved. I told myself I would learn from being punished for the cocaine use and that I would never put myself in that position again. I told myself that life would get better and that my spirits would lift once I had cleared my name and people could see I was an innocent man.

I returned to race-riding on 7 June 2007, not far from Ballydoyle at an evening meeting at Tipperary Junction. My first ride was on a decent horse called The Bogberry and we beat into second place a horse trained by Kevin Prendergast and ridden for all he was worth by a nineteen-year-old kid called Chris Hayes. A nineteen-year-old kid – it was like gazing back at the old me.

As I rode at the outposts of Irish racing, Dylan Thomas won the King George at Ascot with Johnny Murtagh on board and Peeping Fawn, one of Aidan's new breed, was sweeping all before her at Goodwood in the Nassau Stakes, and York in the Yorkshire Oaks. I still got glimpses of old glories. I won on Dylan Thomas in the Irish Champion Stakes at Leopardstown at the beginning of September and it felt even sweeter because it was a rare opportunity to ride a horse like him in a big race again. It felt like I mattered on days like that.

I loved Dylan Thomas anyway, but that win at Leopardstown seemed as if he had given me a precious gift just when I was starting to feel like a beggar. It was the first time a horse had won the race twice and I said, and felt, that he was the best I had ever ridden.

In my other world, my dark world, I was still hoping against hope that the case against me would be thrown out.

The 'lads' at Coolmore – John and Sue Magnier, Michael Tabor and Derrick Smith – helped me enormously in funding my legal case and without them I would have been in serious trouble.

I was taking on a lot of different opponents: the City of London police, the BHA, elements of the racing establishment. It took a lot of doing. This wasn't a race against Frankie Dettori or Ryan Moore. I didn't know how to win this one. I needed help and I was given help. I had a great defence team and even in early September 2007, my barrister, John Kelsey-Fry QC, and Christopher Stewart-Moore were telling me that they were confident there was no case to answer and that the case against me would be thrown out by the presiding judge, Mr Justice Forbes, before it came to trial.

The case against me essentially revolved around the accusation that I had been stopping horses to make money for Miles Rodgers, who had been backing those horses to lose on Betfair. The prosecution's sole expert witness was Ray Murrihy, a senior Australian racing steward, but Mr Murrihy was not versed in the traditions and rules of English racing. He admitted that in his witness statement. He admitted that he mainly knew about Australian racing.

When John Kelsey-Fry and Christopher Stewart-Moore saw that witness statement, they went for a dismissal before the trial. They went in front of Mr Justice Forbes and argued that the case could not and should not go ahead because the prosecution case depended utterly on the fact that I was supposed to have stopped a horse and there was no evidence. Not only had the prosecution's sole expert witness declared that he was not, actually, an expert when it came to UK horse racing, but nor was there any evidence that I had ever spoken to Miles Rodgers or had any contact with him.

Even if I had been in touch with him, I might just have been saying that I thought a particular horse would win a particular race. That is not a criminal offence. There is no criminal offence in saying 'I am tipping this horse'. You have to have a stopped horse for there to be a case and there was zero evidence of that.

Even a money trail wouldn't help build a case, because you could give someone money for giving you tips without it being illegal, although I suppose the amount of money you gave someone would indicate whether or not you were giving more than a tip. You would give more money to someone who was saying they would stop a horse, because the result is therefore known; but, in my case the prosecution didn't have that. They had no money trail at all, so they depended entirely on the proposition that a horse, or horses, had been stopped.

They could then, in theory, have tried to go backwards and say that Miles Rodgers, who I didn't know, was somehow getting this information that I was stopping horses and was somehow getting money to me, but they couldn't tell us how any of that was working.

Kelsey's point to the judge was that when you are look-ing at different strands of evidence, a mathematical formula applies.

He said: 'When I was a schoolboy, nought plus nought plus nought equals nought. You've got no evidence.'

Mr Justice Forbes disagreed. He refused our dismissal application. The case went to trial. At moments like that, I

found myself thinking of what Frank Spencer once said in
the sitcom, *Some Mothers Do 'Ave 'Em*:

> Hooray for British Justice
> It must not be done but seen
> And now I've seen it done to me
> I know how done I've been

CHAPTER 25

One Last Fling

The proceedings against me began in Court 12 of the Old Bailey on 24 September 2007, but then two weeks of legal argument over the admissibility of certain evidence and witnesses delayed the start of my trial. I'd been waiting and waiting for it to begin but now, suddenly, I was praying for it to be delayed just a little longer.

When a pipe burst and flooded Court 12 in the first week of October, my prayers were answered. On Saturday 6 October, I flew in a light plane to a small airport just outside Paris, not to escape justice, but to get myself ready for one last fling before I entered that forbidding world of evidence bundles and ornate wigs and barristers who could tear a man to shreds with words.

My last fling was the Prix de l'Arc de Triomphe on my favourite horse, Dylan Thomas, at Longchamp the next day. Some people had doubts about whether I would be fit, physically or mentally, for such a big test so close to the trial and after such a tortured period of my life. But if Aidan O'Brien had any doubts, he didn't show them.

He was adamant that when Dylan Thomas burst out of the gate at Longchamp, I would be on his back and so I took that plane over with a couple of other jockeys and walked the course on the Sunday morning with Aidan and Seamie Heffernan and some of the lads. I didn't know what was coming when I got back to England. Some people were telling me that if I were to be found guilty, I could be looking at a six-year jail sentence. There are always cheery voices like that around. I was confident I would be found innocent, but I still wanted to make the most of this. I didn't know when, or where, or if, the opportunity would arise again.

This particular Arc, like most big races, had a bit of a back-story for me. A couple of months earlier, I had ridden a horse called Eagle Mountain in the Grand Prix de Paris, an Arc trial. There were only seven runners and I was going well until I had a coming together with the French jockey Stéphane Pasquier, who was on the favourite, Zambezi Sun.

We knew there was going to be no pace in the race and nobody really wanted to make the running. We were all riding hold-up horses but eventually, after about two furlongs, one went on and when you finally get a pacemaker everyone wants to be right behind that front runner. When he kicks, you respond. You have a big advantage if you're right there with him.

I made my move to go right up behind him and so did Stéphane. He popped just in front of me and I clipped his heels, and Eagle Mountain and I went down. He put me on the floor and I got pretty shaken up. I was okay but they put me in the ambulance and took me to the medical room to check me over. Stéphane and Zambezi Sun won the race comfortably, but it was announced that there would be a stewards' inquiry. It didn't look particularly good for Stéphane because in France, if you put someone on the floor, you usually get disqualified.

As I lay in the medical room, feeling sorry for myself and a bit irritated because I thought Eagle Mountain would have won, Stéphane came in to see me and he was crying. He said how sorry he was and how he didn't mean it and he wanted to make sure I was okay. I think he was probably also worried that he was going to lose the race and not do himself any favours with Prince Khalid Abdullah, who owned the Juddmonte horses that Stéphane was contracted to ride.

I wasn't particularly pleased about what had happened. I was still shaken up and I knew I could have been hurt a lot more seriously. But it was an honest racing accident. It was one of those things. He had done it to me this time, but I could just as easily have done it to him. There was nothing malicious in it. I got up and got myself together and went to the stewards' inquiry. I always thought the stewards in France were fairer than anywhere else in Europe because they take each case on its merits. In England, in particular, you often got the feeling they had made up their minds before anybody walked into the inquiry.

Jockeys often try to help each other in the stewards' room. You don't want someone else suspended or fined for nothing, because the result isn't going to change. Sure, if you think you can get a race off somebody, you'd cut his throat for it. But if they're not going to change the result in your favour, you're not going to gain anything by getting someone in trouble.

There was no point in criticising Stéphane. I told the stewards it was a fifty-fifty. We both wanted to be in the same place. He got there before me, I clipped his heel. The stewards pricked their ears up that. 'You clipped his heel?' one of them asked.

I nodded and after that, there was really very little they could do. The stewards had to let Stéphane keep the race. He was obviously grateful and he was still very apologetic. I knew he didn't mean to put me on the floor, but there is no quarter given when you are out there. We said our goodbyes a few minutes later and I headed back to Ireland.

What goes around, comes around, and a few weeks later, we were riding in the Arc, me on Dylan Thomas and Stéphane on Zambezi Sun again. Everything about the Old Bailey trial went out of my mind for those few minutes and the race went smoothly for me. Dylan Thomas travelled really well. He had had a long year and he was tired, but Aidan knew he was still Ballydoyle's best bet. He had run seven times already that year when he arrived at Longchamp but he was as full of heart as always.

Some horses can go over the top when they get tired and run no race. Some can withstand it and some can't. There was never a doubt about whether Dylan Thomas could take it and as we came around the home turn, we were in a lovely position. Song of Hiawatha had set a fast pace and Frankie Dettori and Authorized never got in touch, but Dylan Thomas was comfortable all the way and when we got inside the two-furlong marker, we kicked on.

Just as we kicked, he started to hang violently right and I couldn't hold him. He veered towards Stéphane Pasquier and Zambezi Sun and effectively wiped them out. He didn't unseat Stéphane but I thought I had certainly impeded him.

We overhauled Johnny Murtagh on Soldier of Fortune, but then Richard Hughes and Youmzain came with an incredible run on our outside. They were cutting the gap with every stride and I thought the finishing post would never come but we got there by a head.

I didn't feel any joy. Johnny rode up alongside me and started congratulating me and patting me on the back, but I couldn't celebrate. It was nothing to do with the court case. I knew how bad Dylan Thomas veering across the track must have looked on television and I was convinced that we would be disqualified. All I could do was shake my head. I was sure the race was going to be taken off us. Johnny tried to reassure me but I wasn't having it. I actually began to feel quite resigned to the fact that the stewards would rule against us and that I would be flying back to London empty-handed.

I caught sight of Richard Hughes and he was grinning from ear to ear. He knew I was going to get chucked out and that he was going to win the Arc. Somewhere, I heard Clare Balding's voice coming from a television, saying that the French rules were that if you interfere, you are out. What happens is that you are disqualified from wherever you finished and placed behind the horse that you impeded.

I went back into the paddock and unsaddled. I tried to put on a smile and a brave face, but there is nothing worse than winning a race and getting it taken off you. It's hard enough when it's an ordinary race, let alone the Prix de l'Arc de Triomphe. I just felt empty inside. Everyone was saying 'congratulations', but I knew what was coming next. Sure enough, after a few minutes, there was that familiar metallic ding-dong over the loudspeaker system that heralds an important announcement. They said there was a stewards' inquiry.

That's the sound you don't want to hear when you know

you are the culprit. In the weighing room, the English boys sit together and the French boys sit together and the first person I saw when I came in was Richard Hughes. He was still smiling. He told me afterwards that he had spoken to Youmzain's trainer, Mick Channon, when he dismounted and they were both sure the Arc was theirs.

We went into the stewards' room and the three stewards were sitting behind a big desk, looking at a big screen that was almost as wide as the wall. The form is that the jockeys stand and look at the stewards and the screen and you watch the race unfold together. The stewards waited until everyone came in. I was one of the first into the room and I stood there, looking at the floor. It was two or three minutes before Stéphane Pasquier arrived, but it felt like an hour.

When you finish a race, you go to the toilet, wash your face, get changed and weigh out for the next race. Even though it's an inquiry and you know you're supposed to go straight to the stewards' room, when you know you haven't committed any foul play, as Stéphane did on this occasion, you tend to do your own little bits and bobs before you go in.

You can relax if you're not in the wrong. You're not the accused. You've got nothing to worry about. When you do something wrong, you are in there straight away because you don't want to annoy the stewards even before you start with the inquiry. So after what seemed like an age, Stéphane walked in the door. As he strode across the room, he stared at me and started clapping. He smiled a broad smile. 'Well done, Kieren,' he said. 'I would like to offer you my congratulations on a brilliant race.'

The stewards stared and stared at him. It was as if they couldn't believe what he was doing. I don't know what he said to them then, but he talked animatedly with them in French. They asked me a couple of questions. I said my horse had moved right and I thought I was clear and I thought the best horse won.

But I didn't say a whole lot because Pasquier was talking all the time and stating a case. I still don't know what he said even today but whatever it was, it worked. It was half an hour before the ding-dong sounded again to announce the outcome of the inquiry. When I heard it, my heart almost stopped. 'The result stands,' the announcement said.

I have been in a lot of inquiries and a lot of tight spots and I have never been as relieved as that. I was in the weighing room with the other jockeys when I heard the announcement and there were more congratulations and a bit of laughing and joking. The usual stuff.

A few minutes later, I was riding in a horse-drawn carriage out to the centre of the course for the traditional Arc trophy presentation. The crowd was cheering me from the terraces and, for a moment or two, I felt like a conquering king in a foreign land.

The next morning, I was in the dock at the Old Bailey.

CHAPTER 26

Trial of the Century

And so, for a couple of months, I entered another world. For the arraignment and the swearing in of the jury, I sat in the glass-fronted dock of Court 12 at the Old Bailey with my co-accused and watched and listened as one team of barristers fought to clear me and another tried to put me in jail. In the press, they called it racing's Trial of the Century.

For the rest of the nine weeks in court, I sat with my barristers, John Kelsey-Fry QC and Ian Winter QC and Jane Glass, my criminal solicitor. I was between Ian, who kept me entertained, and Jane, who the *Racing Post* journalist David Ashforth in his daily trial reports nicknamed 'The Legal Blonde'. Kelsey sat in front of us. The press gallery was to my left. Beyond them sat the jury.

Directly in front of us were the other defendants, accompanied by their legal teams, and in the front ranks and to the right were the Crown Prosecution team. Above us all and facing us was the trial judge, Mr Justice Thane Forbes, who entered the court each day from a side door in his bright red robes. Behind and above him was what looked like a plastic replica of the royal coat of arms. The courtroom was very different from Court 13 in the Strand where all those years before I had given evidence in the Top Cees case. That court was all oak-panelled and leather upholstery with an awe-inspiring atmosphere. This court at the Old Bailey was more like a waiting room at a passport office, all ginger furniture and plastic upholstery.

If I were found guilty, I had been told, I could expect six to ten years in prison. I read afterwards that I appeared to be paying more attention to the court proceedings than Fergal Lynch and Darren Williams. Being told you could spend a portion of your life behind bars tends to have that effect on you.

Some of the proceedings were tedious. Anybody who has been involved in a legal case or observed a trial will tell you that. The lawyers leaf through evidence bundles and debate legal argument, often at great length. There are frequent interruptions and pauses. But sometimes the exchanges between a barrister and a witness can be electric. I enjoyed watching those.

I lived in London during the trial. I stayed at the Grosvenor House Hotel on Park Lane some of the time and with a friend of mine who lived in Hendon, in north London, the rest of the time. Proceedings in Court 12 started at 10.30am. Most mornings, there were photographers waiting outside the Old Bailey, trying to take pictures when I walked in.

The courtroom was always crowded with barristers because there were five other defendants – my fellow jockeys Fergal Lynch and Darren Williams, Philip Sherkle, a barman who was an acquaintance of mine, Shaun Lynch, who was

Fergal's brother, and gambler Miles Rodgers. We were all charged with conspiring to defraud the customers of Betfair, the betting exchange company, by betting on horses to lose in 27 flat races between December 2002 and the end of August 2004. I rode in 17 of the supposedly suspect races.

The court was told that Rodgers, a professional gambler from South Yorkshire, had placed a total of £2.12m on those races and was the mastermind of a race-fixing conspiracy that involved the rest of his co-accused. The jury heard that there was an unlawful conspiracy between the defendants that those 27 races under investigation in the case should be fixed. The fixing was not to ensure that certain horses won but that certain horses lost. The City of London police had codenamed their investigation into us Operation Krypton. It cost the taxpayer more than £10m.

In his opening statement, Jonathan Caplan, QC for the prosecution, outlined his case. 'The object of the conspiracy,' he told the court, 'was to wager large amounts of money on a particular horse to lose in each of those races whilst knowing that the jockey was prepared, if necessary, to cheat by stopping the horse.'

Before the emergence of Betfair, this alleged crime could not be committed unless you had a bookmaker's licence. Betfair is a betting exchange which allows punters to bet directly with each other and to back horses to lose as well as to win. The word that was spread around the racing world was that the case against us was strong. That was wrong, but I think the idea had gained credence because many people could scarcely believe that the police would spend so much time and so much money investigating a case if there were not real substance to it.

My barrister, John Kelsey-Fry QC, known by all as 'Kelsey', soon dispelled any illusions as to the strength of the prosecution case. I still remember his brilliant opening speech in which he told the jury that his usual problem when acting for a defendant was looking to find weaknesses in the case. Here, he said, he had a completely different problem, which was trying to find what the prosecution's case was, and that up until that moment he had been unable to identify it. No money changing hands, no meaningful contact between me and Miles Rodgers and no proper evidence of stopped horses.

The truth is that by the time the case came to court, more than three years after I had first been arrested, they had no evidence against me at all. They had nought. In fact, they had less than nought.

Miles Rodgers certainly had less than nought. At least, he had after he'd placed bets that horses ridden by me would lose. That was because I won five of the races the prosecution said I had agreed to lose, an inconvenient truth Mr Caplan found hard to surmount. It turned out Miles Rodgers blew £338,000 betting on races I was supposed to have promised to lose.

Some co-conspirator I was. Mr Caplan had to concede at an early stage that there was no evidence that I had received 'any money or benefit from Rodgers'. So, as had been apparent to my legal team all along, I hadn't gained anything from Rodgers and he certainly hadn't gained anything from me.

Mr Caplan's chosen device for dealing with the fact that I had won in five races that I had apparently agreed to lose was to say that a horse race was 'a dynamic event' and so it was not possible to achieve the desired result all the time. This, of course, suggests that he was alleging I was part of a conspiracy to do something that was not, by his own admission, possible to achieve with any degree of certainty.

The prosecution case did not get off to a good start. Its first witness, David O'Reilly, the 'legal counsel' for Betfair, was forced to concede to the court that he had provided misleading evidence. In a statement presented to the court, O'Reilly had referred to Levitator, on whom I was beaten at Warwick in June 2004, as 'a good example of a drifter' in Betfair's pre-race market.

Data supplied by Betfair showed that the accounts allegedly controlled by Miles Rodgers had laid Levitator from 7/1 out to 11/1. The prosecution contended that Rodgers' willingness to offer long odds about certain horses showed a confidence about the outcome that was not shared by the rest of the market.

Under cross-examination from Peter Kelson QC, representing Rodgers, O'Reilly was gradually made to understand the Betfair data included bets made after the start of the race, and that Rodgers had not taken bets on Levitator at higher than 8/1 before the 'off'.

The significance of this is that the in-running market on Betfair is a quite separate market and clearly identifiable as such. The horse's position in the race, and the way he is running now, affect the odds. If a horse gets a bad start, his odds will lengthen, and if he is in the front rank, his odds will shorten. To compare odds given before the race starts with odds after it has started does not assist in showing a level of confidence that that horse would lose, as David O'Reilly was seeking to do.

Mr Kelson then referred O'Reilly to a Betfair advert, claiming that the firm offered 20 per cent better odds than bookmakers, and advised him that 8/1 is only 23 per cent higher than Levitator's starting price of 13/2.

'Will you now accept,' Mr Kelson said, 'that the assertion in your statement is inaccurate and that in fact this was not a good example at all? In fact it is, regrettably, downright misleading.' O'Reilly admitted that was the case, although he claimed it had been done unintentionally.

The prosecution made great play of text messages between me and Philip Sherkle before races and suggested some of them were coded to mean I was going to lose on a particular horse. It was absurd. I gave Philip Sherkle tips here and there. He was someone I knew. That was all. It seemed like a curious basis for a conspiracy charge but, as someone from the BHA told the press anonymously after the trial was over, I was 'the trophy'. They didn't want to press on without me.

It was later in the trial that the court was told Paul Scotney, the director of security at the BHA, had told trainer Alan Jarvis at a social occasion that he would 'get Kieren Fallon' if it was the last thing he did. It was just one of the reasons why the trial was to become such a major embarrassment for Scotney and a humiliation for the BHA.

Scotney was widely ridiculed for his performance on the stand in the trial. He was evasive and contradictory. He was picked up several times on inconsistencies in his evidence that he had to correct. It seemed to me the defence barristers had a lot of fun with him. I thought they tore him to bits.

He denied that he said he would get me if it were the last thing he did, of course, and he also had to deny that anything could be read into the offer he had made to Acting Detective Inspector Mark Manning to join the BHA. Manning was the main police officer in the case and Scotney admitted that he had offered him a job with the BHA. Peter Kelson QC, who was acting for Miles Rodgers, told the jury that Manning's impartiality was in question because he had been offered a job at the BHA. His credibility was shot early on.

Manning didn't exactly impress in the witness box, either. He was questioned in court about how he had convinced the chief constable of South Yorkshire police to accede to a request to place a bugging device in Miles Rodgers' car and in the car park of his restaurant by exaggerating the scale of the evidence he had.

The problem for the police was that the Jockey Club, who had instigated the police inquiries, only had betting evidence against Miles Rodgers which suggested that he was more confident of placing bets to lose on horses ridden by me, Fergal Lynch and Darren Williams. These bets could be based on nothing more than tips. What the police needed was evidence that we had stopped horses for Rodgers.

As I have said, the Crown Prosecution had no evidence of reward and no evidence of any meaningful contact between myself and Rodgers. They needed some hard evidence if the prosecution was going to get off the ground. They needed to get an order for intrusive surveillance into Rodgers' car. In order for such an application to be successful, the City of London police needed to satisfy the chief constable of South Yorkshire (where Rodgers was based) that the matter they were investigating was a serious crime.

It emerged that in the City of London police's application, Det. Insp. Manning had told South Yorkshire police that the conspiracy had involved Rodgers making a profit of £2m, when in fact that figure referred to his total liabilities on Betfair. Under cross-examination, Manning said to my QC, John Kelsey-Fry, that it was multimillion-pound fraud. Kelsey challenged Manning on that and said the fraud was the amount someone gained from a crime. Manning said he was talking about turnover. He was flustered now.

'Are you telling the court you don't know the difference between turnover and profit?' Kelsey asked Manning, in his most withering voice.

I mean, this was a guy who had worked for the City of London police. He was supposed to be an expert in white-collar crime and he was struggling with the difference between turnover and profit. Between him and Scotney, it started to look very soon as if the prosecution case was a coalition of chaos.

Later, when questioning Manning about his dealings with Murrihy, Kelsey quoted him saying to Murrihy: 'It looks as though in the final run to the post that he is in the lead but not in a desperate hurry to hold that position, and he is almost waiting for the third to come up and pass him on the outside.' He then asked, '... was it your place, to point out things that perhaps looked dodgy to you and ask for his comments on them?'

Manning: 'I don't think after twenty-seven tapes with Mr Murrihy I would be qualifed to call myself an expert, my lord, so "no" is the answer.'

Kelsey: 'I'm just wondering what you were doing in this passage.'

Manning: 'It was clearly an inappropriate comment that I shouldn't have passed ...'

Whatever you think of me, some things will probably occur to you straight away about the bigger picture here and the way the accusations, even to the layman's eyes, were fatally flawed and riven with contradictions and irrationalities from top to toe.

Here's one basic thing about the context of the case against me: just look at the stated time period when I was supposed to be 'stopping' horses, which means riding them in such a way that I was preventing them from winning. The prosecution said it was between December 2002 and the end of August 2004. Well, in 2003, I rode 221 winners, which was more than I had ever ridden before in a single season and would ever ride again. I won the jockeys' championship again that season, too. I had always been obsessed with riding winners. That was why I became a jockey. That was my job. I'm not particularly proud of saying it, but that was actually my life force. And that season, the figures tell you I was more obsessed with it than ever. In the heart of a season like that, why would anybody honestly believe that part of my mind was thinking about riding horses to lose? I suppose, in theory, I could have tried to slip in a few deliberate losses into a record-breaking winning season, but to think that is to be ignorant of the way my mind worked. I wanted to win. That was all I cared about. It was all I ever cared about.

Look, this isn't legal argument. I'm just trying to apply human logic to something. This was the most successful period of my career and they're saying my mind was on trying to lose races. It simply doesn't make any sense.

The same thing applies to the 2004 season. I rode 200 winners that season. Only a few jockeys in the history of flat racing have ridden 200 winners in a season. And yet, again, the accusation was that I was trying to lose races in that period. The allegations against me would have been absurd during any time of my career, but they were especially absurd when I was carrying all before me.

Furthermore, it underestimates the intelligence and professionalism of the trainers I was riding for. Trainers such as Sir Michael Stoute, Michael Bell and Ed Dunlop would not tolerate jockeys not trying on their horses for one moment and they would spot it in a millisecond. The reason the trainers I was riding for were top trainers was because they knew the racing game backwards, and a jockey not trying on one of their horses would be rooted out immediately.

The problem is that to the public, horseracing has an aroma of skulduggery and it is an area of life where innuendo about horses not trying is commonplace. In this context, I remember arriving at Canadian immigration shortly after my arrest to be told by the immigration officer that something was coming up on their computer about me.

He asked if I had had any trouble with the police and I said I was a jockey who had been arrested, but not charged, over stopping racehorses. He immediately stamped my passport and waved me through with the words: 'I always thought that was part of a jockey's job.'

In the circumstances, it wasn't surprising that my defence team ripped the prosecution case to shreds. It had always been our contention that the case should never have come to court and, as it progressed, it grew more and more obvious that my legal team had been right.

I was fortunate to have a brilliant QC representing me in Mr Kelsey-Fry. Kelsey is regarded as the leading criminal barrister of his generation and I knew I was lucky to have him on my side. His arguments were concise and brilliantly constructed and they sliced through the flimsy evidence that had been constructed against me.

It is a peculiarity of my life that I worked for the best trainers in British racing and was represented by the best barristers in the British legal system. For a start, Lord Irvine represented me in my Jockey Club hearing after my altercation with Stuart Webster.

Lord Pannick, who forced the government to hold a parliamentary debate on the triggering of Article 50 in the Brexit debacle and is widely held to be the sharpest barrister of his generation, represented me in my appeal against the BHA's decision to ban me from riding in Britain after I was charged in the race-fixing case.

And Patrick Milmo, who was the co-author of *Gatley*, the standard textbook on libel and slander, was the QC for Jack and Lynda Ramsden and me during the Top Cees libel case against the *Sporting Life*. So I have been served well by the legal profession, even if I wish I hadn't had to use their services quite so often.

Kelsey was interested in horseracing himself. He was very knowledgeable about it, actually, and very early on in the case he made a reference to the build-up to my ride on Dylan Thomas in the Arc a few days earlier. Before the race, I had given an interview to the racing presenter Clare Balding. We had spoken about the chances of Aidan O'Brien's two fancied runners, Dylan Thomas and Soldier of Fortune. I'd suggested the soft ground would count against Dylan Thomas and in favour of Soldier of Fortune and I'd said, half-jokingly, that I wished I could switch to the other horse.

Kelsey mentioned the interview when he was addressing the jury. Anyone watching, he suggested, might construe it as me saying my horse would not win the race and take it as a signal to lay the horse to lose for large money on the betting exchanges. Anyone doing so would, of course, he said, have ended up getting their fingers burned.

Right from the first meeting that Kelsey had had with Christopher Stewart-Moore, they had agreed that there was nothing in the case against me that elevated what I had done beyond giving a few tips here and there. Their point was that any jockey going into a racecourse could say he thinks this will win or that will win. That was the beginning and the end of this case. Or it should have been.

Where was the evidence that took the case beyond me having said to someone: 'I don't think this will win.' How was that a criminal offence? Christopher told me he had started to wonder if he was mad because he really couldn't see that there was a case to answer, but then Kelsey said the same thing. There is nothing illegal about jockeys passing on tips, nor was it against the rules of the BHA. Anyway, most of the phone calls and texts between us were little more than idle chatter and stable gossip.

There was one occasion, when Manning was on the stand, when Darren's barrister, Jim Sturman QC, highlighted how innocent the texting was when he read out one of the texts from Darren to Fergal: 'How's your big blonde bird, you dog?' it read. There was a lot of laughter in the court at that point, but Manning did not see the funny side of it. In fact, he had a sense-of-humour failure, which wasn't surprising in the circumstances. 'That doesn't appear to be part of the conspiracy,' he said.

I'd also pointed out in police interviews that I had frequently exchanged texts with Michael Owen, the England footballer, who is heavily involved in racing and who had become a friend of mine. All of these things were just normal social exchanges between friends. If your lives revolve around racing, you are going to talk to each other about racing.

Fergal and I spoke most days. He was Sir Michael Stoute's second jockey when I was there, so that was normal. We discussed horses. When I was due to ride the Queen's horse, Daring Aim, at Newmarket in July 2004 in one of the races under investigation, I told Fergal that I didn't think she was very good. That was pretty much the end of the conversation, but Daring Aim was one of the horses that Miles Rodgers backed to lose for a reasonable amount of money. She won the race. In fact, not only did we win but Sir Michael came to court to testify about my ride. 'It was a brilliant ride,' he said. 'She was not helping him.'

Bear in mind that Sir Michael had been called by the prosecution when he gave that evidence. He also praised my riding on a horse called Krynica a month earlier at Pontefract, in another of the races under investigation. 'He is squeezing her and encouraging her,' Sir Michael told the jury. 'It is beautiful horsemanship – and she was not very good.'

I don't know how the tips I gave to Philip Sherkle or Shaun Lynch were passed on to Miles Rodgers. I have got no idea. Maybe someone was telling Miles Rodgers that I would be willing to tailor rides to his needs but I don't know that. But if he had been led to believe that he could rely on me to stop horses, then someone was obviously feeding him bad information. That information ended up costing him £338,000.

They showed another race to the court where I rode a horse called Gamut at Newbury for Sir Michael. The eventual winner passed us about half a furlong from the finish.

I kept encouraging, cajoling and pushing Gamut so that he almost got up to win. He was one of the horses I was supposed to have stopped, but Mr Kelsey-Fry made a point to the court when the footage had finished playing.

'Imagine being Miles Rodgers and thinking this man was stopping horses,' Mr Kelsey-Fry said. His implication was that Rodgers ought really to have realised fairly early on that, whatever anyone else was telling him, I wasn't in on any scheme.

I think that in the end even Miles Rodgers began to realise that something was wrong. The police had an audio recording of him talking to Fergal Lynch from his car, which had been bugged, and bemoaning the fact that whenever he was on the verge of making a profit I came along and ruined it for them.

At the time the recording was made, Rodgers had already suffered several big losses on my rides and was struggling to satisfy disappointed investors. He thought things were getting back on an even keel, he said, and then he backed another of my rides to lose. Which it didn't. 'Of course,' he says on the tape, 'along comes the fucking little fella and, bosh, it happens again.'

Even in this slightly surreal context, I was astonished when my ride on Russian Rhythm in the Lockinge Stakes at Newbury in May 2004 was included in the list of my seventeen races that were supposed to be suspicious. I loved Russian Rhythm. I'd won the 1000 Guineas on her and the Coronation Stakes. The idea that anyone could ever believe I might not ride to win on her was baffling to me.

The Lockinge was a huge race, too, a big Group One. The court heard that Rodgers backed her to lose at Newbury. I won. That race alone cost him more than £160,000, apparently. Again, the court was told that Sir Michael Stoute had said I had given his horse a 'tremendous ride' that day. He'd actually taken me out for dinner the evening after that race to congratulate me on what I'd done.

On and on it went. The prosecution pinned a lot of hopes on the jury being swayed by the footage of my ride on Ballinger Ridge, because that was the one race where I was vulnerable to the criticism that my jockeyship was lacking. It was the only one of my alleged conspiratorial rides where the experienced English stewards had decided to hold an inquiry. In evidence, William Nunnelly, the senior stewards' secretary, said that stewards on duty in England 'day in, day out are the finest' in the world, and agreed that they were watching the races the jury was considering. And when the horse's trainer, Andrew Balding, was asked about it, he told the court I had been 'mortified' after the race. As I've mentioned, the court was also shown footage of other jockeys making the same mistake. It happens.

Andrew Balding and Sir Michael Stoute were just two of the trainers who lent me staunch support at the Old Bailey. Michael Bell, Ed Dunlop, his father John, Luca Cumani, Amanda Perrett, Paul Howling, Alan Jarvis and David Loder also spoke out in my favour. Loder mentioned that one of the horses I was supposed to have ridden to lose, Bonecrusher, who finished fifth in a race at Epsom in July 2004, was 'thoroughly unreliable'. All spoke highly of the work I had done for them. They all confirmed I had ridden the horses as instructed on the day.

It might well be said that at this stage of the trial I depended on the kindness of trainers. I could hardly bear to watch while they were on the stand. I was pleased, of course, that they were being so supportive and helping to destroy the prosecution case. I was gratified that they thought so highly of me. But most of all, I was embarrassed. I was embarrassed that these people, the leaders in their field, had had to come to court to help me. I had put them in this position and I hated it.

These were people that I respected and admired and I wanted them to respect me. And here I was sitting beside my barristers in a courtroom at the Old Bailey. I wanted to hide. I felt ashamed. And I felt angry that it had ever come to this.

These people were the experts. They were the gods of racing. Bizarrely, they'd been called as prosecution witnesses. Why hadn't the BHA and the police listened to them before they pursued this folly and forced it into the courts? Instead of listening to proper experts, they had had to go to the other side of the world, to Australia, to get someone to tell them what they wanted to hear about their pathetic evidence. It was their biggest mistake of all.

CHAPTER 27

Beggars Belief

Among the many issues of credibility that the prosecution faced in its attempt to convince the jury that I was guilty of stopping horses, perhaps the greatest of all of them was summed up in a statistic that John Kelsey-Fry outlined to the jury quite early in the trial in Court 12 of the Old Bailey in that autumn of 2007. It was a statistic that made a mockery of the case against me. It was a statistic that seemed to be enough on its own to underline that, despite all the millions the police had spent on Operation Krypton and the years they had spent trying to gather evidence, I had no case to answer.

Because no matter how many times the prosecution said I had been involved in a conspiracy to make horses lose, their case was always dashed on the rock of this statistic: my strike rate, or percentage of winners to rides, was 29.4 per cent when I was supposed to be trying to lose a race and 19 per cent the rest of the time. So in these seventeen supposedly suspect rides that the prosecution had outlined, I had a better win rate than across the rest of my career. A much, much better win rate. In the preamble to the trial, I could never understand how the prosecution would get past that bald fact. It turned out, they never did.

'The jury is being asked to believe,' Kelsey said witheringly and with as much incredulity as he could muster, 'that in races he was allegedly trying to lose, the strike rate of one of the world's best jockeys was actually fifty per cent higher than normal.'

The lengths the prosecution went to in order to try to get around that statistic, though, were increasingly desperate. They found it so hard to get anyone to criticise my rides that they had to go to the other side of the world to recruit someone. They went to Australia, to another racing jurisdiction, where the rules and traditions of racing are different, and enlisted the help of Ray Murrihy, the chief stipendiary steward in New South Wales, in the case against me.

I mean, doesn't that seem a bit random to you? To go all the way to Australia to get an opinion about a case that is based around an Irish jockey riding at UK racecourses. If they couldn't find anyone in Newmarket, or the UK, or Europe, or even the Northern Hemisphere, to give expert evidence against me, maybe they should have realised the game was up. Malcolm Wallis, the Director of Regulation at the Jockey Club, expressed surprise in a witness statement '. . . at the fact Mr Murrihy feels able to come from Australia to give evidence about British racing'.

Their case was already crumbling by then, but that was when it fell apart altogether. The extent of Murrihy's ignorance of racing in the UK, his ignorance of UK tracks and their characteristics, was ruthlessly exposed by Kelsey and his testimony was destroyed.

But even before Murrihy took the stand, the problems the police had had trying to get an expert witness to support their case had been laid bare. In 2006, they had recruited Jim McGrath, the Channel 4 pundit and managing director of Timeform who, coincidentally, had been the expert testifying against me in the Top Cees case. His independence and his knowledge of racing were not in question, but in the event he was not called by the prosecution.

Jim McGrath looked at all the races under discussion and told the police there was nothing wrong with these rides and little that was suspicious. The court was told that he was interviewed by Acting Detective Inspector Mark Manning and three other police officers on 28 March 2006 and asked for his opinion about the 27 races that would later form the indictment against me and the other jockeys. But his opinion was not disclosed to the defence until 4 October 2007, the day the jury was sworn in. In particular, he was asked about the Ballinger Ridge ride and he told them that it would have required too much judgement to be deliberately cheating. He had made similar comments about other rides of mine.

McGrath had pointed out at one stage that I had ridden a horse well, because I had adapted my ride to the fact that my horse wasn't responding to the whip. He had explained that I had stopped using the whip and that it had worked well. One of the policemen said that he didn't agree with Jim and told him he thought I should have hit the horse harder.

It was instructive hearing, in particular, what McGrath had said to Manning about one of my rides and the way Manning had tried to lead him.

'My feeling is that the rider on the day did absolutely everything I would expect them to do,' Jim McGrath said, 'and on three occasions I said to you I did not think it was just a competent ride, but a good ride.'

Mr Manning replied: 'You did, but I'm sure the prosecutor won't ask you to say that.'

'Yes,' Jim McGrath said, 'but I'm sure the defence counsel will.'

McGrath's statement should have been disclosed to my defence team by the police because it contained evidence that assisted me and my fellow defendants. In criminal proceedings, apparently, there are two types of material. One is material that the police are going to use for your prosecution and the other is material that they have got which they are not going to use for your prosecution. It is called 'unused material'. The relevant material that must be disclosed is not just material which assists the prosecution but also evidence which assists defendants. In the event, Mr Caplan on behalf of the Crown conceded that there had been errors in their disclosure process that should not have occurred.

The police are obliged to give you a list of the 'unused material' and a legal team can request to see things that it thinks might be pertinent to the case. So even though the police weren't going to use McGrath's evidence, because it didn't fit their preconceptions, they were supposed to tell us it at least existed. They didn't do that. My legal team only found out about it because there was a reference to it on another document.

Jim McGrath subsequently called my legal team and said that not only did the police not use his evidence but also that he had felt under pressure when they interviewed him. He said the atmosphere had been oppressive. He certainly felt uncomfortable enough to complain to the chief constable of the City of London police and write him a letter. None of this was disclosed before the case.

An expert witness expressly has to state that their duty is to the court and not to either party, so once you have gone to someone and they have given their evidence, the court should be aware of that. You can't just say: 'That's not quite the expert evidence we were hoping for so let's ignore him and then go and try and find another expert witness.'

Mr Kelsey-Fry was scathing about the police conduct and forced the officer in charge of disclosure, Detective Constable Stephen Gibbs, into an embarrassing admission.

'I didn't disclose those notes,' Gibbs said, 'and in hindsight I should have done. Like everyone, I am subject to human fragility. Looking at them now in the cold light of day, I would have done.'

A BBC legal analysis of the trial in its aftermath suggested that it had emphasised that the system of legal disclosure was deeply flawed. It pointed out the police had stored a total of 17,000 items relating to the case on their computer system Holmes (Home Office Large Major Enquiry System).

The police draw up the evidence for the prosecution, and then the police and the Crown Prosecution Service decide what evidence needs to be disclosed to the defence. But according to the system, all the defence can do is demand that anything relevant is disclosed. They had to rely on the judgement and rectitude of the police and the CPS.

In the event, the only expert evidence on which the police were able to rely was that of the Australian steward Ray Murrihy. So now the scene was set for the final and decisive encounter of the trial, that between Kelsey and Murrihy. This was the last throw of the dice for the prosecution and for me it made very tense viewing. The prosecution case had been slowly collapsing under the successive assaults from the six defendants' barristers on each and every aspect.

But what if Murrihy was able to convince the jury that the horses had been stopped? Everything depended on Kelsey's succeeding in this encounter and the degree to which Murrihy was able to withstand his assault. Kelsey had one main objective: to convince the judge, as he had tried to do in the dismissal application, that Murrihy was not an expert on English racing. If he was able to do this, then he was confident that the judge would throw the case out on the basis that there was no case to answer. It would mean that Murrihy's evidence was not sufficiently strong for the jury to be allowed to even consider it.

Murrihy's evidence was seen by many as the key to the case. But it emerged under cross-examination that it was deeply flawed, not just because he admitted he had been judging our rides on the basis of the rules of Australian racing but because, as Kelsey said in the subsequent dismissal application, Murrihy did not '... even purport to offer any conclusion or opinion' on the rides in question. All he said is that he would have held a stewards' inquiry, but he made no comment as to what the outcome of the inquiry would be. A classic example of this related to the high point of the Crown's case, my ride on Ballinger Ridge:

MR MURRIHY: 'I simply don't know whether there was an error of judgement or what it was.'

KELSEY: 'You're not in a position there to contradict the stewards' finding?'

MR MURRIHY: 'I'm not in a position to say whether I agree or disagree with it. I didn't investigate it.

I'm not in a position to say whether the position is
right and to embrace it or to say if it is wrong.'

Again in the context of Ballinger Ridge, in Australia, all
jockeys in a race are required to ride out to the line. In
Britain, by contrast, there is a culture of easing horses down at
the finish to avoid winning by large margins and getting the
horse penalised by the handicapper, which was exactly what
I was thinking about when I was riding Ballinger Ridge.
And that is why Murrihy felt he could not comment on the
finding of the English stewards in the case of Ballinger Ridge.

One of Murrihy's complaints about my riding was that he
did not know whether the horse in question was running to
pattern. In Australia, horses are obliged to employ the same
running style as in their previous race – thus a front runner
must race prominently and a 'hold-up horse' must race from
the back. If a trainer wants to try another method in Australia,
he must tell the stewards who will then alert the racing public.
In the UK, a trainer can give any instructions he wants as long
as they are not inconsistent with the horse doing its best.

Murrihy thought that this was a cheats' charter, but the
point is that, given no trainer was said to be involved in the
conspiracy and that every trainer had said I had ridden the
horse consistently with the instructions given, there was no
way that his evidence could get the prosecution home on the
central point.

The defence also pointed out that Murrihy was a vocal
critic of Betfair in Australia. He admitted that he feared
betting exchanges threatened the integrity of racing, but he
insisted his views on Betfair did not colour his opinion on
the races he was asked to judge.

There were several issues with his evidence, not just the fact that he was ignorant of the ways of British racing. For a start, the jury was initially told by Paul Scotney, the BHA's head of security, that he had only met Murrihy once, in Australia in early 2005, during a tour of a number of foreign racing jurisdictions including Sydney, Hong Kong, Japan and Melbourne.

Later, however, Scotney had to admit in court he had also met Murrihy 'for about half an hour in a public house, O'Neill's on Shaftesbury Avenue, for an extension of our conversation in Australia and to talk over some of the things that we were doing'.

The court was also told there were question marks about the way Murrihy was directed by the police. The correct way of getting expert evidence as to whether someone is cheating is not to say 'that horse there has been laid to lose £100,000, what do you think of the way it has been ridden?'

The correct way would be to say: 'Look at that race and tell me if you can see a horse that isn't trying.' Don't identify the supposedly suspicious ride before the witness has seen the footage. Murrihy denied it, but the court was told by the defence that Murrihy had been prompted by the City of London police in his analysis of the races, and in particular, as we heard earlier, by Acting Detective Inspector Manning.

Mr Kelsey-Fry, referring to a police transcript, had reminded Murrihy of a conversation with an investigating officer in which he was told that 'we're clearly looking for any evidence that might support the fact he wasn't riding to win'. But Murrihy, who was on the stand for a week, said that he had never understood that the police were asking him to 'pull apart' every race. Nor would he have accepted such instructions, he said. 'I called it as I'd seen it,' he said.

Mr Kelsey-Fry would not let Murrihy off the hook. One of the 27 races in question was my ride on Barking Mad at Windsor in August 2004 when I had won from the front. That was an irony. It was one of my rare successes at Windsor, a track I had never come to terms with. According to the transcript of his witness statement, Murrihy told the officer: 'On balance, you would say that going to the front and exposing yourself, having to get a horse beat from the front, wouldn't be the ideal way of doing it.'

Murrihy said that his only reason for calling a stewards' inquiry into Barking Mad's success would have been that I had repeatedly looked over my shoulder when well clear towards the end of the race. There's a phrase for that. It's 'clutching at straws'.

As was the case with Ballinger Ridge, Kelsey emphasised that while the practice of easing down, having checked how far in front you were, was discouraged in Australia, it was an accepted part of British racing culture, not just to protect a winner from punishment by the handicapper, but to protect its welfare.

The interaction between Murrihy and Kelsey was often antagonistic. It was bound to be, I suppose. Murrihy's two-day cross-examination was the crux of the trial in many ways. A barrister knows when that moment comes and a great one rises to the occasion. Kelsey was meticulous. He walked Murrihy through the video of the Barking Mad race and got Murrihy to admit I had ridden the horse well from an awkward draw.

'Bearing in mind his draw and preferred manner of racing,' Kelsey-Fry said, 'Kieren Fallon did everything necessary to ensure the maximum chance of winning, didn't he?'

'I wouldn't disagree with that proposition,' Murrihy said.

Kelsey greeted that with one of his theatrical, long-suffering put-downs, making the jury know that he had had to put them through all that just for a simple admission.

'The answer's yes, then?' he said.

Murrihy said it was.

'Thank you,' Kelsey said with a heavy, exasperated sigh and a look of exaggerated weariness.

Kelsey also undermined Murrihy when he questioned him about the Ballinger Ridge race at Lingfield in March 2004. He reminded Murrihy that he had told the court he had never seen a ride like it before. Kelsey then showed the jury footage of eight different British races in which jockeys snatched defeat from the jaws of victory in a similar way to me on Ballinger Ridge, being punished by the stewards for an error of judgement, without intent.

Kelsey asked whether he would accept that all these riders were guilty of 'horrendous blunders'. But Murrihy refused. He said he needed to know more about the background to each ride.

Sometimes, Murrihy's evidence and his lack of knowledge caused the trial to descend into farce. There was one exchange between him and Kelsey that centred on my ride of the Queen's horse, Daring Aim, at Newmarket in July 2004.

Kelsey pointed out to Murrihy that Daring Aim had been swishing her tail – a well-known sign of reluctance to run any faster under pressure – and asked Murrihy to explain the significance of that. Murrihy looked puzzled.

KELSEY: 'You see the flashing tail?'
MURRIHY: 'Yes.'

KELSEY: 'What does that indicate in a horse?'
MURRIHY: 'You would have to – I'm not being
facetious – ask the individual horse!'
KELSEY: 'Oh, Mr Murrihy! ... How am I going to
ask Daring Aim?'

Murrihy's evidence was a joke. It made me angry. It made me angry that the police thought it was viable for them to use a man who had little knowledge of British racecourses, or where the best draw was, or what the camber was, or what its contours were. They thought they could get away with doing something like that after all the money they had wasted on the case and all the stress they had put all the defendants through. The longer Murrihy was on the stand, the more bizarre I found it that the police should be relying so heavily on him.

Murrihy was also ignorant of the fact that one of the accepted tenets of racing in England is that a jockey must obey the trainer's instructions. Murrihy thought that was wrong, but it was another example of him applying his own personal preferences to a set of circumstances that simply didn't exist in the UK.

So when I rode a horse called Beauvrai for trainer Vince Smith at Yarmouth in August 2004, Smith told me to miss the kick and hold Beauvrai up at the back of the field. He thought that that horse needed to go through horses. He didn't want to lead. He wanted to come through them and his confidence built all the time as he was passing them.

I followed Smith's instructions faithfully and held the horse up to the last minute and we won comfortably. And yet Murrihy thought there was something wrong with that. He told the court that my obeying of the trainer's instructions was 'simply not appropriate'. Kelsey responded by asking him whether he was suggesting that I should have ignored my trainer's instructions. Murrihy said I should have ignored the instructions.

Knowing that this assertion blew a hole as big as the *Titanic* in the prosecution case, Kelsey concluded with the line: 'In that case, Mr Murrihy, I don't have anything further to ask you,' and sat down with the flourish of his gown in the manner of a matador's muleta, having delivered his sword between Mr Murrihy's shoulders.

To be fair to Murrihy, he had never tried to hide his ignorance of the sport in the UK. He didn't even pretend he watched races here regularly. 'I have not said I was an expert in respect of UK racing, yes, that is a fair statement,' he said at one point. And at another stage of the trial, he said defiantly: 'It was not incumbent that I verse myself in UK or other jurisdiction rules.'

Nearly nine weeks of the trial had passed and the prosecution had finally completed their evidence when an application was made for the case to be struck out on the grounds that there was no case to answer. Just beforehand, there was an application by all six defendant barristers that the judge should recuse himself, as they had lost confidence in him conducting the trial fairly following a dispute over whether a contemporary note of Manning's was consistent with Manning's evidence. The judge declined the application saying there were no grounds for him to recuse himself.

After so much false hope, I wasn't sure how much chance there was of it succeeding. There was an interruption to court proceedings and so I went for a drink with my legal team at a pub next to the Old Bailey. I phoned Christopher Stewart-Moore and told him I thought something was happening. All the tension had left their bodies.

I look for rather more obvious clues and there was a bucket of champagne in front of Kelsey. I asked Christopher to ask Kelsey what had happened and he said there was no need. 'You've won, Kieren,' he said to me. 'It's over.'

And so, on Friday 7 December 2007, Mr Justice Forbes directed the jury to return not guilty verdicts on all the defendants. He highlighted the limitations of Murrihy's evidence and his admission he was not an expert in UK racing as being part of the reason for his decision.

'This is an extraordinary admission given that he was purporting to give evidence about twenty-seven races run in the UK according to UK racing rules,' Mr Justice Forbes said of Murrihy's testimony. The bans preventing Fergal Lynch, Darren Williams and me from riding in the UK were immediately lifted by the BHA.

A little while later, I walked out to face the battery of tape recorders and cameras that were thrust in my face. I didn't feel a great sense of triumph, to be honest. I felt tired. And most of all, I felt angry. Look at the pictures of me outside the Old Bailey that day and I look like a seventy-year-old man.

I made a statement to the press. I said I was relieved and delighted but also outraged. I said there was never any evidence against me and that the court had just confirmed that. I said I was devastated at having lost over a year's racing at the top level, at possibly the most important time in my career.

Everybody started making statements then. My solicitors, BCL Burton Copeland, called for two inquiries into the failed prosecution, one into the police testimony and the other into why the CPS proceeded with the case.

'Far from proving Kieren Fallon's guilt,' the firm's statement said, 'the evidence called by the prosecution clearly established that Kieren Fallon had never been a party to the alleged conspiracy.' They said they would also prepare a report on the investigation for the Independent Police Complaints Commission.

The BHA got in on the act, too. Ben Gunn, a BHA regulatory director who did much to initiate the whole mess by passing a file of complaint to police early in 2004, insisted he had no regrets over that decision. Nic Coward, the chief executive, said there would be an internal review.

'The fact that racing's governing body yesterday left its official response to men named Gunn and Coward,' Chris McGrath wrote in the *Independent*, 'made it hard to resist the observation that the race-fixing trial at the Old Bailey had ended not with a bang, but a whimper.'

As for Scotney, it emerged he was yet to be questioned by the BHA about the incident where he vowed to get me if it was the last thing he did. Gunn did at least accept that Scotney's performance as a witness had not been 'as strong as it should have been'.

Scotney left the BHA at the end of 2012. He said the failure of the case against me had been 'a low point' in his time at the organisation. He said errors in the prosecution, including the decision to employ Murrihy, were police misjudgements, rather than the BHA's fault. He said he was looking forward to employing his expertise in other sports.

Mark Manning did not get the job at the BHA that he had been promised. The offer was withdrawn. A decision had been reached, it was said, that Manning might no longer get the level of co-operation he needed from the racing industry after what had come to light during the trial.

Me? I spent a few hours in a bar in High Holborn after the case collapsed. Then Christopher, Kelsey, the rest of the legal team and I moved on to Luciano's restaurant in St James's Street.

Christopher's phone was red hot. The *News of the World* had already been on, offering £350,000 to settle the Fake Sheikh libel case. They knew that once I had been found innocent, Mazher Mahmood's article was indefensible. The *Racing Post* were on, too. They offered £250,000 to settle the case we had against them.

I'm glad I enjoyed it while I could. The celebrations didn't last long.

CHAPTER 28

Father Moore's Well

When I was still a young man, riding for Kevin Prendergast in Kildare, never touching a drop of drink, fighting and laughing and riding winners and feeling like I didn't have a care in the world, I started to wonder if I really wanted to leave Ireland or just stay and enjoy what I had.

I was weighing up the offer to go and ride for Jimmy FitzGerald and live in Yorkshire. I knew it would mean leaving everything behind. I knew it would probably be a turning point in my life. It was a big decision, and for quite some time I didn't know what to do. One day, I went down to a holy well that wasn't far from Kevin's yard at Friarstown. Father Moore's Well is named after a priest who lived in the area at the end of the eighteenth century. He was said to have had healing powers and, before he died, he blessed the well.

Families whose kids are poorly visit it, hoping for some kind of cure. Tourists turn up there every so often, too. I was feeling so conflicted about what to do that I thought I might as well go and see what happened. I got there and I prayed.

'Send me whichever way you want,' I said and the road took me to England. I didn't want to go, really. I don't know why I did it, but a few days after I went to Father Moore's Well, I just got on a plane and that was it. I don't know what would have happened if I'd stayed. Maybe I'd still be mucking out in a yard somewhere.

Maybe I would never have become a jockey. Maybe I would never have become a champion and won the Derby. Maybe I would have lived my life in anonymity. Maybe I would never have seen the inside of a courtroom. Maybe I would never have seen the inside of an addiction clinic. But I got on the plane and I made my choice. And I became a champion. And I became a household name. And I lived a life in the spotlight. And I spent too many hours in courtrooms. And less than twenty-four hours after the collapse of my trial at the Old Bailey, it was announced that I had tested positive again for cocaine.

I tested positive at Deauville in France on 19 August 2007 after I'd ridden Myboycharlie in the Group One Prix Morny. Myboycharlie – you couldn't make that up, could you?

I don't even know if the test was accurate. I tested positive for pure cocaine, apparently, which was unusual. Normally, someone who has taken cocaine tests positive for a metabolite of the drug. Anyway, I was advised not to fight it and to tell the truth, I didn't really have the strength for another legal battle.

At the start of January 2008, I was banned from racing worldwide for eighteen months. I was nearly forty-three. I would be well past forty-four by the time I came back. But I got my head down and got on with the suspension. I went to work for Sir Michael and rode out for him every day. I rode four lots every morning on the Newmarket gallops and let spring turn to summer and summer turn to autumn. I played a lot of squash and a bit of golf and I employed a personal trainer to make sure I didn't go to seed. I did what I could to keep my spirits up, and soon there was another spring and another summer and I was able to race again.

It wasn't easy coming back. It felt a bit like being an apprentice. There were lads in the weighing room I didn't even know because I hadn't ridden in England for so long. Richard Kingscote was one. His career had blossomed so quickly that I had missed the start of it and he was fully established by the time my suspension ended.

I found it difficult coming back. It brought all of the embarrassment of the trial back out into the open again. I was introducing myself to people for the first time since I had seen them in the Old Bailey when they had come to testify on my behalf. I hated that. I felt just as shy as ever.

My relationship with Coolmore was over. That ended the day I was banned. They had stood by me for so long and I will always be grateful for that. The second time I was banned, they didn't have any choice but to end our partnership. They appointed Johnny Murtagh as my successor.

I did okay when I came back, but it took me a long time to get into the rhythm of racing. I got a lot of rides from Luca Cumani, Mark Johnston and Kevin Ryan, in particular. I was grateful for that. I rode 140 winners in 2010 and 154 in 2011 when I was in that three-way scrap for the title with Paul Hanagan and Silvestre de Sousa. But my confidence was never the same. The horses don't run for you the same and I didn't ride them with the same feeling. I knew I'd lost the edge I'd once had over everybody else, especially in the

Classics. I didn't quite have the same boldness. I used to live for the buzz of winning, but that was all gone.

There were still some good moments. In 2014, I won the 2000 Guineas on Night of Thunder, a 40/1 shot trained by Richard Hannon Jr. I got the ride only because Richard Hughes chose to go with Toormore instead and for a little while I felt as though that win gave me a bit of a lifeline. It was my fifth win in the 2000 Guineas and it was to be my last. It was my last Classic victory, too. But I had started riding out for Saeed bin Suroor by then, and that had given me confidence because I was riding good horses again and I loved being out on the gallops.

But I only rode 62 winners that season. I should have been gone before Night of Thunder, but you are always holding on, aren't you? Nobody wants to retire. What do you do? Crack up or drink, usually.

Pat Eddery was the most professional jockey I had ever seen and Walter Swinburn was another one – and look what happened to them. They were two of my idols, yet after retiring from the saddle both had comparatively modest training careers and battled problems, Pat with alcohol dependency and Walter with epilepsy caused by the serious fall he suffered at Sha Tin racecourse in 1996. Both died much too soon, Pat aged sixty-three in 2015 and Walter aged only fifty-five in 2016. I thought I too might struggle with how I found life outside the goldfish bowl.

In the winter of 2015, I thought I'd go to America. When you're not on a roll, you have to change something. I thought that by going back to America, where I learned to ride after my suspension with the Stuart Webster thing, maybe it would all come back. Like magic.

I knew it wasn't happening for me by then, but I didn't want to admit it. I knew it wasn't ever going to happen, too. I knew I wasn't riding as well and that I had lost my confidence. Ever since the Old Bailey case, I had lost confidence in myself.

I wasn't riding for Sir Michael or Aidan any more and Henry had gone, dying nine months after his beloved Frankel's final racecourse victory. I was still riding for good trainers, but they didn't have the same number of horses as the men I'd worked for before or the same quality of horses and it was more and more of a struggle.

I felt less and less confident physically, too. I lost the strength in my legs. The power was gone. I didn't know what was wrong with me. I had blood tests but they didn't find anything. I thought maybe going to America would be a cure for everything. I flew to Los Angeles and bought a big Ram Truck. I slung my golf clubs in the back of it and drove across the country from California to New York, finding rides in races wherever I could.

I stayed in motels and kept myself to myself in between rides. And then I moved on. I drove through Albuquerque because I know that's where a lot of the UFC fighters train. I stopped off and had a drink in a bar and then drove on.

I rode at some of the cathedrals of American racing: at Churchill Downs in Louisville, home of the Kentucky Derby, and Keeneland in Lexington, where the Kentucky Horse Park celebrates all things equestrian; and then in Indiana for a while. I rode work for Wesley Ward a few times. I went out on Judy the Beauty, who was a fine filly; she'd won the Breeders' Cup Filly & Mare Sprint in 2014. I had a ride at Philadelphia Park, which I should have won but I made a mess of it and kicked too soon and lost. It was embarrassing. I don't even want to talk about it. I went up to Belmont and rode there and saw some friends in New York.

Then I headed back west and rode work at Santa Anita. I had a bad fall there, riding round Clocker's Corner on a horse for Ben Cecil, working a half mile. Because of all the medication they're allowed to be on in the States, the horses don't feel their injuries like they do in England and so when an accident happens, it happens fast and sudden and a jockey can be badly hurt.

Just as I was on the point of the turn, my horse broke a leg and fired me into the ground. If I had hit the floor straight on, I would have been in trouble, but I hit it side on and so I was just a bit shaken. It unnerved me, though. I decided I'd come back to England to see the kids and catch up a bit.

Michael O'Callaghan asked me if I'd go and ride for him and I drove over to Kildare just to be polite, really, because he seemed like a nice guy. He showed me around the yard and I rode out for a couple of days and he had some nice horses. He was a lovely guy to work with and I liked the operation he had at Crotanstown.

It's like everything else: you know you should be retiring but you are hanging on and looking for an excuse not to. So I stayed with Michael for a little while and he had several promising two-year-olds and I thought he would have a good year with them. I started riding out. I thought, like you do, that it might pick me up again.

We did well and the filly, Now Or Never, ran third in the Irish Guineas at the Curragh behind Jet Setting and Minding in May 2016. She was a good filly and I enjoyed it when I was riding over there in Ireland. But things weren't the same.

I still didn't feel right. I wasn't rejuvenated or anything like that. There was no switch that was going to get flicked. I'd gone past that.

Then I had a fall at York on 10 June. It was in my last race of four that day and I was on a lovely four-year-old called Vilman, riding for trainer Simon West, who has a small yard up on the edge of the Yorkshire Dales. I had hit the front and gone about a length clear and then he snapped a leg. I was able to hold him up before he went down. I felt it going before it snapped and I think he did, too, poor fella. They start putting the brakes on and you know something bad is coming.

It is a macabre thing, trying to get off a horse that is only on three legs. Its actions are grotesque and sad. I managed to jump off in the end as the other horses were flying by me. Some idiot at the back, with his head down, nearly bowled me over. He just brushed me. If he had hit me, he could have killed me. I don't think he even knew I was there. He was young.

I stood and held that poor little horse while they were putting him down. The stewards came around and put a big screen around us so the public couldn't see it. And this horse was ducking and diving, all over the place, down on his bad leg, the adrenaline going through him.

The vet should just have gone in there and injected him. It took probably ten minutes. It seemed like an hour. I was trying to hold on to this horse and trying to soothe him and be nice to him and then finally they injected him and he dropped. I wouldn't have left him. I held him while he died. As I sat there, I just thought: 'It's time to pack it in.'

I never planned to ride my last race. It was one of those things. My last ride was actually on a horse called Magical

Fire at the Curragh on 26 June 2016. There was some symmetry in finishing where I had begun. We finished fifth out of seven.

And then it happened. I got out of bed and I didn't want to go to work. That's when you know you've had enough. It was one weekend in Ireland, but I guess it had been coming for a while. I had a look at my rides and I knew I'd just be making up the numbers. I didn't want to do that any more. I just wanted to get back to England.

I was in a bad way by then. Earlier in the year, I had been examined by Dr Adrian McGoldrick, chief medical officer to the Irish Turf Club, as part of the annual licensing process, and we had started talking about a variety of things that were bothering me. I told him I didn't feel right. My legs weren't as strong as they had been, I had no appetite, I didn't want to get up early like I used to. He said he thought I was suffering from depression. I thought: 'What am I depressed about? The kids are fine, I've been travelling the world, I still love horses.'

But I was trying to stay riding longer than I should have. I wasn't getting the same rides. I wasn't riding with the same flair that I had been. I wasn't dominating like I used to and I was on a downward spiral and I didn't understand. It wasn't until I sat down with Dr McGoldrick that I understood I had to do something about it.

I got worse before I got better. I didn't want to do anything. I didn't want to eat. I didn't want to see people. I started thinking weird things. I was kind of suicidal. I was thinking of ways. I was thinking about what would be the easiest method of getting away. I didn't want to go on. Even though I had everything, I had nothing. I don't know enough about depression, but I do know it's not very nice. I'm lucky

I'm a weak person and that I don't like pain and I don't like heights, because I think I would have done something if I had had the balls.

Drowning would have been an option because, as you'll recall, I nearly drowned when I was in Australia and it was the most peaceful time of my life. People say it's horrible, drowning, but I was as good as gone that time in Sydney and I didn't feel any pain.

I wasn't strong enough to stay alive for myself, but my kids kept coming over to see me and I thought of them. I'd be gone but what are they going to feel? They'd be the ones who were left behind. I knew I needed help by then and I met Dr McGoldrick at the right time.

I wanted to stop racing. When you are over fifty and you start thinking about stuff, it's time to go. When a jockey begins to lose his nerve, it is dangerous. It's like if you are on a motorway and someone keeps braking in front of you for no reason. You know the ones who have lost their nerve. You can see them jump if the horse swishes its tail or you might be in a race and they won't go for a gap when once they would have hoofed the horse through it. I never got to that stage. I retired instead.

My retirement from the sport was announced on 4 July 2016. There was no press conference or anything like that. I didn't want to talk to the press. I asked Dr McGoldrick if he would field some questions from the media and he told them I was suffering from profound depression and had been for some time.

I think I'd been depressed since the trial at the Old Bailey, but I tried to hide things and cover them up. That's the way it is in Ireland. That's what you're taught to do. If somebody got pregnant, it had to be covered up and shoved away under the carpet. It's the Irish way. We don't like to be seen to be weak. We don't like to be seen to have a failing. If somebody said to me I was depressed, I would have laughed. I didn't think I needed help, but getting help was the best thing I ever did.

I spent six weeks in St Patrick's Hospital in Dublin. There are fancy descriptions for the treatment they provide, but it is a mental hospital, basically. The care I received in there was brilliant. I talked a lot, to a lot of different doctors, and I was put on medication that helped me. It was a relief finally to be addressing the problems I had been suffering quietly from for so long.

It wasn't until I came out of St Pat's that I finally thought I would take some time out. I accepted that my career was over. I had been running around after everybody else all my life, trying to please everybody else, and now I wanted a change. I know I had a great career and I rode for some great people and great trainers, but it was always for somebody else.

When I got back to England, my son Cieren was at the British Racing School in Newmarket, learning his trade as an apprentice. He was doing some work with a former jockey called Michael Tebbutt and Michael asked me what I was doing. I told him I was between plans. He invited me to come and ride out for William Haggas in Newmarket. And I did. And everything was grand. The yard had loads of winners all through the autumn, but then Cieren came to ride at the yard and I found that hard.

I was looking to see what they were putting him on, what he's doing wrong, what he's doing right, where he's going. It was like he was five years old again. I thought the anxiety and the angst was going to start all over again and I didn't want that. There wasn't much I could do anyway. He doesn't listen to me. He asks me something and I tell him the answer and his response starts with 'no, but'. I thought, 'You know what, row your own boat.'

I think I'd be a good teacher but I wouldn't have the patience. I'd be like the old school teacher who wants you to learn and wants you to do it right but wouldn't leave any room for error.

I ride out for Godolphin and Saeed bin Suroor now and I have tried to teach in the yard with some of the kids, because a lot of them come and ask me for advice. I will explain it as nicely as I can and then if they don't get it, I will start getting annoyed. But instead of one of them getting bent around the head, which is what used to happen in my day if we didn't know the answer, I have to walk away.

Somebody told me recently I ought to be a jockey coach but that would mean having to deal with the BHA. At least I'd be imparting some of what I've learned and it wouldn't be lost. They might listen to me, I suppose. Kids don't like a yes man, do they?

Anyway, with Cieren, I was constantly watching what he was doing and what they were telling him. I was watching him and getting frustrated. It was a hundred times worse than when I was getting my first ride myself. A lot of people think he's going to be good and I didn't want to be there, getting in his way. A boy has to find his own way home.

My depression is much better now. The doctors put me on an antidepressant called Sertraline and it seems to be working well. When I wake up in the morning now, I'm smiling. I'm happy. I can't wait to get into Saeed's yard in the morning and annoy all the lads.

I will always ride horses wherever I go and whatever I do. While I have the ability to ride, I will ride. I feel normal on a horse. I don't feel normal anywhere else, but I do when I'm on a horse.

A few weeks ago, I was riding three canters up Warren Hill. It was a beautiful morning and there were just horses and riders and the gallops and the brilliant green of the hill. I looked around for an instant at the lad who was riding along behind me. I thought of Father Moore's Well and the life that lies ahead of him.

INDEX

(the initials KF refer to Kieren Fallon)